KING OF THE Q'S BLUE PLATE BBQ

KING OF THE ★Q'S★ BLUE PLATE BBQ

TED READER ★

THE ULTIMATE GUIDE TO GRILLING, SMOKING, DIPPING AND LICKING

PHOTOGRAPHY BY EDWARD POND

★

AN ANGEL EDITION FOR HOME BOOKS

HOME

A HOME BOOK
Published by the Penguin Group
Penguin Group (USA) Inc.
375 Hudson Street, New York, New York 10014, USA
Penguin Group (Canada), 90 Eglinton Avenue East, Suite 700, Toronto, Ontario M4P 2Y3, Canada
(a division of Pearson Penguin Canada Inc.)
Penguin Books Ltd., 80 Strand, London WC2R 0RL, England
Penguin Group Ireland, 25 St. Stephen's Green, Dublin 2, Ireland (a division of Penguin Books Ltd.)
Penguin Group (Australia), 250 Camberwell Road, Camberwell, Victoria 3124, Australia
(a division of Pearson Australia Group Pty. Ltd.)
Penguin Books India Pvt. Ltd., 11 Community Centre, Panchsheel Park, New Delhi—110 017, India
Penguin Group (NZ), Cnr. Airborne and Rosedale Roads, Albany, Auckland 1310, New Zealand
(a division of Pearson New Zealand Ltd.)
Penguin Books (South Africa) (Pty.) Ltd., 24 Sturdee Avenue, Rosebank, Johannesburg 2196,
South Africa

Penguin Books Ltd., Registered Offices: 80 Strand, London WC2R 0RL, England

While the author has made every effort to provide accurate telephone numbers and Internet addresses at the time of publication, neither the publisher nor the author assumes any responsibility for errors, or for changes that occur after publication. Further, the publisher does not have any control over and does not assume any responsibility for author or third-party websites or their content.

KING OF THE Q'S BLUE PLATE BBQ
Copyright © 2007 by Ted Reader.
Design copyright © 2007 by Angel Editions Inc.
Photography by Edward Pond, with the exception of the following: Page 8, 11 (top), 19 (top),
43 (bottom left), 131, 159, 167 (top), 179, 191, 247—courtesy of Mike McColl.
Cover photography by Edward Pond.
Cover design by Bill Douglas at the Bang.

First American edition: May 2007
Also published in Canada by HarperCollins in 2007.

An application to register this book for cataloging has been submitted to
the Library of Congress.

ISBN 978-1-55788-508-1

PRINTED IN SINGAPORE
10   9   8   7   6   5   4   3   2   1

PUBLISHER'S NOTE: The recipes contained in this book are to be followed exactly as written. The publisher is not responsible for your specific health or allergy needs that may require medical supervision. The publisher is not responsible for any adverse reactions to the recipes contained in this book.

Most Home Books are available at special quantity discounts for bulk purchases for sales promotions, premiums, fund-raising, or educational use. Special books, or book excerpts, can also be created to fit specific needs. For details, write: Special Markets, The Berkley Publishing Group, 375 Hudson Street, New York, New York 10014.

Previous spread: Chef Ted Reader; Opposite: Red chilis
ready for picking; Following spread: Balsamic Glazed
Sausage-and-Pepper Stuffed Ribs (p. 154)

To the crew of Team Barbecue: Global Gluttony

Pamela — Director of Operations, my true love. Your love, support and guidance have given me and our team the drive to go for the very best in food, fun and flavor. I love you.

Pit Boss "6 Guns" McColl — "Smoke 'em if you got 'em" is true to your passion for creating great food.

"Jo Jo" Lusted — Thanks for rounding out this perfect team. As Corporate Chef of Teddy's Island BBQ, you are the "Queen of the Q." Watch out guys, this lady can Q with the best.

Finally, to all the other chefs, foodies, friends and BBQ fanatics, you know who you are. Thanks for all your support.

Get Sticky!

CONTENTS

TED READER'S WORLD

WELCOME TO TED'S WORLD. Working with Ted is an experience like no other, and we want to tell you a bit about his excitement, passion and devotion to great food and fun.

With his signature spiky hair, sunglasses and flame-covered chef's jacket, Ted Reader is the complete opposite of what many of us expect a chef to look like. When Joanne arrived for her interview with him, she found out that Ted didn't act like any other chef, either. Ted asked her two questions: "Do you like tequila?" and "Do you like cats?" He then informed her of the only two rules in Ted's World: No. 1 There must always be a bottle of tequila in the freezer. No. 2 Never, ever, let the cats out. Everything else is open to interpretation, imagination and adventure. Having understood the rules, Joanne was presented with a giant 20-oz steak, some lobster tails and a log of goat's cheese. Ted said that he'd be back for lunch in one hour. She cooked lunch, no cats escaped, we had tequila and she had the job.

We never know what to say when someone asks us what we do for a living. Mike once tried to explain it to a chef friend, Olaf Mertens. Olaf's response to some of Mike's stories: "Only in Ted Reader's World!" Ted's World is a place where you really don't know what to expect on a daily basis. In Ted's World, you set up kitchens in fields, on street corners, in backyards and on beaches. You are able to cook on over 100 different types of grills and smokers, try over 80 different types of tequila, be the personal chef for a professional race car driver. Mike has been working for Ted for over four years and he notes that some days we don't cook at all; instead we are experimenting, brainstorming crazy — delicious — new ideas. Only in Ted's

World are you asked for a hundred ideas for things to do with ketchup or what can you do with ranch dressing, other than make a salad. There is definitely no training program, just a lot of trial and error.

The other question we're asked all the time is, "Where do you come up with your recipe ideas?" Ted is wildly creative, with a passion for anything over-the-top. He loves to eat and explore food. Ted has always encouraged us to go beyond the everyday stuff and ask, "Why not?" Why not use grilled cheese sandwiches as burger buns (Teddy's Grilled Cheese Beef Burger, p. 106), make your own hot sauce (Dragon BBQ Sauce, p. 255), or bake a cake on the grill (Pineapple Rum Upside-Down Cake, p. 224). There are no limits when it comes to inventing new, tasty dishes.

We fed over 20,000 people last summer and every time we cook the same old thing, it changes a little. We take it one step further to see what will happen. Many of our recipes come from events, BBQ demo classes and dinner parties. Seeing what people like to eat, what really gets them fired up, always inspires us. As well, for the most part, we work with ingredients and equipment that are familiar to just about everyone. Our kitchen is one that most people would feel at home in, and we have the same grocery store as everyone else. Ted knows that most bottled barbecue sauces are similar (though he would definitely recommend his King of the Q Smokin' Beer BBQ Sauce or his King of the Q Pineapple Rum BBQ Sauce!) — it all depends on personal taste, and whatever you have in the fridge will usually work just fine. That's why, in our recipes, we often just say to use any good gourmet barbecue sauce, or any kind of dressing you like.

Just about anything can inspire Ted to come up with something new, and he is always thinking up a dozen new projects — like his restaurant, Teddy's Island BBQ. It takes a moderately insane chef to open a restaurant and a brilliantly insane chef to open one in the Dominican Republic, which Ted has done. Teddy's Island BBQ

abounds not only with Ted's passion for great food but for what he is truly all about — having fun and loving life.

One day Ted told us he wanted to do a barbecue cookbook that would cover every kind of grilling, smoking and planking, would include over 200 recipes, lots of great tips and advice, and tons of pictures — something different from anything else out there. And here it is: *King of the Q's Blue Plate BBQ*, a shining example of what it's like to be a part of Ted Reader's World. He always finds a way to grill the un-grillable and explain it in a simple, fun way that everyone can understand. As well as including the best BBQ recipes anywhere (at least, in our opinion!), *Blue Plate BBQ* just happens to be a compilation of countless crazy adventures and unforgettable times with Ted. And to those of you opening this book for the first or the fiftieth time, we hope that the recipes and the good times you create along with them truly leave you feeling fantastic.

Chefs Joanne Lusted and Mike McColl

INTRODUCTION

GETTING READY FOR GRILLING, GLAZING, DIPPING AND LICKING

BARBECUING IS MY PASSION. It's also my profession, so I take it pretty seriously. This means that I've made quite a study of the various kinds of grilling and smoking machines and the different types of cooking methods. These days there are hundreds of different types and styles of grills, and it can be tough to pick which one is right for you. That's why I have over 75 grills and smokers in my backyard! With a little ingenuity, you can make great barbecue using just about any kind of heat source. But for fanatics like me, each kind of machine or method is going to offer its own appeal for different cooking situations. Although I use all of my grills, the ones that get fired up the most are my Napoleon propane grills, which also use charcoal; my ceramic charcoal grill-smokers by The Big Green Egg and Primo; my Bradley Digital Electric Smoker; my open firepit; and my big rig #52.

The natural gas or propane grill is what most people have at home. A gas flame ensures steady heat, and this type of grill allows you to cook everything from hamburgers to delicate fish. It's the all-purpose machine. It is also the best grill on which to bake desserts. When you're baking, precise temperature control is a must, and these grills allow you to carefully gauge and maintain an even temperature. The Big Green Egg is a specialty piece of equipment based on an ancient Japanese design. Its ceramic construction allows for something like convection cooking, and it cooks quickly and well. It also converts, to function as a smoker. The Egg is a great grill-smoker, for grillers

who want to ease into smoking. There are also many similar types of ceramic grill-smokers out there. My other favorite is the Primo Kamado, which, like the Egg, is a gem to work with.

A Bradley smoker is a convenient and easy smoker. Because it is electric, it allows for easy temperature and time control. It also uses a wood puck feed system — it's a set-it-and-forget-it type of smoker and it allows for cold and hot smoking, which means you can smoke both hearty beef and delicate chocolate.

Most people don't have open firepits in their backyards, and I wouldn't recommend one unless you have a lot of experience. Safety is always a priority. The open pit is the closest thing to a true barbecue method, however, and nothing can beat it for the flavor it imparts to food — especially great big pieces of grilled meat. If you're thinking about creating your own open-pit grill, do your research carefully, check with the fire department and then go for it!

I like to grill year-round, but for those of you who pull your barbecue out of the garage as soon as the snow melts, here are a few things to keep in mind before you start grilling.

Position your grill where you want to cook: close enough to the kitchen so you don't have to run back and forth, but far enough from

Previous spread: Ribs, hot off the grill
Above (left to right): Beef tenderloin on
the grill; a selection of meat thermometers

the house so you won't fill the family room with smoke or set the roof on fire. Bring everything you need out to the grill: You should try never to leave the barbecue unattended. It's like the military: Keep to your post and watch over your food. You'll have better results, and you'll really get to know your grill.

If your grill has been sitting around in the garage for a few months, give it a thorough cleaning. More than likely, your grill still has grease on it, which might have attracted rodents or spiders.

Another concern? Spiders can get into the Venturi tubes — the tubes that feed propane from the tank to the grill on a gas barbecue. In order to clean the tubes, you'll need a Venturi tube–cleaning brush. Follow the manufacturer's instructions to access them.

Every season you should also install new foil grease catchers underneath the grill — nearly every barbecue has such a spot. Using paper towels and an everyday grease-cutting household cleaner, clean and polish the entire unit so it sparkles.

A clean grill is a tasty grill and a safe grill. Grease buildup can lead to flare-ups and grease fires. Always clean your grill before and after use with a stiff wire brush. If you barbecue on a regular basis, you should go through two or three grill brushes a year. Finally, rub a light

Above (left to right): Fresh mushrooms await grilling; smoked beef brisket coating of cooking oil onto the grids every time you grill, to prevent food from sticking and to make cleanup easier.

Before lighting the grill, check all your connections to and from the source of propane. Turn on the tank and light one burner at a time. Close the lid until the barbecue reaches the desired temperature and then start cooking.

A lot of people ask: How hot should the grill be?
Here's a quick-and-handy reference.

★ High heat — around 500° to 650°F, or higher — is for searing steaks and chops.
★ Medium-high heat — around 400° to 500°F — is the temperature for most grilling, including meats and vegetables.
★ Medium heat — around 300° to 400°F — is the temperature for grilling hamburgers and sausages.
★ Medium-low heat — around 200° to 250°F — is the temperature for more delicate grilling, including some fish.
★ Low heat — less than 200°F — works best for roasting, rotisserie cooking and very lean foods. Low and slow. At this temperature, your grill works more like an oven.

TOOLS OF THE TRADE: THE MUST-HAVE ACCESSORIES
When I teach a class or present a demo, people often mistake me for a plumber, because I carry around a giant toolbox — the kind you find at most hardware stores. Instead of tap washers and wrenches, mine is filled with skewers, tongs, and other essential tools of the trade.

Among those tools are my knives: In my kit, you'll find a filleting knife, a chopping knife, a boning knife, a paring knife, a carving knife and — most important — a chef's knife or French knife. I always wash my knives by hand and store them in a knife block to protect the blades. Another way I keep my blades sharp is by using a wooden cutting board for dicing, slicing and chopping. (Take note that

Opposite: A selection of Ted's tools of
the trade: basting brush, tongs and knives

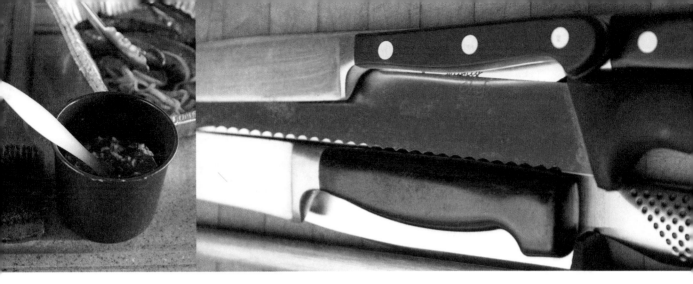

a dull knife is dangerous: It requires more force to cut through food and is more likely to slip.)

One of the other most important "tools" I rely on is a pair of well-insulated gloves. Because grilling involves high heat and flames, run-of-the-mill oven mitts just won't cut it. I use a modified pair of welder's mitts that extend well above the wrist, to protect my arms from grease spatters and flare-ups.

A comfortable pair of tongs is a basic necessity. You can pick up a good pair at any restaurant supply store or at your local barbecue dealer. I like metal restaurant tongs because they're sturdy, have a lot of flexibility and have excellent "grip" to better hold on to food. Another accessory I rely on is a Cajun injector — a large reusable syringe that allows you to inject marinades or melted butter (love the butter!) and, therefore, flavor right into whatever you're cooking.

No grill kit would be complete without a set of "mops" and brushes. You can get a specialty food mop, or something similar, in the kitchen section of your hardware store. For basting, I prefer a silicone brush, because it's easy to use and easy to clean.

Finally, I always have an assortment of grill baskets and grill toppers at the ready. Special baskets for delicate vegetables and fish and a grill-top wok are invaluable for making sure food doesn't fall apart or slip through the grill.

THE ORIGINS OF BARBECUE

The origins of barbecue are ancient, and theories abound as to the history of the word itself.

Bon Appétit magazine suggests that the word comes from an extinct tribe in Guyana, whose many culinary delights included "cheerfully spit-roasting captured enemies." The *Oxford English Dictionary* suggests a similarly Caribbean lineage and pinpoints the word as Haitian in origin.

Some food historians claim that the word comes from the French phrase *barbe à queue*, meaning "from beard to tail," the preferred method of spit-roasting entire hogs. Still other sources suggest that the word comes from 19th-century advertisements for combination bar, beer, pool and eating establishments, playfully dubbed bar-beer-cues.

Perhaps the most reasonable explanation stems from the Spanish word *barbacoa*, which was adapted from a word in Taino, an extinct language of the Arawak tribe. *Barbacoa* roughly translates as "a wooden rack on which meat is roasted over flames." Indigenous to the Dominican Republic and some other Caribbean islands, the Arawak Indians had several words that are the basis for the Spanish *barbacoa*: *ba* from *baba* (father), *ra* from *yara* (place), *bi* from *bibi* (beginning) and *cu* from *guacu* (the sacred fire), or "the beginning place of the sacred fire father." In the Dominican Republic, it is thought that the Taino word *barabicu* means "the sacred fire pit" and *barabicoa* means "the stick stand with four legs and many sticks on top to place the cooking meat." I recently opened my first restaurant, Teddy's Island BBQ, in the Dominican Republic — the perfect place to continue the barbecue tradition.

IN THE DOMINICAN REPUBLIC, IT IS THOUGHT THAT THE TAINO WORD *BARABICU* MEANS *"THE SACRED FIRE PIT."*

RUBS
PASTES AND
MARINADES

ALL GREAT GRILLED food needs a little rubbin' and lovin' to get things seasoned right. Rubs, pastes and marinades are the heart of barbecue — the flavorful elements that turn mere sustenance into edible art.

Seasoning rubs are principally dry blends of spices and herbs, applied directly to whatever you want to flavor. Pastes and marinades have wet elements that often help to tenderize. My signature rub, Bonedust Seasoning, can be used to season just about any meat or fish, and my Amazing Steak Spice and my Bayou Bite Cajun Seasoning, both of which won silver medals at the 2005 American National BBQ Association's Awards of Excellence, also add tons of flavor. Make a big batch of both of these rubs and have them at the ready.

Barbecue wouldn't be barbecue without the use of these fabulous marinades and pastes that add pungent or piquant boosts to plain old chicken breasts, pork loin, steak and seafood. So, before you grill, smoke or plank, make sure to rub, dunk and smear 'em!

BONEDUST SEASONING RUB

This is my signature seasoning mix, and I guarantee you'll love it! Bonedust can be used on everything from ribs to popcorn.

1/2 cup paprika
1/4 cup chili powder
3 tbsp salt
2 tbsp ground coriander
2 tbsp garlic powder
2 tbsp curry powder
2 tbsp hot mustard powder
2 tbsp sugar
1 tbsp freshly ground black pepper
1 tbsp dried basil
1 tbsp dried thyme
1 tbsp ground cumin
1 tbsp cayenne pepper

Makes about 2 1/2 cups

In a medium bowl, combine all ingredients; mix well. Store in an airtight container in a cool, dry place, away from heat and light.

BETTER BUTTER BURGER SEASONING RUB

This flavored butter makes burgers unbelievably good.

4 tbsp Bonedust Seasoning
(see above)
2 tbsp Butter Buds Natural Butter Flavor Granules*
1 tbsp coarsely ground black pepper
2 tbsp kosher salt
1 tbsp dried minced onion
1 tbsp dried minced garlic
1 tsp mustard powder
1 tsp dried chives
1 tsp dried parsley flakes

Makes about 1 cup

In a small bowl, mix together all ingredients. Store in an airtight container in a cool, dry place, away from heat and light.
Note: Butter Buds or other butter-flavored granules can be found in the spice section of many grocery stores.

AMAZING STEAK SPICE RUB

Amazing as a dry rub for steak. It's like a Montreal-style spice, only more amazing.

In a medium bowl, combine all ingredients. Store in an airtight container in a cool, dry place, away from heat and light.

1/2 cup kosher salt
1/4 cup coarsely ground black pepper
1/4 cup coarsely ground white pepper
1/4 cup mustard seeds
1/4 cup cracked coriander seeds
1/4 cup garlic powder
1/4 cup onion powder
1/4 cup crushed red pepper flakes
1/4 cup dill seeds

Makes about 2 1/2 cups

BAYOU BITE CAJUN SEASONING RUB

This rub works well with grilled poultry and meats and can be used anywhere you'd like a little extra heat!

In a small bowl, combine all ingredients. Store in an airtight container in a cool, dry place, away from heat and light.

2 tbsp salt
2 tbsp paprika
2 tbsp cayenne pepper
1 tbsp granulated sugar
1 tbsp hot mustard powder
1 tbsp freshly ground black pepper
1 tbsp garlic powder
1 tbsp onion powder
2 tsp ground cumin
1 tsp dried oregano
1 tsp dried thyme
1 tsp dried sage
1 tsp ground coriander

Makes about 1 cup

MEDITERRANEAN-STYLE RUB

This Mediterranean-style rub is like French-kissing a Greek goddess, if you know what I mean. It makes chicken, fish, pork and vegetables heavenly.

In a large bowl, combine all ingredients; mix well. Store in an airtight container in a cool, dry place, away from heat and light.

1/4 cup dehydrated garlic flakes
1/4 cup kosher salt
3 tbsp sugar
2 tbsp red pepper flakes
2 tbsp MSG-free chicken stock powder
2 tbsp dehydrated onion flakes
1 tbsp freshly ground black pepper
1 tbsp dried parsley
1 tbsp dried basil
1 tbsp dried marjoram
1 tbsp coarsely ground fennel seeds
2 tsp dried thyme
2 tsp cayenne pepper

Makes about 1 cup

Previous spread: Amazing Steak Spice Rub
Opposite: Making Bonedust Seasoning Rub

INDONESIAN CINNAMON RUB

This heady spice mix goes well with meat and chicken.

1/4 cup ground cinnamon
2 tbsp sugar
2 tbsp ground cumin
2 tbsp ground allspice
1 tbsp ground cloves
1 tbsp ground ginger
1 tbsp garlic powder
1 tbsp salt

Makes about 1 cup

In a small bowl, combine all ingredients; mix well. Store in an airtight container in a cool, dry place, away from heat and light.

TANDOORI RUB

This rub gives a great Indian flavor to poultry and meat.

1/4 cup paprika
2 tbsp ground cumin
1 tbsp cayenne pepper
1 tbsp ground coriander
1 tbsp ground cardamom
1 tbsp ground cinnamon
1 tbsp freshly ground black pepper
2 tsp salt
1 tsp ground cloves

Makes about 1/2 cup

In a small bowl, combine all ingredients; mix well. Store in an airtight container in a cool, dry place, away from heat and light.

COCHIN CURRY MASALA SEASONING RUB

Another intensely flavored Indian seasoning; the turmeric in this mix also gives meat a great golden color.

1/4 cup ground cumin
3 tbsp turmeric
1 tbsp salt
1 tbsp ground ginger
1 tbsp ground coriander
1 tbsp freshly ground black pepper
1 tbsp mustard powder
2 tsp ground cinnamon
2 tsp crushed red pepper flakes
1 tsp ground fennel seed
1 tsp grated nutmeg
1 tsp ground mace

Makes about 3/4 cup

In a small bowl, combine all ingredients; mix well. Store in an airtight container in a cool, dry place, away from heat and light.

Opposite (left to right): Indonesian Cinnamon Rub; Ted applies Sweet Rib Rub to a steak

COMPETITION RIB RUB

This classic spice rub is the secret weapon I always take into rib competitions.

In a large bowl, combine Bonedust Seasoning, pepper, garlic powder, cayenne pepper, salt and white pepper; mix well. Slowly incorporate brown sugar into spice mix, about 1/2 cup at a time, blending by hand until thoroughly combined. Store in an airtight container in a cool, dry place, away from heat and light.

1/2 cup Bonedust Seasoning (p. 22)
1/2 cup freshly ground black pepper
1 cup garlic powder
1 tbsp cayenne pepper
1/4 cup kosher salt
1 tbsp freshly ground white pepper
2 cups brown sugar, firmly packed

Makes about 4 cups

SWEET RIB RUB

Sweet 'n' spicy — the best mix for ribs!

In a small bowl, combine all ingredients. Store in an airtight container in a cool, dry place, away from heat and light.

1/2 cup brown sugar, firmly packed
1/4 cup kosher salt
1/4 cup dehydrated garlic flakes
2 tbsp coarsely ground black pepper
1 tbsp red pepper flakes
1 tbsp ground coriander
2 tsp ground ginger
1 tsp hot mustard powder
1 tsp powdered orange drink mix
1/2 tsp cayenne pepper

Makes about 1 1/2 cups

FIERY AND FLAVORFUL: USING HOT CHILIS AND FRESH HERBS

Chili peppers and fresh herbs are key ingredients in many of my pastes and marinades. Chilis add the spicy hit that is so key to great barbecue, while having a variety of fresh herbs on hand really allows you to get flavorful with your food.

Handle hot chili peppers with care. It's best to wear a pair of latex gloves when chopping, since 90 per cent of the "heat" is located in the seeds and the white ribs and membranes. Be very careful not to touch your face or rub your eyes afterward: Capsaicin, the compound that makes peppers hot, can be painfully irritating.

When buying fresh herbs, the rule of thumb is to clean, trim and chop all at once, instead of cleaning and chopping a small handful each time you cook. Rather than letting leftover herbs rot, the prepped herbs can be kept in a resealable plastic bag in the fridge and used as needed. Chopped fresh herbs can also be frozen.

I use fresh herb mixtures — usually a combination of three or four herbs — in many of my recipes. My favorite herb blends are:
★ Parsley, sage, rosemary and thyme (great for meat and poultry)
★ Parsley, dill and chives (great for fish and vegetables)
★ Coriander, flat-leaf parsley and Thai basil (great for meat, poultry and fish)
★ Tarragon, parsley, oregano and thyme (great for poultry and fish)

HAVING A VARIETY OF FRESH HERBS ON HAND REALLY ALLOWS YOU TO GET FLAVORFUL WITH YOUR FOOD.

SMOKED SALT STEAK RUB

Savory and smoky, this rub is all that a great steak needs.

Special equipment: Smoker

Smoked Salt
2 cups coarsely ground sea salt

Rub
1/2 cup smoked salt
1 tbsp cracked black peppercorns
2 tbsp garlic powder
1 tbsp crushed red pepper flakes
2 tsp sugar
1 tbsp dried basil
1 tsp cumin seeds
1 tsp mustard seeds

Makes about 1 1/2 cups

To prepare the Smoked Salt: Spread an even layer of sea salt onto a foil-lined smoke rack. Place rack in a preheated 125°F smoker and smoke for 2–3 hours, or until salt is a smoky brown color. Transfer to a container and let cool. Cover and store in a cool, dry place, away from heat and light.

To prepare the Rub: In a small bowl, combine 1/2 cup smoked salt, pepper, garlic powder, pepper flakes, sugar and basil; mix well and set aside. In a heavy saucepan over medium heat, toast cumin and mustard seeds for about 1 minute, or until seeds are golden brown. Remove from heat and let cool. Add toasted seeds to smoked salt mixture; mix well to combine. Store in an airtight container in a cool, dry place, away from heat and light.

F@$#'N JERK RUB

Rub this jerk on pork, chicken and fish. Note that ground habanero pepper can be purchased through the Internet or at specialty food shops — add slightly more or less, to adjust the heat to your taste.

2 tbsp onion powder
2 tbsp ground allspice
1 tbsp brown sugar, firmly packed
1 tbsp freshly ground black pepper
1 tbsp garlic salt
2 tbsp cayenne pepper
2 tbsp dehydrated chives
1 tbsp ground habanero chili pepper
1 tbsp kosher salt
1 tsp mustard powder
1/2 tsp ground nutmeg
1/4 tsp ground cinnamon

Makes about 1/2 cup

In a small bowl, combine all ingredients; mix well. Store in an airtight container in a cool, dry place, away from heat and light.

Tips for using marinades:
Different foods will need to marinate for specific lengths of time:

★ Fish and seafood — 20 minutes
★ 4 to 6 oz portions of poultry — up to 4 hours
★ Whole birds — up to 24 hours
★ Beef, pork, lamb — 4–8 hours
★ Tougher cuts of meat such as brisket or flank steak — 24–48 hours, or up to 2–3 days

HERBED SEA SALT RUB

This simple rub, with lots of fresh herbs, is terrific on beef, veal, lamb and chicken.

In a small bowl, combine all ingredients; mix well. Store in an airtight container in the refrigerator for up to 1 week.

1/2 cup coarsely ground sea salt
1 tbsp chopped fresh chives
1 tbsp chopped fresh thyme
1 tbsp chopped flat-leaf parsley
1 tsp freshly ground black pepper

Makes about 3/4 cup

BONEDUST BURN BBQ PASTE

Rub this fiery paste onto your favorite cut of meat or steak before grilling. Feel the burn, baby, feel the burn!

In a small bowl, combine all ingredients. Mix well to form a paste. Store in an airtight container in the refrigerator for up to 1 week.

2 tbsp Bonedust Seasoning (p. 22)
2 canned chipotle peppers, minced
2 Scotch bonnet peppers, minced
2 tbsp sambal oelek chili sauce
2 cloves garlic, minced
1 green onion, minced
2 tbsp chopped flat-leaf parsley
2 tbsp extra-virgin olive oil
1 tsp chili oil (optional)

Makes about 1/2 cup

Bonedust Burn BBQ Paste

ESPRESSO BLAST PASTE

1/2 cup espresso coffee beans
6 cloves garlic, minced
1/2 cup mixed chopped fresh herbs
(flat-leaf parsley, coriander,
sage, thyme)
1/4 cup cracked black peppercorns
1/4 cup extra-virgin olive oil
2 tbsp molasses
2 tbsp balsamic vinegar
1 tbsp brown sugar, firmly packed
Salt

Makes about 2 cups

Crushed espresso beans add a great roasted flavor to this seasoning mix. Rub some on your favorite thick, juicy steak... Oh, baby!

If you don't have a coffee grinder, crush the coffee beans by spreading them on a baking tray lined with parchment paper, then use a heavy-bottomed frying pan to crush. Transfer crushed beans to a medium bowl and add remaining ingredients. Store, refrigerated, in a sealed container for up to 2 weeks.

SESAME GINGER PASTE

1/4 cup chopped fresh Thai basil
1/4 cup chopped fresh coriander
3 green onions, finely chopped
2 Thai chili peppers, finely chopped
4 tbsp grated fresh ginger
3 tbsp sesame seeds
2 tbsp soy sauce
2 tbsp rice wine vinegar
2 tsp kosher salt
1 tsp coarsely ground black pepper
1 tsp sesame oil

Makes about 1 1/2 cups

A paste with Asian zest, this is great on richly flavored fish such as salmon and swordfish.

In a medium bowl, combine all ingredients; mix well. Store in an airtight container in the refrigerator for up to 1 week.

MARGARITA PASTE

1/4 cup fresh lime juice
1/2 bunch chopped fresh coriander
2 jalapeño peppers, seeded
and minced
2 large cloves garlic, minced
2 tbsp extra-virgin olive oil
2 tbsp kosher salt
1 tbsp cracked black peppercorns
1 tsp grated lime zest
1 tsp prepared yellow mustard
1 tsp brown sugar, firmly packed

Makes about 1 cup

Rub this lime-flavored paste onto your favorite cut of meat.

In a small bowl, combine all ingredients; mix well to form a paste. Store in an airtight container in the refrigerator for up to 1 week.

CHARDONNAY HERB MARINADE

Use this marinade with chicken or turkey, fish or shellfish, pork or beef. It also doubles as a great dressing for grilled vegetables and salads.

In a large bowl, combine all ingredients; mix well. Store in an airtight container in the refrigerator for up to 1 week.

4 cloves minced garlic
1 green onion, chopped
1 red chili pepper, seeded and minced
2 cups Chardonnay
1/2 cup mixed chopped fresh herbs (Thai basil, flat-leaf parsley, thyme and coriander)
1/2 cup freshly squeezed orange juice
3 tbsp extra-virgin olive oil
2 tbsp grain mustard
2 tbsp rice wine vinegar
1 tsp grated fresh ginger
1 tsp coarsely ground black pepper

Makes about 3 cups

HOT BBQ FISH DRIZZLE MARINADE

This drizzle adds more than a little zip to your grilled seafood. It's also great on grilled chicken and steaks.

In a small bowl, combine all ingredients; mix well. Store in an airtight container in the refrigerator for up to 1 week.

1 habanero chili pepper, seeded and minced
1/4 cup Sriracha hot chili sauce
1/4 cup sambal oelek chili sauce
1/4 cup rice vinegar
2 tbsp Vietnamese fish sauce
1 tbsp chili oil

Makes almost 1 cup

MI PHO #1 MARINADE

I have become a regular at a local Vietnamese place called Mi Pho #1, which makes the best noodle soup in Toronto. This marinade was inspired by the hot-sour-salty-sweet flavors of the soup.

In a small bowl, combine all ingredients; mix well. Store in an airtight container in the refrigerator for up to 1 week.

2 green onions, finely chopped
1 Thai chili, seeded and minced
1/2 bunch Thai basil, finely chopped
1/2 cup good-quality soy sauce
2 tbsp hoisin sauce
1 tbsp sambal oelek chili sauce
1 tbsp Sriracha chili sauce
1 tbsp brown sugar, firmly packed
1 tbsp extra-virgin olive oil
1 tsp red wine vinegar
1/2 tsp Thai fish sauce
Juice of 1 lime

Makes about 1 cup

JACK AND A COKE MARINADE

1 can Coca-Cola
4 cloves garlic, minced
2 oz Jack Daniel's whiskey
2 tbsp extra-virgin olive oil
2 tbsp Worcestershire sauce
Dash hot pepper sauce
1 tbsp chopped flat-leaf parsley
1 tbsp chopped fresh sage
Pinch ground cinnamon

Makes about 1 1/2 cups

This sweet marinade, with just a hit of spice, is great for beef short ribs, brisket and rib steaks.

In a medium bowl, combine all ingredients; mix well. Store in an airtight container in the refrigerator for up to 1 week.

CABERNET MARINADE

2 cups Cabernet Sauvignon
6 cloves garlic, minced
1 tbsp coarsely ground black pepper
2 tbsp mixed chopped fresh herbs (rosemary, thyme, flat-leaf parsley)
2 tbsp extra-virgin olive oil
1 tbsp balsamic vinegar
1 tsp Worcestershire sauce

Makes about 2 1/2 cups

Use as a marinade for chicken, fish, shellfish, pork or beef.

In a medium bowl, combine all ingredients; mix well. Store in an airtight container in the refrigerator for up to 1 week.

LUTHER'S SHEEP DIP MARINADE

2 jalapeño peppers, seeded and diced
2 bay leaves
1 large yellow onion, minced
2 cups apple cider vinegar
1 (12 oz) bottle beer (preferably dark ale)
1/4 cup balsamic vinegar
1/4 cup Worcestershire sauce
1/4 cup Bonedust Seasoning (p. 22)
2 tbsp freshly ground black pepper
1 tbsp salt

Makes about 3 1/2 cups

This is my good buddy and fellow chef Luther's old family recipe. Originally, it was used to marinate lamb, but it is great with any meat or poultry.

In a large bowl, combine all ingredients; mix well. Store in an airtight container in the refrigerator for up to 1 week.

PINEAPPLE RUM MARINADE

A great marinade for shellfish, chicken and pork. The Scotch bonnet pepper adds a lot of heat. Use a milder chili, if you prefer.

In a medium bowl, combine all ingredients; mix well. Store in an airtight container in the refrigerator for up to 1 week.

4 cloves garlic, minced
1 green onion, minced
1 Scotch bonnet pepper, seeded and minced
1/2 bunch fresh coriander, chopped
1 cup pineapple juice
1/2 cup dark rum
2 tbsp extra-virgin olive oil
1 tsp salt
1 tsp cracked black peppercorns

Makes about 2 cups

BIG YELLA MUSTARD MARINADE

I remember making beef short ribs with my dad, using a version of this mustard marinade. It rocks!

In a large bowl, combine all ingredients with 1/4 cup water; mix well. Store in an airtight container in the refrigerator for up to 1 week.

4 cloves garlic, minced
2 green onions, minced
1 small onion, diced
2 cups prepared yellow mustard
1 cup honey brown lager
1 oz Southern Comfort
2 tbsp white vinegar
2 tbsp extra-virgin olive oil
1 tbsp chopped fresh sage
1 tsp black mustard seeds, toasted
1 tsp red pepper flakes

Makes about 3 1/2 cups

Big Yella Mustard Marinade

GRILL-ROASTED GARLIC MARINADE

When I was traveling in Gilroy, California, the sweet smell of garlic in the air inspired this incredibly delicious grill-roasted garlic marinade.

In a food processor, purée the Grill-Roasted Garlic until smooth. In a medium bowl, combine the puréed garlic and all remaining ingredients; mix well. Store in an airtight container in the refrigerator for up to 1 week.

2 heads Grill-Roasted Garlic (p. 219)
1 cup tomato juice
1/2 cup white balsamic vinegar
1/4 cup chopped fresh basil
1/4 cup chopped fresh thyme
1/4 cup chopped fresh oregano
1/4 cup chopped flat-leaf parsley
2 tbsp extra-virgin olive oil
1 tsp kosher salt
1 tsp cracked black peppercorns
1 tsp hot pepper flakes

Makes about 2 cups

BLOODY CAESAR MARINADE

Ribs, steaks and chicken taste unbelievably good with this spicy marinade. Any pepper-flavored vodka will do.

In a medium bowl, combine all ingredients; mix well. Store in an airtight container in the refrigerator for up to 1 week.

1 green onion, minced
2 cups Clamato juice
1/2 cup Inferno Pepper Pot Vodka
2 tbsp extra-virgin olive oil
1 tbsp chopped fresh dill
1 tbsp Worcestershire sauce
1 tbsp prepared horseradish
2 tsp celery salt
1 tsp hot pepper sauce
1 tsp kosher salt
1 tsp cracked black peppercorns

Makes about 3 cups

MOJO MARINADE

This tangy citrus marinade is a recipe from ex–Toronto Blue Jays manager Carlos Tosca. It is great on chicken or fish.

In a large bowl, combine all ingredients; mix well. Store in an airtight container in the refrigerator for up to 1 week.

1 head fresh garlic, finely minced
1 cup Seville orange juice (or 1/2 cup each of orange juice and lime juice)
1/4 cup fresh lemon juice
1/4 cup vegetable oil
3 tbsp chopped fresh oregano
1 tsp salt
1/2 tsp ground cumin
Freshly ground black pepper

Makes about 1 1/2 cups

Bloody Caesar Marinade

STARTERS

WHEN I GO out to eat I much prefer to sample a variety of appetizers, rather than just focusing on a main course. Appetizers allow you to graze on many of the chef's goods, and serving grilled and smoked appetizers is also a great way to entertain. I think starters are one of the best ways to let your grillin' imagination run wild. As either appetizers, hors d'oeuvres or snacks, these tasty treats allow for lots of variety and experimentation. From chicken "lollipops" and Bloody Caesar Shrimp to wings and Planked Figs with Goat Cheese and Pancetta, these dishes are sure to get your guests excited — and long before the main event.

My recommendation is to prepare appetizers well ahead of time. Many of these recipes allow you to do most of the prep work in advance, or they can even be finished in advance and reheated. Once your guests arrive, just throw the prepped food on the grill and feed the hungry — they will be amazingly grateful. Remember: Make it fun and they will come.

PLANKED FIGS WITH GOAT CHEESE AND PANCETTA

Special equipment: 1 untreated cedar plank, soaked in cold water for 1 hour

4 slices pancetta
1/2 cup crème de cassis liqueur
1 tbsp cracked black peppercorns
12 medium to large black or green figs, halved lengthwise
1 cup crumbled goat cheese
1/2 cup crumbled Stilton cheese
1 green onion, chopped
1 tbsp chopped fresh sage
Salt and freshly ground black pepper
Drizzle of honey

Serves 8 to 12

Fresh figs are especially good for this dish, but you can substitute dried figs in a pinch.

Preheat grill to medium-high (about 400°F). Grill pancetta until crisp, about 2–3 minutes. Remove from heat and set aside.

Pour crème de cassis into a large, shallow dish. Sprinkle with peppercorns. Place figs, cut side down, onto cassis-and-pepper mixture. Marinate for 20 minutes.

Meanwhile, in a bowl, combine goat cheese, Stilton, green onion and sage. Season with salt and pepper and set aside.

Remove figs from marinade and place, cut side down, on cedar plank. Transfer plank to grill, close lid and plank-bake for 10–12 minutes, or until figs are soft and heated through. Reduce grill temperature to low. Turn figs over and spoon goat cheese mixture onto them. Top with grilled pancetta, close lid and continue to bake until cheese is hot and gooey, about 3–5 minutes.

Remove planked figs from grill to a platter and serve immediately, drizzled with honey.

WISCONSIN CHEESE SPREAD

1 cup cream cheese
1/2 cup mayonnaise
2 cups shredded sharp cheddar cheese
1 to 2 tsp Bonedust Seasoning (p. 22)
1 tbsp mixed chopped fresh herbs (parsley, chives, thyme, oregano)

Makes about 4 cups

While traveling through Wisconsin one summer, I came across a cheese shop that used blocks of cheese to depict military artifacts such as hand grenades and F-18 fighter jets. It was a wild place, and on top of all that it had the most awesome cheese spread. This is my version of what I ate in Wisconsin.

In a food processor, combine cream cheese, mayonnaise and 3 tbsp water until smooth. Add cheddar cheese, Bonedust Seasoning and herbs; continue processing until smooth. (If the mixture is too thick, add 1–2 tbsp hot water.) Spread cheese on fresh bread, garlic bread, crackers, toast or muffins.

Previous spread: BBQ Chicken Lollipops
Opposite: Grilled figs and
wheels of brie ready for planking

STILTON-STUFFED CEDAR-PLANKED BRIE WITH BLACKCURRANT RELISH

Why do this? Why not! Bacon and blue cheese can only make a simple brie taste fantastic.

To prepare the Blackcurrant Relish: In a medium saucepan over medium heat, combine all ingredients. Cover with cold water. Slowly bring mixture to a rolling boil. Reduce heat to low, cover and simmer for 15 minutes, stirring occasionally, until thickened. Remove from heat and set aside until needed.

To prepare the Stilton-Stuffed Cedar-Planked Brie: Preheat grill to high (about 500°F). Using a small paring knife, scoop out a 1/2-in-deep well in the center of each wheel of Brie, leaving about a 1/4-in rim. Place half the scooped-out cheese in a mixing bowl and either eat the remaining scooped-out cheese or store in the refrigerator for another day. In the bowl with the Brie, add Stilton, bacon, onion, parsley and cracked black peppercorns. Mix well to incorporate. Pack cheese mixture into the wells in the center of both wheels of Brie and place on plank, pressing lightly to secure. Top with Blackcurrant Relish.

Transfer plank to grill, close lid and plank-bake for 10–15 minutes, or until Brie softens, bulges and turns golden.

Remove Brie-topped plank from grill and place on another (unused) plank in the center of the table. Serve with a fresh baguette and lots of napkins.

Special equipment: 1 untreated cedar plank, soaked in cold water for 1 hour

Blackcurrant Relish
2 cups blackcurrants
3/4 cup sugar
1 tsp cracked black peppercorns
1/4 tsp ground nutmeg
1 sprig savory
1/2 cinnamon stick

Stilton-Stuffed Cedar-Planked Brie
2 (125 g) wheels Brie cheese
1 cup crumbled Stilton cheese
1/4 cup diced Triple-Smoked Bacon (p. 238)
2 green onions, thinly sliced
1 tsp chopped fresh flat-leaf parsley
1 tsp cracked black peppercorns
1/4 cup Blackcurrant Relish

Serves 8 to 10

GRILL-BAKED HAVARTI CHEESE WITH PASSION FRUIT TOPPING

Passion fruit is sweet and tart and goes really well with this gooey grilled Havarti cheese.

Passion Fruit Topping

1/4 cup passion fruit pulp
1/2 cup passion fruit juice
1/4 cup passion fruit preserves
2 oz dark rum
1 tbsp grated fresh ginger
Juice of 1 lime
Salt and freshly ground black pepper

4 passion fruit
1 green onion, finely chopped
1 cup cubed Havarti cheese
1/4 cup finely chopped fresh coriander
2 tbsp brown sugar, firmly packed

Serves 4

To prepare the Passion Fruit Topping: In a small bowl, combine passion fruit, juice, preserves, rum, ginger and lime juice. Mix well and season with salt and pepper.

Slice base of each passion fruit so that it will stand evenly on grill. Slice off tops and reserve. Spoon out passion fruit pulp, leaving about 1/2 inch on bottom and sides. Eat the scooped-out pulp, or discard.

Preheat grill to medium (400°F). In another bowl, combine remaining ingredients; mix well to combine. Liberally stuff this mixture into hollowed-out passion fruit and cover with reserved tops. Reduce grill temperature to low and place stuffed fruit onto grill. Grill-bake with lid closed until cheese is soft and bubbling, about 10–12 minutes. Halfway through grilling time, remove tops and spoon Passion Fruit Topping over fruit. Return tops to fruit, cover and continue grilling until fully baked. When done, remove fruit from grill to a platter and serve.

BBQ BRISKET DIP

Barbecued brisket is tender and delicious. So is this dip.

3 cups shredded and coarsely chopped BBQ Beef Brisket (p. 122)
4 green onions, sliced
1 cup chopped grilled white onions
1 tbsp mixed chopped herbs (p. 26)
1 tbsp hot pepper sauce
1/2 cup barbecue sauce
1/2 cup ranch dressing
1/2 cup sour cream
1 (8 oz) pkg softened cream cheese
1 large egg
1/2 cup grated Parmesan cheese
1 cup shredded mozzarella cheese

Serves 4 to 8

In a large bowl, combine brisket, green onion, grilled onions and fresh herbs. Add hot sauce and barbecue sauce; mix and set aside.

In a separate bowl, combine ranch dressing, sour cream, cream cheese and egg. Whisk together until smooth. Add 1/4 cup Parmesan cheese and all the mozzarella; whisk until well incorporated.

Preheat grill to medium (about 350°F). Place brisket mixture in an oven- or grill-proof pan or casserole dish. Spread cream cheese mixture evenly over top. Sprinkle with remaining 1/4 cup Parmesan cheese. Transfer brisket dip to grill, close lid and bake for 10–15 minutes, or until brisket is hot and cheese topping is golden brown and bubbling. Serve immediately with grilled garlic bread.

Stuffed Portobello Mushrooms

STUFFED PORTOBELLO MUSHROOMS

You may have some extra grilled mushroom-and-cheese mixture leftover from this recipe. If you do, just freeze it for later use as a spread for grill-toasted garlic bread.

In a large bowl, soak portobello mushrooms in hot water, about 20 minutes. Meanwhile, in a small bowl, combine breadcrumbs and Parmesan cheese and set aside.

Preheat grill to medium (about 350°F). Remove portobello mushrooms from water and drain. Transfer to a large bowl with oyster mushrooms, cremini mushrooms and onion, and toss with 1/4 cup oil, 2 tbsp vinegar and steak spice. Transfer to a grill basket and grill mushrooms and onions until lightly charred and tender, about 10–12 minutes.

Remove vegetables from grill and let cool. Pick 4 of the best-looking portobello mushroom caps and set aside. On the bias, thinly slice remaining portobellos — each cap should yield 8 slices — and set aside. Thinly slice grilled onions and oyster and cremini mushrooms and place in a bowl. Add cream cheese, herbs and mozzarella, and mix well; season with a splash of vinegar, and salt and pepper to taste.

Place 1 ball of bocconcini cheese on the center of each of the 4 reserved portobello caps. Divide grilled mushroom-and-cheese mixture into 4 equal parts and mound over top of bocconcini balls. Fan 8 slices of grilled portobello mushroom over the top of each mound and cover with reserved breadcrumb mixture. Transfer stuffed portobello caps onto a medium-low grill (about 300° to 325°F) and grill for 8–12 minutes, or until lightly charred and the cheese is hot and gooey. Serve immediately.

8 portobello mushroom caps
4 cups hot water
1/4 cup fresh breadcrumbs
1/4 cup Parmesan cheese
1/2 lb large oyster mushrooms
1/2 lb cremini mushrooms
1 large onion, quartered
1/4 cup + 1/4 cup extra-virgin olive oil
2 tbsp + 2 tbsp balsamic vinegar
2 tbsp Amazing Steak Spice (p. 23)
1/2 cup softened cream cheese
2 tbsp mixed chopped fresh herbs (p. 26)
2 cups shredded mozzarella cheese
4 small balls bocconcini cheese
Salt and freshly ground black pepper

Serves 8

GET OUTSIDE

Barbecuing is not only the best way to cook just about anything, it's also the perfect excuse to throw an outdoor, backyard party. Cooking on the grill is inclusive: Anyone can help with chopping up simple ingredients or take over flipping burgers or steaks, and everyone wants to take a peek inside a smokin' grill.

Whether fancy or casual, an outdoor bash, with lots of great food, cold drinks and good friends, is the perfect way to celebrate. And the best part is, cooking up good things on the grill allows you to take part, rather than be stuck in the kitchen!

Here are my tips on outdoor entertaining:

★ KISS — Keep it simple, sexy! Relax, have fun. Cook food you know.
★ Preparation is key. Do as much as you can ahead of time.
★ Get your guests involved. Give them a pair of tongs or set them to chopping. Everyone enjoys food they've had a hand in preparing.
★ Hire us as your caterer! Give us a call at 416-Go-Away and let us do the work!
★ Have lots of cold beverages on hand: juice, pop and lots of water, as well as alcoholic drinks, if you like. Speaking of which...

Here is my tip for the quickest way to chill beer:

★ Fill an ice tub with 24 beers
★ Top with 10 lb of ice
★ Pour in a couple of gallons cold water (use your garden hose)
★ Now add 2 cups of salt
★ Wait 8 to 10 minutes and ya got cold beer

BARBECUE BRINGS PEOPLE TOGETHER. JUST TRY TO KEEP THEM AWAY WHEN YOU'RE PLANKING SOMETHING DELICIOUS.

BEEF JERKY

Tangy Mi Pho #1 Marinade gives classic jerky a kick.

Special equipment: Smoker

1 lb beef eye of round, chilled
2 cups Mi Pho #1 Marinade (p. 31)
1/4 cup brown sugar, firmly packed
2 tbsp Amazing Steak Spice (p. 23)

Serves a whole bunch of protein-munching BBQ fanatics

Chill beef in freezer for 15 minutes. Using a carving knife or meat slicer, slice into 1/4-inch-thin slices across the grain.

In a medium bowl, combine Mi Pho #1 Marinade and brown sugar. Dip each slice of beef into marinade and lay in a large casserole dish. Pour remaining marinade over top. Cover and refrigerate for 3–4 days, turning meat daily.

Prepare barbecue smoker, following the manufacturer's instructions, for smoking at approximately 150°F. Remove beef from marinade, discarding leftover liquid. Lightly pat each beef slice with paper towel to remove excess marinade. Arrange slices in a single layer on wire smoker rack. Place a bowl of ice in the smoker to keep the smoke cool. Smoke jerky for 6–8 hours, or until beef is lightly smoked and dry, replenishing ice as needed.

Remove jerky from smoker and cool completely. Serve immediately, or transfer to an airtight container and refrigerate for up to 6 weeks.

DRUNKEN GOLD MINER WINGS

The honey-mustard-and-ground-nut coating makes eating these wings a sticky, crunchy experience.

In a small bowl, combine honey, mustard and butter. Mix well and set aside.

Preheat grill to medium (about 350°F). Trim wing tips from wings and cut through the joint to separate winglets from drumettes. Using a Cajun injector, inject each wing piece with a little Yukon Jack whisky. In a large bowl, toss injected wings with Sweet Rib Rub. Transfer to a grill basket and grill wings for 10–12 minutes, each side, turning every 5–6 minutes, or until fully cooked, golden brown and crisp.

When cooked, carefully remove wings from grill basket and transfer to a big bowl. Toss with honey-mustard mixture. Add ground beer nuts, toss again and serve.

Special equipment: Cajun injector

1/4 cup honey
2 tbsp Dijon mustard
2 tbsp butter
3 lb jumbo chicken wings (about 36)
8 oz Yukon Jack whisky
4 tbsp Sweet Rib Rub (p. 25)
3/4 cup ground beer nuts

Serves 4 to 8

BBQ CHICKEN LOLLIPOPS

These spicy drumettes are lollipops for grown-ups (see photo on p. 36).

Using a sharp knife, slice around the knuckle of each drumette to loosen the skin and meat from the bone. Scrape and push the meat down the length of the bone, forming a lollipop-like ball of chicken at the end. Place chicken "lollipops" in a large bowl and toss with Bayou Bite Cajun Seasoning and oil. Set aside.

Preheat grill to medium (about 350°F). Grill chicken lollipops for 10–12 minutes, turning every 5–6 minutes, until fully cooked, golden brown and crisp. Transfer to a bowl and toss with barbecue sauce, lemon juice, butter, fresh herbs and hot sauce. Serve immediately with your favorite dip.

2 lb chicken drumettes (about 24 pieces)
2 tbsp Bayou Bite Cajun Seasoning (p. 23)
2 tbsp vegetable oil
1/2 cup spicy barbecue sauce
1 tbsp fresh lemon juice
3 tbsp butter
1/4 cup mixed chopped fresh herbs (p. 26)
Dash or two hot pepper sauce

Serves 4

CHICKEN AND PEPPER JACK TORTILLA TORTE

This cheesy grilled tortilla torte is easy and delicious.

Special equipment: Cajun injector

3 (6 oz) chicken breasts, grilled
and sliced
2 oz Tequila Anejo
1 tbsp Margarita Paste (p. 30)
1 large red bell pepper
1 cubanelle pepper
1 medium sweet white onion
2 tbsp extra-virgin olive oil
Salt and freshly ground black pepper
1/2 cup softened cream cheese
1 cup grated pepper Jack cheese
2 cups grated cheddar cheese
1/4 cup ranch dressing
2 tbsp fresh breadcrumbs
2 jalapeño peppers, seeded and diced
2 tbsp chopped fresh coriander
Salt and freshly ground black pepper
5 (8 in) flour tortillas
2 tbsp extra-virgin olive oil, for
grilling the torte

Serves 8

Preheat grill to medium-high (about 400°F). Using a Cajun injector, inject each chicken breast with tequila. Rub injected chicken breasts with Margarita Paste, ensuring all breasts are completely coated. Season peppers and onion with oil, salt and pepper. Grill peppers and onion, turning occasionally, for 3–4 minutes, or until skins begin to blister and onion is lightly charred. Remove from grill and cool slightly before thinly slicing. Set aside in a large bowl.

Place chicken breasts on grill, and grill for 8–12 minutes, turning once, until fully cooked. Remove chicken breasts from heat and cool slightly before slicing thinly. Add to vegetables in bowl, and set aside.

In another bowl, combine cream cheese, pepper Jack cheese, cheddar cheese, ranch dressing, breadcrumbs, jalapeño peppers and coriander; mix well. Add cream cheese mixture to vegetables and chicken and combine. Season with salt and pepper to taste.

To assemble the torte, place a tortilla in the bottom of a 7-in springform pan. Spread evenly with a quarter of the chicken-cheese mixture. Top with another tortilla and spread with an even layer of chicken-cheese mixture. Repeat procedure with remaining tortillas and chicken-cheese mixture. When done, wrap torte tightly with plastic wrap and place a heavy weight on top. Refrigerate for 6–8 hours or overnight, until set.

Preheat grill to medium-high (about 400°F). Remove weight, plastic wrap and pan. Cut torte into 8 wedges and bake on foil-lined grill for 3–4 minutes, each side, or until heated through and filling is gooey. Serve with lots of salsa and guacamole.

24-HOUR JACK DANIEL'S SALMON GRAVLAX

When cold smoking, I like to run a hook through the tail section of the salmon to hang it in the smoker. This ensures an even smoke and allows any excess fat to drip off the fish.

Place salmon, skin side down, on a 2-in-deep baking sheet. Rub steak spice into the fish, pressing spices to adhere. Spread the dill evenly over the salmon. Drizzle 1/2 oz Jack Daniel's over the salmon and dill.

    In a small bowl, combine salt and brown sugar. Sprinkle the salt-and-sugar mixture evenly over the salmon, making sure to cover the entire fish. Drizzle remaining 1/2 oz Jack Daniel's over salt-and-sugar mixture. Cover with plastic wrap and place another baking sheet over top; weight it with a heavy tin or brick. Refrigerate for 24 hours.

    When fully cured, remove salmon from refrigerator. Unwrap and scrape away salt, sugar and dill mixture. Briefly rinse under cold water to remove excess cure and pat dry with paper towel.

    Prepare smoker for cold smoking (about 125°F), following manufacturer's instructions. Cold smoke salmon gravlax for 3 hours.

    Remove from smoker and serve, or transfer to an airtight container and refrigerate for up to 1 week — or freeze for up to 2 months.

Special equipment: Smoker

1 (1/2 to 2 lb) boneless Atlantic salmon fillet, skin on and scaled
2 tbsp Amazing Steak Spice (p. 23)
1 bunch fresh dill, washed
1 oz Jack Daniel's whiskey
3/4 cup kosher salt
3/4 cup brown sugar, firmly packed

Serves 8 to 10

BLOODY CAESAR SHRIMP

If you can't find infused vodka at your local liquor store, substitute regular vodka.

Using a Cajun injector, inject shrimp with vodka. In a large bowl, add Bayou Bite Cajun Seasoning to shrimp and toss to coat evenly. Thread 6 shrimp onto each skewer and spray with nonstick cooking spray. Arrange kebabs in a shallow glass dish. Pour Bloody Caesar Marinade over kebabs. Marinate, covered and refrigerated, for 15–20 minutes, turning once.

    Preheat grill to medium-high (about 375° to 400°F). Remove kebabs from dish and discard liquid. Grill kebabs for 1–2 minutes, each side, basting liberally with melted butter, until fully cooked and lightly charred.

    Remove shrimp kebabs from grill and sprinkle with dill and a little melted butter. Serve immediately.

Special equipment: Cajun injector
4 bamboo skewers, presoaked in water for 1 hour

1 1/2 lb shrimp (about 24), peeled and deveined — tails on
4 oz Inferno Pepper Pot Vodka
2 tbsp Bayou Bite Cajun Seasoning (p. 23)
1 1/2 cups Bloody Caesar Marinade (p. 35)
6 tbsp melted butter
1 tbsp chopped fresh dill

Serves 4 to 8

LAMB SPIEDINI WITH CORIANDER AND MINT PESTO

Spiedini **is an Italian term for grilled kebabs. Tender lamb goes perfectly with Coriander and Mint Pesto.**

Cut lamb shoulder into 1/2-in cubes, trimming the meat. Thread 8 cubes of lamb onto each skewer and place in a shallow pan. Pour Grill-Roasted Garlic Marinade over lamb, cover and marinate in refrigerator for 24 hours.

To prepare the Coriander and Mint Pesto: In a food processor, pulse mint, coriander, garlic, ginger and nuts. With the machine running, add oil in a steady stream until liquid emulsifies. Season with salt and pepper to taste and set aside.

Remove lamb skewers from marinade, discarding any excess liquid, and season with kosher salt and cracked peppercorns.

Prepare charcoal grill, according to manufacturer's instructions. When coals reach the white ash stage, grill spiedini for 2–3 minutes each side, turning once, until fully cooked and lightly charred.

Remove lamb from grill and serve immediately with Coriander and Mint Pesto for dipping.

Special equipment: 24 (8 in) bamboo skewers, presoaked in water for 1 hour

3 lb boneless lamb shoulder
2 cups Grill-Roasted Garlic Marinade (p. 35)

Coriander and Mint Pesto
1/2 bunch fresh mint leaves
1/2 bunch fresh coriander leaves
8 cloves garlic
1 tbsp chopped fresh ginger
1/4 cup ground macadamia nuts, peanuts or almonds
1/2 cup extra-virgin olive oil
Salt and freshly ground black pepper

2 tbsp kosher salt
2 tbsp cracked black peppercorns

Serves 6 to 8

GRILLED CRAB GUACAMOLE DEVILED EGGS

Guaranteed, the best deviled eggs you've ever eaten.

Place eggs in a large pot and cover with cold water. Bring to a boil over high heat. Cover pot and remove from heat. Let stand for 9 minutes. Drain eggs and run under cold water for 10 minutes. Peel eggs, being careful not to break the whites. Cut the eggs in half lengthwise. With a small spoon, carefully remove yolks and place in a bowl. Arrange egg whites on a cookie sheet lined with paper towel and set aside.

Mash yolks with a fork, or press through a fine sieve. In another bowl, mash avocado and combine with crabmeat, mayonnaise, coriander, mustard, lemon juice and yolks. Season with salt and pepper and a dash of cayenne pepper. Spoon mixture into each of the egg whites, piling it high. Wrap a half-slice of bacon around the middle of each stuffed egg, securing with a toothpick.

Preheat grill to medium-high (about 400°F). Place grill topper, holding bacon-wrapped deviled eggs, onto grill and close lid. Grill-roast eggs for 5–8 minutes, or until bacon is hot and crisp. Serve immediately.

12 extra-large eggs
1 avocado, peeled, pitted and mashed
1/2 cup lump crabmeat
1/4 cup mayonnaise
1 tbsp chopped fresh coriander
1 tbsp Dijon mustard
1 tbsp fresh lemon juice
Salt and freshly ground black pepper
Pinch cayenne pepper
12 slices bacon, parcooked until just crisp and cut in half

Makes 24 deviled eggs

STEAK-WRAPPED SHRIMPSICLES WITH HONEY BROWN SUGAR BBQ SAUCE

"Shrimpsicle" is a fancy name for jumbo shrimp that has been wrapped in beef tenderloin and grilled on a skewer, resembling a savory Popsicle when done!

To prepare the Honey Brown Sugar BBQ Sauce: In a bowl, whisk together brown sugar, barbecue sauce, 1/4 bottle of beer, coriander and jalapeño pepper. Season with generous pinch of Bonedust Seasoning and salt and pepper to taste.

Using a Cajun injector or syringe, inject each shrimp with some of the remaining beer; season with Bonedust Seasoning. Set aside.

Preheat grill to medium-high (about 400°F). Freeze beef for 15 minutes before thinly slicing into 1- to 2-oz slices. Wrap each shrimp with 1 or 2 slices of beef, pressing firmly around the middle so the beef adheres. Brush with oil and season each with a pinch of Bonedust Seasoning. Skewer the shrimp onto wooden chopsticks or soaked bamboo skewers.

Grill beef-wrapped shrimp for 3–4 minutes each side, until the shrimp are just cooked through and the beef is lightly charred. Baste with Honey Brown Sugar BBQ sauce and serve immediately.

Special equipment: Cajun injector
16 chopsticks or bamboo skewers, presoaked in water for 1 hour

Honey Brown Sugar BBQ Sauce
1/4 cup brown sugar, firmly packed
1/4 cup gourmet barbecue sauce
1 (12 oz) bottle honey brown lager
1 tbsp chopped fresh coriander
1 jalapeño pepper, minced
Bonedust Seasoning (p. 22)
Salt and freshly ground black pepper

2 lb beef tenderloin
16 jumbo shrimp, peeled and deveined
2 to 3 tbsp vegetable oil
2 to 3 tbsp Bonedust Seasoning (p. 22)

Serves 8

SAVORY GOAT CHEESE AND ONION TOASTS

Perfect as a light appetizer, and perfectly simple.

Preheat grill to medium-high (about 400°F). In a medium bowl, toss quartered onions with steak spice and 2 tbsp oil. Transfer to grill basket and grill for 12–15 minutes, or until tender and lightly charred. Remove from grill and slice.

Melt butter in a heavy sauté pan over medium-high heat. Add grilled onion slices and garlic; stir to coat with butter. Continue cooking, stirring occasionally, for 10–15 minutes, or until onions are a deep golden brown.

Brush cut sides of baguette with remaining oil and season with extra steak spice. Transfer to grill and lightly toast for 2–3 minutes. Remove from grill and spread goat cheese and onions on each cut side of toasted baguette. Top with crumbled feta cheese, chives and salt and pepper to taste. Place baguette halves on top rack of grill and heat for 4–5 minutes, or until cheese has melted. Slice baguette halves into 4 to 6 pieces and serve immediately.

1 large Spanish onion, quartered
1 large red onion, quartered
2 tsp Amazing Steak Spice (p. 23)
2 tbsp + 2 tbsp extra-virgin olive oil
2 tbsp butter
4 cloves garlic, minced
1 large French baguette, cut in half lengthwise
1 cup softened goat cheese
1/2 cup crumbled feta cheese
2 tbsp chopped fresh chives
Salt and freshly ground black pepper

Serves 4 to 6

STUFFED JALAPEÑO PEPPERS

These cheesy stuffed peppers are delicious, and just spicy enough.

1/2 cup fresh breadcrumbs
1/4 cup grated Parmesan cheese
24 jalapeño peppers (about 1-in in diameter and 3-in long)
1 cup shredded Beer-Can Chicken (p. 168) or plain roasted chicken
1 cup cream cheese, softened
1 cup shredded mozzarella cheese
2 green onions, chopped
1/4 cup chopped fresh coriander
1/2 cup diced red onion
1 tbsp Bonedust Seasoning (p. 22)
Salt and freshly ground black pepper
Dash hot pepper sauce
8 slices bacon, parcooked and cut into 3 pieces

Serves 8 to 12

In a small bowl, combine breadcrumbs and Parmesan cheese.

Preheat grill to medium (about 350° F). Slice tops off jalapeños and remove seeds and membranes. Be careful not to cut holes in the peppers. Set aside.

In a large bowl, combine remaining ingredients, except bacon. Mix well. Transfer mixture to a large, resealable plastic bag. Carefully snip off 1/2-in of one corner of the bag on a diagonal to form a piping bag. Pipe filling into the cavity of each pepper. Press lightly to ensure that pepper is full. Dip top of stuffed jalapeño into breadcrumb mixture, ensuring that filling is completely covered with mixture. Place one piece of bacon over top of stuffed jalapeño and skewer both ends of bacon through sides of pepper with a toothpick to secure. Set peppers onto a foil-lined baking sheet. Transfer to grill, close lid and grill-bake for 15–20 minutes or until outsides of peppers begin to blister, filling is hot and bubbling, and bacon is crisp.

Remove tray from grill and cool for 2–4 minutes before serving.

JO'S MARGARITA LOBSTER TAILS

When I first interviewed my chef Joanne, the only test I put her through was to make lunch. I gave her some ingredients, an hour and a half, and no instructions. This is what she made — it was the beginning of a delicious friendship.

Preheat grill to medium-high (about 400°F). Turn lobster tails upside down, so that the underside is exposed. Using kitchen shears, cut the underside of the tail, where the hard and soft parts of the shell meet. Don't cut through fins of tail. Repeat on other side of tail. Carefully peel the hard outer shell away from the meat, leaving fin portion of the tail intact.

To devein the lobster tail, lay tail on the cutting board. Using a small paring knife, make a shallow incision starting at the fin end of the tail (until a dark-colored vein is exposed), and work your way down to the opposite end. Using your paring knife, cut the vein away from the fin and discard vein. Rinse tail under cold running water. Repeat with all remaining lobster tails.

In a large bowl, combine remaining ingredients; mix well. Reserve 1/4 cup of this marinade, set aside, then place prepared lobster tails in the bowl. Cover with plastic wrap and marinate in refrigerator for 15 minutes.

After marinating, remove lobster from fridge. Insert sharp end of bamboo skewer into flesh end of tail, pushing skewer through until sharp end touches fin. Repeat with remaining lobster tails. Discard used marinade.

Place skewered lobster tails on a well-seasoned grill. Grill each for 3–4 minutes. Turn and cook an additional 3–4 minutes, basting continually with some of the reserved marinade.

Remove and serve immediately with the reserved marinade and wedges of lime.

Special equipment: 6 wooden chopsticks or bamboo skewers, presoaked in water for 1 hour

6 (3 to 4 oz) frozen lobster tails, thawed, peeled and deveined
6 oz lime juice
2 oz tequila
Zest of 1 lime
1 tbsp chopped fresh coriander
1 red bell pepper, finely diced
1 jalapeño pepper, seeded and diced
2 cloves garlic, minced
3 oz extra-virgin olive oil
Sea salt and cracked black peppercorns to taste

Serves 6

REDNECK PULLED PORK CHOWDER

Pulled pork is so good, it deserves to be a soup, too.

8 plum tomatoes

1 large red bell pepper

1 large onion

3 slices smoked bacon, diced

2 tbsp chili oil

3 cloves garlic, minced

3 jalapeño peppers, seeded and diced

1 cup beer

1 cup tomato juice

1 (16 oz) can crushed tomatoes

4 cups Smoked Chicken Stock (p. 261)

2 cups thinly sliced cabbage

3 cups Smoked Pulled Pork (p. 128)

1/2 cup barbecue sauce

2 tbsp Bonedust Seasoning (p. 22)

Salt and freshly ground black pepper

2 tbsp chopped flat-leaf parsley

Serves 8

Preheat grill to high (about 500°F). Grill tomatoes, pepper and onion on grill for 8–10 minutes, until skin is blistered and charred. Remove from grill and set aside to cool. Remove skins from tomatoes and pepper. Coarsely chop tomatoes, pepper and onion and set aside.

In a large pot over medium-high heat, fry bacon in chili oil until just crisp. Add grilled onions, garlic and jalapeños and sauté, stirring, for 5 minutes. Deglaze with beer, by stirring brown bits up from bottom of pot. Add tomato juice, crushed tomatoes and Smoked Chicken Stock. Bring to a boil, stirring occasionally. Add reserved chopped charred tomatoes and pepper and cabbage, and return to a boil. Reduce heat to medium-low and simmer for 15 minutes. Add pulled pork and barbecue sauce, stirring to incorporate, before adding Bonedust Seasoning and salt and pepper to taste. Simmer 15–20 minutes longer. When finished, add parsley and serve, garnished with a dollop of sour cream and croutons.

GREAT WHITE NORTH CLAM CHOWDER

This is New England clam chowder with a BBQ twist.

2 lb steamer clams, rinsed well

1/2 cup + 1 cup lager beer

1 lb peameal bacon

2 tbsp butter

1 cup diced celery (1/2-in dice)

1 cup diced onion (1/2-in dice)

1 cup diced leek (1/2-in dice)

2 cups peeled and diced Yukon Gold potatoes (1/2-in dice)

1 cup diced butternut squash (1/2-in dice)

1/2 cup grilled corn kernels

4 to 6 cups Smoked Chicken Stock (p. 261)

1 bay leaf

1 tsp chopped fresh thyme

1 cup whipping cream

Salt and freshly ground black pepper

Serves 6 to 8

In a large pot, combine clams and 1/2 cup of beer. Cover, bring to a boil and steam for 6–8 minutes, or until clams open. Remove from heat and let cool, discarding any unopened clams. Remove clam meat from half the shells, reserving remaining clams in their shells for garnish. Discard empty shells.

Preheat grill to medium-high (about 400°F). Grill peameal bacon for 1–2 minutes per side. Remove from grill, dice and set aside.

In a large pot, over medium-high heat, melt butter. Add grilled bacon and sauté for 1–2 minutes, stirring. Add celery, onion, leek, potatoes, squash and corn and sauté for 3–4 minutes to soften. Add remaining beer, Smoked Chicken Stock, bay leaf and thyme and return to a boil. Reduce heat and simmer for 30 minutes, or until potatoes and squash are fully cooked and tender and chowder has thickened. Add cream and clam meat, and heat through, stirring constantly; season with salt and pepper to taste. Ladle into bowls and garnish with reserved clams in shells.

GRILLED PORTOBELLO MUSHROOM SOUP

Grilling the mushrooms gives this classic soup added flavor.

Combine beer, 1 cup of water, steak spice and oil, and pour into a shallow roasting dish. Add portobello mushrooms and immerse in marinade. Soak for 1 hour.

Preheat grill to medium-high (about 400°F). Remove portobello mushrooms from marinade, discarding liquid, and place on grill. Grill for 4–5 minutes per side. Remove from grill and set aside, allowing to cool slightly. In a large bowl, combine onions, cremini mushrooms and potatoes with oil and Bonedust Seasoning. Transfer vegetables to a grill basket and grill for 8–10 minutes, or until tender and lightly charred. Remove from grill and let cool slightly.

Slice grilled portobello mushrooms into thin strips. Place grilled onions, potatoes, cremini mushrooms and half of the grilled portobello slices in a medium-sized soup pot. Add Smoked Chicken Stock and bring to a boil over medium-high heat. Reduce heat and simmer for 30 minutes, or until potatoes are cooked through. Using a hand blender, purée mixture until smooth. Add cream and heat through. Remove from heat and season with salt and pepper to taste. Serve garnished with reserved portobello slices and cheddar.

2 (12 oz) bottles beer
1 tbsp Amazing Steak Spice (p. 23)
2 tbsp vegetable oil
8 portobello mushrooms, cleaned
2 medium onions, peeled and sliced into 1/2-in rings
1 lb cremini mushrooms
2 large Yukon Gold potatoes, quartered
1 tbsp vegetable oil
1 tsp Bonedust Seasoning (p. 22)
8 cups Smoked Chicken Stock (p. 261)
1 cup whipping cream
Salt and freshly ground black pepper
1/2 cup crumbled aged white cheddar

Serves 8

DRINKS

NO BOOK ON BARBECUE would be complete without the perfect drinks to accompany all your delicious grillin' endeavors. I'm always experimenting on the grill, and coming up with great drinks that complement barbecue is something I really enjoy.

Drinks can make the perfect meal that much better, and though you might not think it, you'll be surprised at how useful your grill can be in concocting exciting drinks!

There are lots of options for BBQ-inspired drinks — whether cocktails or a serious Coke float for grown-ups. For wowing guests at your next cocktail party, serve drinks made with grilled vegetables as garnishes. Grilled fruit, such as pineapple (my favorite), also works well as both a garnish and a base for tasty drinks. Apples, peaches, pears, grapes and strawberries work well on the grill, but watch out for melons, as they tend to get mushy.

TEDDY'S BBQ MARTINI WITH GRILLED ONION AND CORN GARNISH

Special equipment: 2 bamboo skewers, soaked in water for at least 1 hour

Grilled Onion and Corn Garnish
4 cocktail onions
2 canned baby corn cobs
Salt and freshly ground black pepper

2 oz bourbon
4 oz vodka
2 dashes Tabasco brand chipotle pepper sauce
Grilled Onion and Corn Garnish

Makes 2 martinis

When it comes to bourbon in my martinis, I prefer Woodford Reserve.

To prepare the Grilled Onion and Corn Garnish: Preheat grill to high (about 500°F). Thread 1 cocktail onion, 1 baby corn and second cocktail onion onto each skewer. Coat skewered onions and corn liberally with nonstick cooking spray and season with salt and pepper to taste. Place skewers on grill and cook for 2–3 minutes, each side, until vegetables are tender and lightly charred.

Place two martini glasses in freezer to chill. Drizzle bourbon into each chilled glass. Fill a cocktail shaker with ice and add vodka and Tabasco; cover and shake vigorously. Strain the vodka-Tabasco mix into chilled glasses. Garnish with Grilled Onion and Corn skewers.

BBQ BLOODY CAESAR

Special equipment: 2 bamboo skewers

4 fire-roasted tomatoes (for method see p. 250), coarsely chopped
4 oz vodka
2 oz Jack Daniel's whiskey
1 cup Clamato juice
2 big splashes Worcestershire sauce
2 big splashes Tabasco sauce
2 tbsp prepared horseradish
Salt and freshly ground black pepper
Bonedust Seasoning (p. 22)
2 small store-bought pickled pepperoncini
2 lime wedges

Makes 2 Caesars

The fire-roasted tomatoes add a delicious, smoky flavor to this Caesar. If you prefer Virgin Caesars, just omit the vodka and whiskey and tipple to your heart's content.

In a blender, combine fire-roasted tomatoes, vodka, Jack Daniel's, Clamato juice, Worcestershire and Tabasco sauces, and horseradish. Blend thoroughly; season with salt and pepper to taste. Pour enough Bonedust Seasoning into a saucer to cover the surface. Run a lime wedge around the rim of each of two large glasses and dip rims into Bonedust Seasoning. Fill glasses with ice and pour blended mixture into glasses. Garnish each with a skewered pepperoncino and a wedge of lime.

BBQ Bloody Caesar

VANILLA FLOAT FOR GROWN-UPS

Use premium or homemade ice cream for these sophisticated floats and indulge, just before your afternoon delight.

Pour 2 oz vanilla cognac and 1 oz of Jack Daniel's into each of 2 large milkshake-style glasses. Fill with Coca-Cola and add 1 or 2 scoops of ice cream. Garnish with vanilla beans and serve with parfait spoons and straws.

4 oz vanilla cognac liqueur
2 oz Jack Daniel's whiskey
2 cans Coca-Cola or vanilla Coca-Cola
2 to 4 large scoops vanilla ice cream
2 vanilla beans, for garnish

Makes 2 floats

PEANUT BUTTER AND GRILLED BANANA MILKSHAKE

Use canned whipped cream for this recipe — it's perfect for a banana–peanut butter milkshake and a hell of a lot easier than whipping cream by hand.

Preheat grill to medium-high (about 350°F). Peel bananas and place on grill; cook for 4–5 minutes, turning once, until lightly charred and heated through. Remove from grill and let cool completely. Wrap and chill in refrigerator.

In a blender, combine chilled grilled bananas, ice cream, liqueur, schnapps, peanut butter and milk. Blend until smooth. Transfer milkshake mixture to large chilled glasses and garnish each with 1/2 cup whipped cream, a drizzle of melted Smoked Chocolate, roasted peanuts and biscotto. Serve immediately with great big straws.

2 large bananas, just ripe
4 scoops vanilla ice cream
1 oz banana liqueur
2 oz butterscotch schnapps
2 tbsp smooth peanut butter
2 cups whole milk
1 cup whipped cream, canned
2 oz Smoked Chocolate (p. 228), melted
12 roasted peanuts, crushed
2 biscotti

Makes 2 milkshakes

KILLER SANGRIA

1 lemon
1 lime
1 orange
24 oz port
8 oz Grand Marnier
8 oz brandy
16 oz soda water

Serves 6

There are rules to this recipe: Consume at your own risk, and only if you plan to spend the next day in bed or not employed in any way.

Slice lemon, lime and orange into 1/4-in wheels and place in large pitcher or punch bowl; add port, Grand Marnier and brandy. Stir and refrigerate until ready to serve.

To serve, fill 6 highball glasses two-thirds full with ice. Pour enough sangria over ice so that it is also fills two-thirds of each glass. Finish with some soda water and garnish with sangria-soaked slices of lemon, lime and orange.

PASSION FIZZ

2 passion fruit (when ripe, skin appears wizened and shriveled)
6 slices English cucumber
6 raspberries
16 oz sparkling water

Makes 2 fizzes

For all of you Foofie Foo Foos out there, this is about as dainty and delicate as I get.

Fill 2 highball glasses two-thirds full with ice. Cut passion fruit in half and scoop out flesh with a spoon. Add scoop of passion fruit to each highball and top with 3 cucumber slices and 3 raspberries. Fill glasses with sparkling water and serve.

CRÈME BRÛLÉE MARTINI

2 oz + 1 oz vanilla cognac liqueur
1/4 cup sugar
4 oz whole milk
1 oz Butter Ripple Schnapps
1 tbsp Skor pieces

Makes 2 martinis

You'll need a mini-blowtorch, 1 cocktail shaker and several martini glasses for this vanilla-flavored dessert-tini.

Pour 2 oz of vanilla liqueur into one saucer and sugar into another saucer. Dip each rim of 2 martini glasses into liqueur and then into sugar, making certain that the entire rim of each glass is well coated. Using a mini-blowtorch, lightly "char" the rim of each glass very carefully until the sugar is golden brown and crunchy, like the top of a crème brûlée. Set aside.

In a cocktail shaker, combine milk, schnapps and remaining vanilla cognac liqueur and ice. Vigorously shake and pour into rimmed glasses. Garnish with Skor pieces.

Measuring Butter Ripple Schnapps
for the Crème Brûlée Martini

SALADS
AND
DRESSINGS

SALAD MIGHT NOT be the first thing that comes to mind when you think of barbecuing, but salads are actually some of the best, and simplest, types of dishes to prepare on the grill. With meats and fish, you have to make sure you get the timing and temperature just right — veggies are a lot more forgiving. Anything from a quick grill to a real searing intensifies their natural flavors.

Fire-roasting beets gives them a smoky, sweet flavor. Grilled carrots and onions will transform any greens into a robust, energy-filled treat. And grilled tomatoes and chilis are the underpinnings of a funky hot salad dressing.

To me, a summer picnic or backyard barbecue wouldn't be complete without the addition of a grilled salad. So be adventurous. Grill your vegetables and make some awesome salads. Who knows? You may stumble upon the perfect summer treat.

MY BIG FAT GREEK SALAD

1 large red onion, diced
1 red bell pepper, cut into 8 wedges
1 yellow bell pepper, cut into 8 wedges
1 green bell pepper, cut into 8 wedges
1 pint grape tomatoes, halved
1 English cucumber, sliced
4 pieces feta cheese,
cut into 1/2-in cubes
1 cup kalamata olives
1/2 cup My Big Fat Greek
Dressing (p. 78)

Serves 8

Greek salad is always a huge hit at any event, and this version is especially good.

In a large bowl, combine all ingredients other than dressing; toss gently. Drizzle My Big Fat Greek Dressing over salad; toss again and serve.

GRILLED SWEET PEPPERS WITH YOGURT RANCH DRESSING

4 large red bell peppers
1 large Spanish onion
1 tbsp Bonedust Seasoning (p. 22)
2 tbsp extra-virgin olive oil

Yogurt Ranch Dressing
1/2 cup plain yogurt
1/4 cup mayonnaise
1/2 cup crumbled goat cheese
Juice of 1 lemon
2 tbsp extra-virgin olive oil
1 tbsp dried oregano
2 tbsp cracked black peppercorns
1 tsp minced garlic
Salt

Serves 6 to 8

My Greek Texan buddy, Eddy Zervoudakis, made this recipe for me one day at his home. We ate, we drank, he passed out. Watch that ouzo.

Preheat grill to medium-high (about 400°F). Cut peppers in half, lengthwise, through the middle. Remove the seeds and stem. Cut each pepper half into 4 wedges. Slice onion into 1/2-in-thick slices. In a large bowl, toss peppers and onion with Bonedust Seasoning and oil. Transfer vegetables to a grill basket and place over direct heat on grill. Grill peppers and onion for 5–8 minutes each side, or until lightly charred. Remove from grill and arrange vegetables on a serving platter.
To prepare the Yogurt Ranch Dressing: In a medium bowl, whisk together all dressing ingredients. Spoon over grilled vegetables and serve.

FIRE-ROASTED BEET AND PEAR SALAD

The combination of beets and pears is particularly delicious, but remember to wear rubber gloves when you work with beets, otherwise your fingers will end up stained red.

Preheat grill to medium heat (about 350°F). Peel beets and cut into 1/2-in-wide sticks. Wrap beet sticks in foil and roast on grill until tender, about 45–60 minutes. Remove from grill and carefully open foil pouch. Set aside.

Slice pears in half through stem and then slice in half again. Remove core. Place pears onto preheated oiled grill and grill for 3–4 minutes, turning several times, until tender and lightly charred. Remove pears from grill and set aside.

In a small bowl, whisk together remaining ingredients, except cheese.

In a serving bowl, combine grilled beets and pears. Pour in honey-orange dressing and toss. Garnish with blue cheese and serve immediately.

2 beets, blanched
2 pears
1 tbsp honey
1/4 cup freshly squeezed orange juice
2 tbsp vegetable oil
2 green onions, thinly sliced
1 tbsp chopped fresh rosemary
1 tbsp apple cider vinegar
Salt and freshly ground black pepper to taste
1/2 cup crumbled blue cheese

Serves 6

GRILLED CARROT AND ONION SALAD WITH ORANGE RUM DRESSING

1/2 tsp salt
6 carrots, peeled and trimmed
1/2 cup orange marmalade
1/4 cup freshly squeezed orange juice
3 tbsp unsalted butter
2 tbsp apple cider vinegar
Juice of 1 lemon
2 oz dark rum or Grand Marnier
Pinch of freshly grated nutmeg
Salt and freshly ground black pepper
1 large onion, quartered
2 tbsp extra-virgin olive oil
2 tbsp chopped fresh basil
1 tbsp chopped fresh mint
1/4 cup golden raisins
2 cups trimmed sugar-snap peas

Serves 4 to 6

Grilling makes carrots sweet and delicious. And just about any root vegetable would work in this recipe — try parsnips or Jerusalem artichokes for variety.

Preheat grill to medium-high (about 400°F). Add salt to a pot of boiling water; parboil carrots for 3–4 minutes, or until tender but still crunchy in the center. Remove from pot and let cool slightly.

In a large saucepan, add marmalade, orange juice, butter, vinegar, lemon juice, rum and nutmeg. Place saucepan on grill and bring to a simmer, stirring occasionally. Move pan to side of grill, away from direct heat. Season with salt and pepper to taste, and continue simmering.

Brush carrots and onion with oil; season with salt and pepper to taste. Grill carrots and onion until lightly charred and tender, about 5–8 minutes, turning occasionally. Remove vegetables from grill and let cool slightly.

Remove saucepan from grill and set aside; cover to keep warm.

Slice carrots on an angle into 1-in-thick slices. Slice onion and toss in a large bowl with carrots. Add fresh herbs, raisins and sugar-snap peas to bowl. Mix gently to combine.

Pour hot orange-rum dressing over vegetables. Stir and let sit for 5 minutes before serving.

GRILLED FENNEL WITH FIRE-ROASTED PEPPER PESTO AND PECORINO CHEESE

Grilled fennel loses some of its licorice taste and becomes quite sweet — a great counterpoint to pesto and sharp pecorino cheese.

Fire-Roasted Pepper Pesto

2 red bell peppers
2 cloves garlic
1/4 cup toasted pine nuts
1/4 cup grated Parmesan cheese
2 tsp fresh lemon juice
1 tbsp chopped fresh basil
1 tsp crushed red pepper flakes
2 tbsp extra-virgin olive oil
Salt and freshly ground black pepper

Grilled Fennel

3 fresh fennel bulbs, trimmed of stalk and root
1/4 cup extra-virgin olive oil
Salt and freshly ground black pepper
1 1/2 cups grated Pecorino Romano cheese

Serves 8

To prepare the Fire-Roasted Pepper Pesto: Preheat grill to medium-high (about 400°F). Place bell peppers directly over heat and roast for 8–10 minutes, until skin blisters and blackens. Transfer to a bowl and cover with plastic wrap. Let peppers steam in covered bowl for 2 minutes before removing blackened skin and seeds. Transfer peppers to a food processor. Add garlic and process until puréed. Add pine nuts, Parmesan cheese, lemon juice, basil, red pepper flakes and olive oil; process until smooth. Season with salt and pepper to taste and set aside.

To prepare the Grilled Fennel: Slice fennel bulbs, lengthwise, into 5 or 6 slices each. Brush with olive oil and season with salt and pepper to taste. Grill fennel slices 3–5 minutes each side, or until tender and lightly charred. Reduce grill temperature to low. While still on the grill, top each fennel slice with 1 tsp of pepper pesto. Sprinkle liberally with Pecorino Romano cheese. Close grill lid and grill until cheese melts. Remove from heat and serve immediately.

GRANDPA'S HOT DOG SALAD

My grandpa created this recipe while attempting to grill onions and sausages. It's delicious eaten on its own or served in a wrap, pita or hot dog bun.

1/4 cup vinegar
2 tbsp grain mustard
1/4 cup ketchup
1/4 cup garlic oil
2 tbsp extra-virgin olive oil
1 ear of corn, sliced into 2-in rounds
1 red onion, quartered
1 white onion, quartered
2 bell peppers, seeded and chopped
3 cloves garlic, minced
4 jumbo hot dogs
2 bratwurst sausages
2 chorizo sausages
2 andouille sausages
16 mini smoked sausages
1 cup cubed cheddar cheese

Serves 8

Preheat grill to medium (about 350°F). In a medium bowl, combine first 5 ingredients to make dressing. Mix well and set aside.

Place corn, onions, peppers and garlic in grill basket. Grill vegetables for 10–15 minutes, or until tender, turning twice. Remove from grill and transfer to a large bowl.

Cut several large incisions in jumbo hot dogs. Place hot dogs and assorted sausages on grill. Grill, turning occasionally, for 6–8 minutes, or until heated through and lightly charred. Remove from grill and immediately cut each hot dog and the larger sausages into bite-sized pieces. Add still-warm grilled hot dog and sausage pieces to vegetables in bowl. Toss with dressing and top with cubed cheddar cheese; toss again, allowing cheese to melt slightly before serving.

T-BONE'S DIABLO SLAW

Coleslaw, amped up and on fire.

1 small head green cabbage, cored and shredded
1 small head red cabbage, cored and shredded
2 medium red onions, sliced
2 large carrots, peeled and grated
1 large English cucumber, seeded and sliced
2 red bell peppers, stem and seeds removed, thinly sliced
3 jalapeño peppers, seeded and chopped
2 1/2 cups grated Asiago cheese
3/4 cup ranch dressing
3/4 cup mayonnaise
1/4 cup spicy barbecue sauce
1/4 cup apple cider vinegar
4 cloves garlic, minced
3 tbsp Bayou Bite Cajun Seasoning (p. 23)
Salt and freshly ground black pepper

Serves 12

In a large mixing bowl, combine all ingredients except for salt and pepper. Mix for 2–3 minutes to thoroughly combine; season with salt and pepper to taste. Cover with plastic wrap and refrigerate for 2 to 3 hours before serving.

UNFORGETTABLY DELICIOUS PURPLE POTATO SALAD

Purple potatoes give this a cool look, but good old Yukon Golds will also do just fine.

Place potatoes in a large pot and cover with cold water. Bring to a boil and add salt. Reduce heat to medium-low and simmer potatoes for 15–20 minutes, or until tender. Drain and let cool in a large bowl before roughly mashing.

In a medium bowl, whisk together mayonnaise, mustard, oil, cheese and lemon juice to make dressing; season with salt and pepper to taste.

Add chopped eggs, olives, jalapeño peppers, green onion and onion to smashed purple potatoes. Pour dressing over potato mixture and stir well to combine; store in refrigerator until ready to serve.

1 1/2 lb Peruvian purple potatoes or mini Yukon Golds
2 tsp salt
3/4 cup mayonnaise
2 tbsp Dijon mustard
1/4 cup extra-virgin olive oil
1/4 cup grated Parmesan cheese
1 tbsp fresh lemon juice
Salt and freshly ground black pepper
4 hard-boiled eggs, peeled and chopped
3/4 cup sliced green olives
2 jalapeño peppers, seeded and finely chopped
2 green onions, thinly sliced
1 small onion, diced

Serves 4

SWEET-AND-SOUR SLAW

This sweet, tangy slaw is great with ribs.

In a large bowl, combine all ingredients; toss together to mix well. Cover with plastic wrap and refrigerate for 2–3 hours before serving.

1 head red cabbage, cored and thinly sliced
1 small red onion, thinly sliced
1 red bell pepper, seeded and thinly sliced
2 green onions, thinly sliced
1/4 cup diced fresh pineapple
1/4 cup pineapple jam
3 tbsp apple cider vinegar
2 tbsp vegetable oil
2 tbsp sultana raisins
1 tbsp hot pepper sauce
1 tbsp chopped flat-leaf parsley
Salt and freshly ground black pepper to taste

Serves 6 to 8

T-Bone's Diablo Slaw

CUCUMBER SLAW

1 English cucumber, seeds removed, julienned into 2-in-long strips

1 (6 in) piece daikon radish, julienned

2 shallots, finely diced

1 tbsp chopped capers

1 tbsp prepared horseradish

1 tbsp chopped fresh flat-leaf parsley or dill

1/2 tsp sugar

1 tbsp white vinegar

1 tbsp extra-virgin olive oil

Salt and freshly ground black pepper

Serves 4

Try this cool and refreshing slaw with spicy ribs, Indian-flavored chicken or planked salmon.

In a medium bowl mix together all ingredients; cover and refrigerate to chill.

MY THAI NOODLE SALAD

1 lb pad thai rice noodles (banh pho)

1 tbsp sesame oil

1/2 lb boneless, skinless chicken thighs

2 cups Mi Pho #1 Marinade (p. 31)

1 lb (16 to 20) shrimp, peeled and deveined

1 block firm tofu, cut lengthwise into slices about 1-in thick

1/2 cup Spicy Peanut Dressing (p. 78)

2 cups bean sprouts

4 green onions

1/2 cup chopped fresh coriander

1 cup cashews, roasted

Serves 4

Serve with lime wedges and your favorite hot sauce.

Place noodles in a large bowl; cover with cold water and soak for 1 hour. When fully soaked, drain well and toss with sesame oil.

Meanwhile, place chicken thighs in a large, resealable bag and pour in 1/2 cup of the Mi Pho #1 Marinade. Seal and refrigerate for 1 hour.

In two other resealable plastic bags, marinate shrimp and tofu separately, each in 1/2 cup of marinade. Seal and refrigerate until ready to use.

Preheat grill to medium-high (about 400°F). Remove chicken from marinade, discarding used liquid, and grill for 3–4 minutes, each side, until fully cooked. Set aside and let cool slightly before cutting into 1-in chunks.

Remove tofu slices from marinade, reserving marinade, and grill for 2–3 minutes, each side, until lightly charred. Set aside and let cool slightly before cutting into 1-in chunks.

Remove shrimp from marinade, discarding used liquid, and grill for 2–3 minutes, each side, or until cooked through and lightly charred. Transfer grilled shrimp to a medium bowl and add grilled chicken and tofu chunks. Pour in reserved tofu marinade, cover with plastic wrap and refrigerate.

To assemble salad, toss noodles with Spicy Peanut Dressing and divide among 4 plates. Top with chicken, tofu and shrimp mixture. Add bean sprouts, green onion, coriander and cashews and serve.

FIRE-ROASTED TOMATO, ONION AND PASTA SALAD

I like to use alphabet-shaped pasta for this, but that's just me. Penne or rigatoni would also work well.

Bring a large pot of water to a boil; stir in pasta and salt. Cook for 5–6 minutes, or until pasta is al dente. Drain and transfer to a large bowl. Stir in 3 tbsp garlic oil and let cool.

In a large mixing bowl, combine basil, Grill-Roasted Garlic, vegetable oil, vinegar, lemon juice, and salt and pepper to taste. Mix well and set aside.

Preheat grill to medium (about 350ºF). Toss tomatoes and red onions in remaining 3 tbsp garlic oil and season with salt and pepper to taste. Grill tomatoes and red onions until lightly charred and tender, about 10–12 minutes. Remove from grill and let cool slightly. Chop tomatoes into large chunks and slice onions into 1/2-in segments. In a large bowl, toss chopped grilled tomatoes, grilled red onions, green onion, pasta and dressing. Mix well, season with salt and pepper, garnish with grated parmesan and serve.

2 cups alphabet pasta
1 tsp salt
3 tbsp + 3 tbsp garlic oil
2 tbsp chopped fresh basil
1/4 cup Grill-Roasted Garlic (p. 219)
1/2 cup vegetable oil
1/4 cup white balsamic vinegar
2 tbsp fresh lemon juice
Salt and freshly ground black pepper
6 plum tomatoes, cut in
half lengthwise
2 red onions, peeled and cut
into wedges
4 green onions

Serves 4 to 6

Below: Fresh onions and tomatoes for Fire-Roasted Tomato, Onion and Pasta Salad (left); the finished salad (right)

PINEAPPLE RUM VINAIGRETTE

Grilled marinated pineapple makes a delicious vinaigrette.

Place pineapple slices in a small bowl and add rum; marinate for 1 hour.

Preheat grill to medium-high (about 400°F). Grill pineapple slices, reserving rum, for 3–5 minutes on each side, until lightly charred and tender. Remove from grill, cool slightly and finely chop.

In a medium bowl, combine chopped pineapple, reserved rum, pineapple juice, vinegar, honey, red pepper flakes, green onion, shallot, ginger and coriander. Slowly add the oil in a thin stream, whisking constantly to form a smooth emulsion. Season with cayenne pepper, and salt and pepper to taste. Transfer to a container, cover and refrigerate until needed.

3 slices fresh pineapple (1/2-in thick)
1/4 cup spiced rum
1/4 cup pineapple juice or white grape juice
3 tbsp white wine vinegar
3 tbsp honey
1 tsp crushed red pepper flakes
1 green onion, finely chopped
1 tbsp chopped shallot
2 tsp grated fresh ginger
1 tbsp chopped fresh coriander
1/2 cup extra-virgin olive oil
Pinch of cayenne pepper
Salt and freshly ground black pepper

Makes about 3 cups

PICO DE GALLO VINAIGRETTE

Pico de gallo, **which translates from Spanish as "rooster's beak," is a salsa of diced tomatoes, onion and chili peppers. This salsa vinaigrette is the perfect accompaniment to a simple salad of crisp lettuce, sliced tomatoes, onions and grilled peppers. It makes for a great marinade, too!**

In a large bowl, combine all ingredients; whisk until well combined. Transfer to a container, cover, and refrigerate until needed.

1 medium cubanelle pepper, finely diced
1 small Vidalia onion, finely diced
3 firm plum tomatoes, seeded and diced
1/4 cup chopped fresh coriander
2 green onions, chopped
2 jalapeño peppers, seeded and minced
2 tsp sugar
2 tsp kosher salt
1 tsp cracked black peppercorns
1/2 cup fresh lime juice
1/2 cup cane vinegar or white vinegar
1 cup vegetable oil

Makes about 4 cups

A selection of dressings: (from left) Pineapple Rum Vinaigrette, Pico de Gallo Vinaigrette, My Big Fat Greek Dressing

VANILLA MAPLE VINAIGRETTE

1 vanilla bean, cut in half and seeded
1 shallot, finely chopped
3 tbsp maple syrup
3 tbsp vegetable oil
3 tbsp champagne vinegar or white wine vinegar
1 tbsp Dijon mustard

Makes about 1 cup

A truly sexy dressing: Serve this as part of a romantic dinner, when you're hoping things will heat up — only for adults of consenting age.

In a medium bowl, combine vanilla bean and seeds with remaining ingredients. Add 2 tbsp warm water and mix well. Transfer to a container, cover, and refrigerate until needed. Remove vanilla bean before serving.

MY BIG FAT GREEK DRESSING

1/4 cup extra-virgin olive oil
1/4 cup diced kalamata olives
1/4 cup crumbled feta cheese
2 tbsp red wine vinegar
1 tbsp fresh lemon juice
1 tbsp chopped garlic
1 tbsp chopped fresh oregano
1 tbsp chopped flat-leaf parsley
Salt and freshly ground black pepper to taste

Makes about 1/2 cup

Serve this dressing on My Big Fat Greek Salad (p. 66). Cook a lamb on the front lawn. Invite some friends and drink some ouzo.

In a medium bowl, combine all ingredients; mix well. Transfer to a container, cover, and refrigerate until needed.

SPICY PEANUT DRESSING

1/4 cup chunky peanut butter
1/2 tsp sesame oil
1/4 cup unsweetened coconut milk
2 tbsp rice vinegar
2 tbsp soy sauce
2 tbsp mirin
1/2 cup warm water
1 tbsp chopped coriander
Juice of 1 lime
2 cloves garlic
1 red chili pepper, seeded and minced
1 tbsp vegetable oil
Salt and freshly ground pepper

Makes about 1 cup

Nutty and spicy, this dressing is perfect for My Thai Noodle Salad (p. 74), and also, believe it or not, is great on chicken or turkey dogs.

Microwave peanut butter for 10–20 seconds to soften.
    In a medium bowl, whisk together the softened peanut butter, sesame oil, coconut milk, vinegar, soy sauce, mirin, water, coriander, lime juice, garlic, and chili. Slowly add the oil in a thin stream, whisking constantly to form a smooth emulsion. Season with salt and pepper to taste. Transfer to a container, cover, and refrigerate until needed.

SPINACH AND BACON DRESSING

Serve this with grilled radicchio, endive and escarole.

Wash spinach well and remove stems; blanch by immersing in a pot of boiling water for 10 seconds. Remove from pot and briefly plunge leaves into a bowl of ice-cold water. Using your hands, gently squeeze spinach to drain as much excess liquid as possible. Finely chop spinach.

In a large bowl, combine spinach with green onion, parsley, garlic, onion and red pepper; set aside.

In another bowl, whisk together cream cheese, mayonnaise, mustard, honey, lemon juice, Parmesan cheese and vinegar until smooth. Fold in spinach mixture and diced bacon; season with salt and pepper to taste. Transfer to a container, cover, and refrigerate until needed.

1 lb fresh spinach
2 green onions, minced
1/4 cup chopped flat-leaf parsley
1 clove garlic, minced
1/2 small Vidalia onion, diced
1/2 small red bell pepper, seeded and finely diced
1/2 cup softened cream cheese
1 cup mayonnaise
2 tbsp Dijon mustard
1/4 cup honey
1 tbsp fresh lemon juice
1/4 cup grated Parmesan cheese
2 tbsp white wine vinegar
4 slices bacon, cooked crisp and diced
Salt and freshly ground black pepper

Makes about 4 cups

GRILLED SWEET ONION AND BLUEBERRY VINAIGRETTE

This vinaigrette also makes a delicious marinade for portobello mushrooms. The blueberries and honey add a sweet dimension to the mushrooms' earthiness. Just marinate the mushrooms for about 15 minutes, then grill.

Preheat grill to medium (about 350°F). Brush onion with a little oil and season with salt and pepper; grill 4–5 minutes each side, until lightly charred and tender. Remove from grill, finely dice and set aside.

In a food processor or blender, combine 1/2 cup blueberries, lemon juice, vinegar, honey and mustard; process until smooth. Transfer to a large bowl and add diced onion, thyme, peppercorns and sea salt; mix well. Slowly add 1 cup oil in a thin stream, processing to form a smooth emulsion. Stir in remaining blueberries. Transfer to a container, cover, and refrigerate until needed.

1 medium Vidalia onion, quartered
2 tsp + 1 cup extra-virgin olive oil
Salt and freshly ground black pepper
1/2 cup + 2 tbsp frozen blueberries, thawed
2 tbsp fresh lemon juice
1/2 cup balsamic vinegar
1/4 cup honey
1 tbsp Dijon mustard
2 tbsp chopped fresh thyme
1 tbsp cracked black peppercorns
1 tsp sea salt

Makes about 1 1/2 cups

SANDWICHES

I LOVE A GOOD SANDWICH, and I'm all for eating with your hands — it's what getting sticky is all about! But a sandwich is more than just portable food. I like to think of sandwiches as a fun and surprising way to entertain. Most people don't expect sandwiches for dinner, but sophisticated, delicious sandwiches such as Provolone, Pancetta and Grilled Rapini Panini and Grilled Mahi Mahi and Scallop Baguette Sandwich will change their minds.

Of course, nothing beats biting into a big-ass sandwich, like a Grilled Chicken Tikka Naanwich with Cucumber Mint Raita or a Big Turkey Cutlet Sandwich with Fire-Roasted Tomato Salsa, and having the juices run down your chin (and do a triple back flip!) to land on your belly. It's always chin-dripping time in my sandwich chapter.

GRILLED BEEF TENDERLOIN LETTUCE WRAPS

Fire-Roasted BBQ Dressing
3 plum tomatoes
1 small onion, quartered
1 tsp Bonedust Seasoning (p. 22)
1 clove garlic, minced
1 anchovy fillet
1 1/2 tbsp prepared horseradish
1/8 cup apple cider vinegar
1/2 cup gourmet barbecue sauce
1/8 cup tomato juice
1/4 cup extra-virgin olive oil
1 tsp chopped fresh oregano
Salt and freshly ground black pepper

1 1/2 lb beef tenderloin
2 tbsp + 1 tbsp Amazing Steak
Spice (p. 23)
2 medium Vidalia onions, with root
ends and skin
1 head radicchio, washed
3 tbsp Fire-Roasted BBQ Dressing
1 cup crumbled Gorgonzola cheese
1/4 cup roasted cashews
2 tbsp kosher salt
2 tbsp coarsely ground black pepper
1 head iceberg lettuce, outer leaves
removed, cored and washed
6 fresh basil leaves

Serves 6

Inspired by Asian cold rolls — tender grilled beef is dressed and wrapped in crunchy lettuce leaves.

To prepare the Fire-Roasted BBQ Dressing: Preheat grill to medium-high (about 400°F). Brush tomatoes and onion with a little oil and season with Bonedust Seasoning. Grill tomatoes and onion for 8–10 minutes, turning occasionally, until charred and tender. Remove from grill and transfer to a food processor. Add remaining ingredients and process until smooth. Transfer to a container, cover, and refrigerate until needed.

Preheat grill to high (about 500°F). In a shallow glass dish, season tenderloin with 2 tbsp Amazing Steak Spice, pressing gently so that seasoning adheres to meat. Grill tenderloin for 5–6 minutes, turning occasionally, until lightly charred on all sides and medium-rare inside. Transfer from grill to a container and let cool. Once cooled to room temperature, cover loosely with plastic wrap and store in freezer for 2 hours, or until frozen.

Once frozen, remove grilled tenderloin from freezer. Using a mandoline or meat slicer, shave beef into about 36 slivers. Place shaved tenderloin on a parchment-lined tray, cover with plastic wrap and refrigerate until needed. Preheat grill to medium-high (about 400°F).

Peel Vidalia onions and cut into wedges, leaving root end attached. Spray with nonstick cooking spray, season with remaining tbsp of Amazing Steak Spice and set aside. Peel off outer layer of radicchio and discard. Separate radicchio leaves and toss in a bowl with Fire-Roasted BBQ Dressing.

Grill seasoned onion wedges until lightly charred and tender, about 5–6 minutes. Grill radicchio until lightly charred and softened, about 1–2 minutes per side. Remove radicchio and onion wedges from grill and let cool. Slice off root ends from onion wedges and set wedges aside.

In a small bowl, combine Gorgonzola and cashews, add salt and pepper and set aside.

To assemble, place iceberg lettuce leaves on plates or on 1 large serving platter; each leaf should curve upward, to resemble a bowl. Line each leaf bowl with grilled radicchio, 3 slices of beef, a grilled onion wedge and some of the Gorgonzola-cashew mixture. Garnish each with 1 basil leaf and serve immediately.

SURF-AND-TURF SLIDERS

I love "sliders" — mini sandwiches that slide right into your belly! Here is one of my favorite kinds.

Freeze beef tenderloin for 15 minutes, to make it easier to slice. Using a sharp knife, slice chilled beef into 1 1/2- to 2-oz slices. Place each slice in between sheets of plastic wrap and, using a mallet or rolling pin, lightly pound or roll into a circle about 1/8-in thick. Preheat grill to medium-high (about 400°F). Wrap dinner roll halves in aluminum foil, creating a pouch, and place on grill to toast.

Meanwhile, wrap each shrimp with 1 slice of beef, pressing firmly where ends meet to secure. Brush with oil and lightly coat with Better Butter Burger Seasoning, gently pressing with a spatula so that spices adhere. Grill beef-shrimp wraps, basting with barbecue sauce, for 3–4 minutes on each side, or until shrimp is just cooked and beef is lightly charred.

Remove toasted rolls from foil pouch and place 2 halves on each of 4 plates. On each of the bottom halves, stack a lettuce leaf, tomato slice, onion slice, 1 grilled beef-wrapped shrimp, 2 slices of bacon and 1 slice of cheese. Cover with tops of rolls and serve with plantain chips on the side.

1 lb beef tenderloin
8 small dinner rolls, sliced in half
8 jumbo shrimp, peeled and deveined
2 tbsp vegetable oil
2 tbsp Better Butter Burger Seasoning (p. 22)
1/4 cup gourmet barbecue sauce
8 lettuce leaves
8 slices tomato
8 slices red onion
16 slices cooked bacon
8 slices Manchego cheese

Serves 4

PROVOLONE, PANCETTA AND GRILLED RAPINI PANINI

Pancetta, a salt- and spice-cured Italian bacon; provolone, a mild smoky-flavored cow's milk cheese; and panini, crusty Italian rolls, make this sandwich delicious.

Preheat grill to medium (about 300°F). Lightly spray pancetta with nonstick cooking spray and grill for 2–3 minutes, each side, until slightly crisp. Remove from grill and cool slightly.

Meanwhile, brush the inside of the buns with oil and rub with garlic. Top bottom half of each panini with 2 slices of provolone. Add 1/4 cup of chopped Grilled Rapini and top with 2 slices pancetta and remaining cheese. Season filling with salt and pepper to taste.

Cover each bottom half with top half of panini to form a sandwich. Transfer prepared sandwiches to a grill basket and press down slightly, ensuring each remains intact. Grill sandwiches in baskets, turning once, for 4–5 minutes, or until bread is lightly charred and golden brown and filling is heated through. Carefully remove sandwiches from basket and let cool slightly. Cut in half and serve immediately.

4 slices pancetta
2 panini, cut in half lengthwise
3 tbsp extra-virgin olive oil
2 cloves garlic, sliced in half
1/2 lb sliced provolone cheese (about 8 slices)
1/2 lb Grilled Rapini (p. 216), roughly chopped
Salt and freshly ground black pepper

Serves 2

GRILLED EGGPLANT AND ROASTED GARLIC HUMMUS PITA

2 cups canned chickpeas, rinsed and drained

1/2 cup + 2 tbsp extra-virgin olive oil

1/4 cup puréed Grill-Roasted Garlic (p. 219)

2 tbsp tahini

Juice of 1/2 lemon

Salt and freshly ground black pepper

2 tbsp chopped fresh basil

1 cup crumbled feta cheese

1 large eggplant

1 medium red onion

3 tbsp Mediterranean-Style Rub (p. 23)

2 large pitas

Handful of baby spinach

Dash of hot sauce

Serves 4

Tahini, a traditional Middle Eastern ingredient available at most food stores, is a thick paste made from sesame seeds.

In a food processor, combine chickpeas, 1/2 cup oil, garlic purée, tahini and lemon juice; process until smooth. Season with salt and pepper to taste and transfer hummus to a bowl. Stir in basil and feta cheese and set aside.

Preheat grill to medium-high (about 400° to 450°F). Cut top off eggplant and discard; slice eggplant lengthwise into 1/4-in-thick strips. Peel onion and slice into 1/4-in rings. Lightly brush eggplant and onion slices with remaining 2 tbsp oil and season with Mediterranean-Style Rub. Grill vegetables until lightly charred and tender, about 5–7 minutes, and set aside.

Cut pitas in half to form 4 pockets. Grill each pocket for 1–2 minutes, or until lightly toasted and warm. Fill each pocket with 2–3 slices of grilled eggplant, hummus, grilled onions and baby spinach. Drizzle with hot sauce and serve.

GRILLED MAHI MAHI AND SCALLOP BAGUETTE SANDWICH

2 tbsp + 1 tbsp olive oil

2 cloves garlic, minced

1 Scotch bonnet pepper, minced

4 jumbo scallops

4 (2 to 3 oz) mahi mahi fillets

Juice of two limes

4 to 6 sprigs fresh dill

1 baguette, cut in half lengthwise

1 ripe avocado, pitted and halved

1 to 2 tbsp mayonnaise

Serves 4

Scotch bonnet peppers are exceedingly hot. Substitute jalapeño pepper, if you'd prefer something a little less fiery.

Preheat grill to medium-high (about 400°F). In a bowl, combine 2 tbsp oil, garlic and Scotch bonnet pepper. Mix well and set aside.

Slice scallops in half, into 8 medallions. Place mahi mahi fillets in the center of a 12 x 12-in sheet of foil. Top with scallop medallions, oil-and-chili mixture, lime juice and a few sprigs of dill. Bring foil ends together and seal to form a pouch. Carefully place pouch on grill, close lid, and steam for 15–20 minutes, turning once, until seafood is fully cooked.

Brush baguette with remaining 1 tbsp oil and grill for 3–4 minutes, turning once, until lightly toasted. Remove from grill. Scoop out avocado halves and smear avocado onto bottom half of baguette.

Remove foil pouch from grill and open carefully to avoid steam. Transfer seafood to avocado-smeared baguette. Garnish with tomato, lettuce, onions, sprouts, or whatever you like. Top with second baguette half, which you have spread with mayonnaise. Slice evenly into 4 sandwiches and serve with a big green salad.

Grilled Mahi Mahi and Scallop Baguette Sandwich

GRILLED CHICKEN TIKKA NAANWICH WITH CUCUMBER MINT RAITA

This sandwich is made with naan, a delicious Indian flatbread found in ethnic food stores and bakeries.

Cucumber Mint Raita

1 ripe tomato

1 medium English cucumber, peeled, halved and grated

2 cloves garlic, minced

1/4 cup chopped fresh mint

Pinch of cayenne pepper

1/2 tsp ground cumin

2 tbsp fresh lemon juice

1 cup plain yogurt

1/2 cup sour cream

1/2 cup diced red onion

Salt and freshly ground black pepper

4 (6 oz) boneless, skinless chicken breasts

2 tbsp + 1 tbsp Cochin Curry Masala Seasoning (p. 24)

2 cloves garlic, minced

2 green chili peppers, seeded and minced

4 tsp grated fresh ginger

1 cup plain yogurt

1/4 cup vegetable oil

2 tbsp fresh lemon juice

2 tbsp chopped fresh coriander

4 naan

1/2 cup extra-virgin olive oil

Salt and freshly ground black pepper

1/2 cup Cucumber Mint Raita

2 cups shredded iceberg lettuce

Serves 4

To prepare the Cucumber Mint Raita: With a sharp knife, lightly score tomato skin and blanch in boiling water for 5–10 seconds. Cool and peel off skin. Finely chop skinned tomato and set aside. In a medium bowl, mix together the chopped tomato, cucumber, garlic, mint, cayenne pepper, cumin, lemon juice, yogurt, sour cream and onion; season with salt and pepper to taste. Cover with plastic wrap and refrigerate for 1 hour.

Rub chicken breasts with 2 tbsp Cochin Curry Masala Seasoning, pressing gently so that spices adhere to meat. In a bowl, whisk together the garlic, green chili pepper, ginger, yogurt, oil, lemon juice and coriander. Pour over chicken, turning to coat. Cover and marinate for 2–4 hours in refrigerator.

When chicken is fully marinated, preheat grill to medium-high (about 400°F). Remove chicken from marinade and place on grill. Spoon a little extra marinade over chicken and grill for 18–20 minutes, or until chicken is fully cooked.

Meanwhile, brush both sides of naan with olive oil. Season with remaining Cochin Curry Masala Seasoning and salt and pepper to taste. Grill-toast naan for 1–2 minutes, each side, until lightly golden. Remove from grill and cut in half; spread each of 4 halves with 1 tbsp Cucumber Mint Raita. Top each with shredded lettuce, chicken, a little more raita and remaining naan half.

BIG TURKEY CUTLET SANDWICH WITH FIRE-ROASTED TOMATO SALSA

When you're feeling super hungry, this big-ass sandwich feeds one nicely. For regular eaters, it feeds up to 8.

To prepare the Fire-Roasted Tomato Salsa: Preheat grill to medium (about 350°F). Grill onion and tomatoes for 6–10 minutes, or until tender and slightly charred. Transfer to a cutting board and let cool before coarsely chopping. In a bowl, combine chopped onion and tomato, garlic, Bonedust Seasoning, oil, herbs, tomato sauce and olives. Mix well and set aside for 30 minutes, to allow flavors to meld.

Meanwhile, season turkey fillets with Mediterranean-Style Rub, gently pressing with a spatula so that spices adhere to meat. Grill seasoned fillets for 2–4 minutes each side, basting with barbecue sauce until crisp and fully cooked. Remove from grill and set aside.

To assemble sandwich, cut top from loaf of bread. Scoop out two-thirds of the inside from bottom half of loaf. Brush inner surface of hollowed-out half with oil and season with salt and pepper to taste. Line with grilled turkey cutlets, mozzarella cheese and Fire-Roasted Tomato Salsa. Replace top half of loaf and slice into 4 sandwiches. Serve immediately.

Fire-Roasted Tomato Salsa
1 large onion
4 plum tomatoes
2 cloves garlic, minced
1 tsp Bonedust Seasoning (p. 22)
1 tbsp extra-virgin olive oil
1/4 cup mixed chopped fresh herbs (p. 26)
1/2 cup Fire-Roasted Tomato Sauce (p. 250)
1/4 cup sliced black olives

8 (2 to 3 oz) turkey fillets
3 tbsp Mediterranean-Style Rub (p. 23)
1 cup gourmet barbecue sauce
1 large loaf of crusty Italian bread
1/4 cup extra-virgin olive oil
Salt and freshly ground black pepper
1/2 cup shredded mozzarella cheese

Serves 4

WASABI TUNA TACO WITH AVOCADO SALSA

The most delicious tuna is lightly seared on the outside and very rare on the inside. Even better is seared fresh tuna served with fiery-hot wasabi and avocado in a taco!

In a small bowl, combine avocado, tomato, coriander, lime juice and oil. Mix together and add Bonedust Seasoning to taste; set aside.

Preheat grill to high (about 500°F). Season tuna with Herbed Sea Salt Rub, gently pressing so that spices adhere to steaks. Grill tuna for 1–2 minutes on each side, until outside is seared but inside is just rare. Remove from grill and cool slightly before thinly slicing.

In a small bowl, combine wasabi powder and 1 tbsp cold water. Mix well to form a paste; set aside.

To assemble, line bottom of each taco shell with 1/4 cup shredded lettuce. Top each with the prepared avocado-and-tomato salsa, several slices of grilled tuna and a dollop of wasabi paste. Serve immediately with wedges of fresh lime.

1 ripe avocado, peeled and diced
3 small ripe plum tomatoes, seeded and diced
2 tbsp chopped fresh coriander
2 tbsp fresh lime juice
1 tbsp extra-virgin olive oil
Bonedust Seasoning (p. 22)
4 (6 oz) fresh tuna steaks
2 tsp Herbed Sea Salt Rub (p. 29)
1 tbsp wasabi powder
8 hard taco shells
2 cups shredded iceberg lettuce
4 lime wedges

Serves 4

PLANKED SALMON ROLL-UPS WITH HONEY MUSTARD DUNK

These roll-ups are the perfect use for leftover salmon.

To prepare the Honey Mustard Dunk: In a small bowl, combine mustard, honey, lemon juice and Jack Daniel's; mix well and season with salt and pepper to taste. Cover with plastic wrap and refrigerate until needed.

Preheat grill to medium-high (about 400°F). Flake salmon into a medium bowl. Add cream cheese, onion, dill and lemon juice; season with salt and pepper to taste.

On a clean, flat surface, spread 1/2 cup of salmon-and-cream-cheese mixture evenly on each tortilla. Tightly roll tortillas, tucking in ends as you roll. Spray tortillas with nonstick cooking spray and season with Herbed Sea Salt Rub. Grill roll-ups for 5–6 minutes or until lightly charred on all sides. Remove from grill and let cool for 2–3 minutes before slicing.

When ready, slice roll-ups into 1-in-thick pinwheels. Secure with toothpicks and serve with Honey Mustard Dunk.

Honey Mustard Dunk
1/2 cup Dijon mustard
3 tbsp honey
1 tbsp fresh lemon juice
1 oz Jack Daniel's whiskey
Salt and freshly ground pepper

1 lb Ultimate Planked Salmon (p. 188)
8 oz cream cheese
1 medium red onion, finely diced
1 tbsp chopped fresh dill
Juice of 1 lemon
Salt and freshly ground pepper
4 (10 in) flour tortillas
2 tbsp Herbed Sea Salt Rub (p. 29)

Serves 8 to 12

QUESADILLAS

QUESADILLAS ARE ONE of the oldest and simplest types of food in the Americas. A flat bread of corn or flour is folded around delicious ingredients and grilled or fried.

As part of our catering work, we make dozens of different kinds of quesadillas, and as much as we love sandwiches, quesadillas are something different and special. They're just a bit more versatile — we've learned that they really are the perfect fast, easy vehicle for just about anything you want to make. They are also incredible comfort food.

My chef Joanne, in particular, creates the most inspired and delicious concoctions, including Planked Salmon Quesadillas and the inspired Drunken Chicken Quesadilla. All are loaded with ooey and gooey fillings. Give 'em a try: These are perfect for dinner, brunch, lunch, or cut into bite-sized pieces as party hors d'oeuvres.

CALGARY STAMPEDE BEEF BRISKET QUESADILLA

1 cup cooked, smoked and shredded Beef Brisket (p. 122)
1 1/2 cups shredded mozzarella cheese
1 tbsp chopped fresh thyme
1/4 cup hickory barbecue sauce (I recommend King of the Q Smokin' Beer BBQ Sauce)
10 (6 in) flour tortillas
2 tbsp Bonedust Seasoning (p. 22)

Serves 10 as an appetizer or 5 as a main course

While at the Calgary Stampede, I had the chance to taste some succulent Alberta beef, including smoky beef brisket. It inspired me to make this recipe for some local cowboy buddies of mine.

Preheat a lightly oiled grill to medium (about 350°F). In a large bowl, combine beef, cheese, thyme and barbecue sauce. Mix until moist and sticky. Place 1/4 cup beef mixture on right half of each tortilla, leaving a small space around the edges. Fold tortilla over from left to right, forming a half-moon shape. Firmly press down so that the filling sticks. Spray both sides of the quesadillas with nonstick cooking spray and sprinkle with Bonedust Seasoning. (At this stage, you can cover quesadillas with plastic wrap and refrigerate for up to 6 hours.) Grill quesadillas for 3–4 minutes, each side, until lightly charred and crisp. Remove from grill and let cool for 2–3 minutes. Once filling has cooled, cut into 2–3 wedges each. Serve immediately with your favorite smoky barbecue sauce for dipping.

DRUNKEN CHICKEN QUESADILLA

1 fully cooked Beer-Can Chicken, (p. 168), chilled and shredded (about 4 cups)
2 cups shredded mozzarella or Monterey Jack cheese
1 cup shredded cheddar cheese
3 green onions, thinly sliced
2 tbsp chopped fresh coriander
1/2 cup ranch dressing
1/4 cup gourmet barbecue sauce
10 (8 in) flour tortillas
1 tbsp Bonedust Seasoning (p. 22)

Serves 10 as an appetizer or 5 as a main course

My Beer-Can Chicken, boozy and flavorful, makes this quesadilla especially good.

Preheat a lightly oiled grill to medium (about 350°F). In a large bowl, combine all ingredients except for the tortillas. Mix until moist and sticky. (If the mixture is dry, add a little more dressing.)

Place one-tenth of the chicken mixture on right half of each tortilla, leaving a small space around the edges. Fold tortilla over from left to right, forming a half-moon shape. Firmly press down so that the filling sticks. Spray both sides of quesadilla with nonstick cooking spray and sprinkle with Bonedust Seasoning.

Grill for 2–3 minutes, each side, until lightly charred and crisp. Remove from grill and let cool for 2–3 minutes. Once filling has cooled, cut each into 2–3 wedges. Serve immediately with extra barbecue sauce for dipping.

Drunken Chicken Quesadilla

DO THE MASHED POTATO CHEDDAR QUESADILLA

1 1/2 cups day-old Cedar-Planked
Mashed Potatoes (p. 213)
1 cup shredded cheddar cheese
1/4 cup chopped green onions
1/4 lb bacon, fully cooked and diced
(about 1/2 cup)
10 (8 in) flour tortillas
2 tbsp Bonedust Seasoning (p. 22)
1/2 cup sour cream

Serves 10 as an appetizer or 5 as a main course

Here's a great way to use up leftover mashed potatoes. Serve these cheesy treats as an appetizer, or with salad for a great main course.

Preheat a lightly oiled grill to medium (about 350°F). In a bowl, combine potato, cheese, green onion, bacon and Bonedust Seasoning. Mix thoroughly.

Place 1/4 cup of potato mixture on right half of each tortilla, leaving a small space around the edges. Fold tortilla over from left to right, forming a half-moon shape. Firmly press down so that the filling sticks. Spray both sides with nonstick cooking spray and sprinkle with Bonedust Seasoning. (At this stage, you can cover with plastic wrap and refrigerate for up to 6 hours.)

Grill quesadillas for 3–4 minutes, each side, until lightly charred and crisp. Remove from grill and let cool for 2–3 minutes. Once filling has cooled, cut into 2–3 wedges each. Serve immediately with sour cream or your favorite barbecue sauce for dipping.

GRILLED ONION, VEGETABLE AND GOAT CHEESE QUESADILLA

2 cups diced grilled vegetables
(sweet onions, pepper, mushrooms,
zucchini, for example)
1 1/2 cups shredded
mozzarella cheese
1/2 cup goat cheese
1 tbsp chopped fresh basil
3 tbsp mayonnaise
3 tbsp grain mustard
3 tbsp Amazing Steak Spice (p. 23)
10 (8 in) flour tortillas
2 tbsp Bonedust Seasoning (p. 22)

Serves 10 as an appetizer or 5 as a main course

Any grilled vegetables will do when making this recipe: Use whatever you have on hand.

Preheat a lightly oiled grill to medium (about 350°F). In a bowl, combine grilled vegetables, mozzarella and goat cheese, basil, mayonnaise and mustard. Season with 1 tbsp steak spice. Place 1/4 cup of mixture on right half of each tortilla, leaving a small space around the edges. Fold tortilla over from left to right, forming a half-moon shape. Firmly press down so that the filling sticks. Spray both sides with nonstick cooking spray and sprinkle with Bonedust Seasoning. (At this stage, you can cover quesadillas with plastic wrap and refrigerate for up to 6 hours.)

Grill quesadillas for 3–4 minutes, each side, until lightly charred and crisp. Remove from grill and let cool for 2–3 minutes. Once filling has cooled, cut into 2–3 wedges each. Serve immediately with your favorite barbecue sauce for dipping.

PLANKED SALMON QUESADILLA

These salmon quesadillas are not to be missed.

Preheat lightly oiled grill to medium (about 350°F). In a large bowl, combine salmon, mozzarella, cream cheese, green onion, dill, lemon juice and 1/4 cup sour cream; season with salt and pepper to taste. Spoon 1/4 cup of mixture onto right half of each tortilla, leaving a small space around the edges. Fold tortilla over from left to right, forming a half-moon shape. Firmly press down so that the filling sticks. Spray both sides with nonstick cooking spray and lightly sprinkle with Bonedust Seasoning. (At this stage, the quesadillas can be refrigerated, covered, for up to 6 hours.)

    Grill for 3–4 minutes, each side, until lightly charred and crisp but not burnt. Remove from grill and let sit 2–3 minutes. Once filling has cooled slightly, cut into 2–3 wedges each. Serve with extra sour cream for dipping.

8 oz (about 1 cup) flaked Ultimate Planked Salmon (p. 188)
1 cup shredded mozzarella cheese
1/4 cup softened cream cheese
2 green onions, thinly sliced
2 tbsp coarsely chopped fresh dill
1 tbsp fresh lemon juice
1/4 cup + 1/2 cup sour cream
Salt and freshly ground black pepper
10 (8 in) flour tortillas
2 tbsp Bonedust Seasoning (p. 22)

Serves 10 as an appetizer or 5 as a main course

SMOKIN' BBQ PORK QUESADILLA

My chefs and I took the ever-popular pulled pork sandwich, grilled it, and turned it into an even tastier snack.

Preheat a lightly oiled grill to medium (about 350°F). In a medium bowl, combine all ingredients except for the tortillas. Mix until moist and sticky.

    Place 1/4 cup of pork mixture on right half of each tortilla, leaving a small space around edges. Fold tortilla over from left to right, forming a half-moon shape. Firmly press down so that the filling sticks. Spray both sides with nonstick cooking spray and sprinkle with Bonedust Seasoning. (At this stage, you can cover quesadillas with plastic wrap and refrigerate for up to 6 hours.)

    Grill quesadillas for 3–4 minutes, each side, until lightly charred and crisp. Remove from grill and let cool for 2–3 minutes. Once filling has cooled, cut into 2–3 wedges each. Serve immediately with your favorite barbecue sauce for dipping.

1 cup Slow-Smoked Pulled Pork (p. 128)
1 1/2 cups shredded mozzarella cheese
1/4 cup chopped green onions
2 tbsp chopped fresh rosemary
3 tbsp ranch dressing
3 tbsp gourmet barbecue sauce
10 (8 in) flour tortillas
2 tbsp Bonedust Seasoning (p. 22)

Serves 10 as an appetizer or 5 as a main course

Smokin' BBQ Pork Quesadilla

BURGERS

PATIENCE IS A VIRTUE, especially when it comes to grilling burgers. Too many people try to rush things: I like to call these people flippers and pushers. Flipping and pushing dries out the meat and takes away the flavor.

The flavor in burgers and dogs comes from their fat content, so choose a good medium ground over lean ground. To get the juiciest results from your medium ground you need to preserve the fat, which means flipping only once — when one side of the meat is done. You'll know it's ready when your spatula slides under the meat easily and comes away from the grill without sticking.

Always grill your burgers until they're well done, in order to eliminate any bacteria that might exist. And when grilling burgers and sausages, keep the lid open: With the lid closed, you increase the risk of flare-ups. Do all this, and the result will be the best burgers you've ever tasted. Get juicy, get sticky, get messy!

LUDICROUS BURGERS

Nothing beats a burger. There just isn't anything like biting into a juicy burger piled high with lots of good things. Burgers are another type of food I love to experiment with. My own personal mission is to create the ultimate, tastiest burger — what I like to call the Ludicrous Burger.

For years I've been making burgers that blow people's minds; then at a charity event for the Elliott Foundation (an organization that benefits children's charities) I cooked up a pair of Ludicrous Burgers that were auctioned off for $1,500 each! With two 8 oz all-beef patties, eight different kinds of cheese, caramelized onions, sausages, homemade bacon and a fried egg, these burgers were held together with a gooey grilled cheese sandwich top and bottom. Get creative and create your own Ludicrous Burger!

As out-there as the Ludicrous Burger is, there are lots of tips that apply to everyone looking to make better burgers.

★ Think outside the box when looking for buns. You can use just about anything to sandwich around your burger.

★ Have tons of condiments and toppings on hand. The more, the better, and don't be afraid to try new things.

★ Keep the meat cold. It's easier to mix your ingredients and form the patties when the ground meat is nice and cold. Once you've formed your patties, put them back in the refrigerator and let them rest for a bit: They'll grill better and taste better, too.

★ Concentrate on the meat itself. The best-quality meat you can afford makes the best-quality burger. And pay attention when you season it — all the effort you put into making the meat mixture juicy and flavorful will be worth it in the end.

★ Grill burgers over high heat to start, then turn the heat down and let them cook slowly.

THIS MIGHT JUST BE THE MOST EXPENSIVE BURGER EVER SOLD.

PRIME RIB BURGER WITH HORSERADISH CREAM AND YORKSHIRE PUDDING BUNS

Special equipment: Meat grinder

Yorkshire Pudding Buns

3 large eggs
1 cup whole milk
1 cup all-purpose flour
1/2 tsp salt
Freshly ground black pepper
2 tbsp chopped fresh chives
1 tbsp chopped flat-leaf parsley
1/2 cup Crisco vegetable shortening

Horseradish Cream

1 tbsp vinegar
1/4 cup sour cream
2 tbsp softened cream cheese
3/4 cup mayonnaise
1/2 cup freshly grated horseradish
2 tbsp chopped fresh chives
Dash of hot pepper sauce
Salt and freshly ground black pepper

2 lb boneless prime rib
1 medium onion, minced
6 cloves garlic, minced
2 tsp salt
1 1/2 tsp cracked black peppercorns
2 tsp hot mustard powder
2 tbsp Better Butter Burger
Seasoning (p. 22)
4 Yorkshire Pudding Buns
1/2 cup melted butter

Serves 4

The most succulent-tasting cut of beef is the rib steak, so isn't it a crime to grind up such beautiful meat? Well, yes, but sometimes you just want a seriously full-flavored, amazingly juicy burger.

To prepare the Yorkshire Pudding Buns: Whisk eggs in a large bowl until just blended. Gradually whisk in milk. Sift flour, salt and pepper into egg mixture; add herbs and whisk again until smooth. Cover with plastic wrap and refrigerate batter for 30 minutes.

Preheat grill to medium-high (about 400°F). Place a large muffin tin on the grill and heat for 10 minutes. Scoop about 1 1/2 tbsp of shortening into 4 muffin molds. Close grill lid and allow fat to get very hot, about 5 minutes. Reduce heat to low and carefully pour 3/4 cup of batter into each mold. Close lid and bake for 25–30 minutes, until puddings are golden brown and crisp. (Resist the urge to open grill lid: If you do, the puddings won't rise.) Remove from grill, cool slightly.

To prepare the Horseradish Cream: In a small bowl, whisk together vinegar, sour cream, cream cheese and mayonnaise until smooth. Add horseradish, chives and hot sauce, and salt and pepper to taste. Set aside.

Preheat grill to medium-high (400° to 450°F). Cut the prime rib of beef into 1- to 2-in chunks. Spread chunks evenly on a parchment-lined cookie sheet and store in freezer for 10–15 minutes to chill.

When fully chilled, remove beef from freezer and, using the large grind plate of your meat grinder, grind once. Change grind size to small and grind meat a second time. Add onion and garlic to grinder and pass the meat through once more. Transfer meat mixture to a bowl and add salt, pepper, mustard powder and Better Butter Burger Seasoning to mixture. Mix with your hands, being careful not to overmix. Divide into 4 equal portions. Form into balls, then gently press each into a patty, about 1/2-in thick. Grill patties 4–5 minutes, each side, for medium- to well-done.

Just before burgers are ready, slice Yorkshire Pudding Buns in half and brush insides with melted butter. Grill, cut side down, for 2–3 minutes, or until buttered side is crisp and golden brown. Serve burgers on grill-toasted Yorkshire Pudding Buns with Horseradish Cream.

SOUTHWEST MOLTEN BURGER

Stuffing a disk of flavored butter into a patty takes a little practice, but the end result will blow your guests away. Make sure to warn people that these burgers have a molten filling, and have plenty of napkins at the ready.

To prepare the Chili Butter: Combine all Chili Butter ingredients in a food processor and process until smooth. Transfer Chili Butter to a sheet of plastic wrap. Spread butter evenly on wrap and, lifting one end, roll into a 1 1/2-in-wide tube. Twist ends of plastic wrap to tighten butter tube and store in freezer overnight or for at least 2 hours.

To prepare the Chipotle and Roasted-Garlic Aioli: Combine all aioli ingredients in a food processor; process until smooth. Transfer to a container and store in refrigerator, covered, overnight or for at least 2 hours before using. (Aioli, in an airtight container, will keep up to 2 weeks in the refrigerator.)

To prepare the Chili Rub: In a small bowl, combine all ingredients. Mix well and set aside.

In a large glass bowl, combine ground beef, 1/4 cup water and Better Butter Burger Seasoning. Mix lightly with your hands; be careful not to overmix the beef. Divide into 4 equal portions and form into balls. Remove prepared Chili Butter roll from freezer, unwrap and slice off four 1/4-in-thick disks. (Set unused Chili Butter aside to soften.) Poke your thumb into the middle of each ground beef ball to create a hole, and insert a frozen Chili Butter disk. Using your hands, push beef mixture back into place around butter, so that it is thoroughly encased. Gently flatten beef balls into patties, about 3/4-in thick, ensuring that the butter is still completely sealed within.

Preheat grill to medium (about 350°F). Coat patties lightly with mustard and sprinkle with prepared Chili Rub. Spray grill with nonstick cooking spray. Grill patties for 4–5 minutes, each side, or until just firm to the touch. If using, place slices of cheese on top of each patty 2 minutes before burgers are done. Transfer burgers to a platter, tent with foil and let sit for 2–3 minutes.

Meanwhile, smear buns with softened Chili Butter, sprinkle with a little garlic powder and toast for 30–60 seconds on the grill. Remove buns to 4 plates and generously slather with prepared aioli. Place a patty on bottom half of each bun; top with a big dollop of guacamole and cover with remaining bun. Serve immediately.

Chili Butter
1/2 cup butter
2 chipotle peppers in adobo sauce
2 tbsp ancho chili powder
1 head Grill-Roasted Garlic (p. 219)
1/2 tsp salt

Chipotle and Roasted-Garlic Aioli
1 1/2 cups good quality mayonnaise
1 head Grill-Roasted Garlic (p. 219), squeezed out of its skin
1 tsp ground cumin
1 tbsp chopped chipotle peppers in adobo sauce

Chili Rub
2 tbsp ancho chili powder or any other chili powder
1 tbsp garlic powder
1 tbsp onion powder
1 tsp freshly ground black pepper
1 tsp ground chipotle peppers (substitute cayenne pepper if you can't find ground chipotles)
1 tsp dried oregano
1 tsp dried parsley

1 1/2 to 2 lb ground chuck (20 per cent fat content)
1 tsp Better Butter Burger Seasoning (p. 22)
4 disks Chili Butter
1 tbsp prepared yellow mustard
4 slices Jack cheese (optional)
4 hamburger buns
Chili Butter to coat buns
Garlic powder
Guacamole

Serves 4 to 8

CHEESY STUFFED BURGER DOGS

These novelty cheese-string-stuffed hamburger dogs are surprisingly delicious; serve with mustard, relish, ketchup, sauerkraut, sliced onions, sliced pickles, chili peppers and whatever else you like to nosh on.

1 lb regular ground beef
1/2 lb lean ground pork
1/4 cup Vidalia onion, finely diced
2 tbsp Bonedust Seasoning (p. 22)
1 tbsp Dijon mustard
1 tbsp Worcestershire sauce
1 tsp minced garlic
Salt and freshly ground black pepper
6 hot dogs
3 mozzarella cheese strings
(about 21 g each), halved lengthwise
Gourmet barbecue sauce
6 hot dog buns

Serves 6

In a large bowl, combine beef, pork, onion, Bonedust Seasoning, mustard, Worcestershire sauce and garlic; season with salt and pepper to taste. Using your hands, mix well to incorporate. Cover with plastic wrap and refrigerate for 1 hour.

When chilled, cover a flat surface with 6 10 x 6-in sheets of plastic wrap. Remove meat from refrigerator and evenly spread a 6 x 4-in rectangle, with a thickness of about 1/2 in, on each plastic sheet.

Place a hot dog and a cheese string half along length of one side of meat rectangle and, using the plastic wrap as a guide, lift up and tightly roll, molding the meat around the hot dog and cheese. The roll should be about 2 inches in diameter. Twist plastic wrap to tighten and seal the ends of the meat roll. Repeat with remaining meat mixture and cheese strings to form 6 burger dogs. Refrigerate burger dogs, still in plastic wrap, for 30 minutes, to allow rolls to set.

Preheat grill to medium (about 350°F). Remove burger dogs from refrigerator and unwrap. Grill for 10–12 minutes, or until fully cooked, turning occasionally and basting with barbecue sauce during the last 2–3 minutes of grilling time. Place hot dog buns, cut side down, on grill and toast for 3–4 minutes or until golden brown. Remove grilled burger dogs from grill and place 1 in each toasted hot dog bun. Serve immediately with extra barbecue sauce and garnish with your favorite condiments.

REGIS AND KELLY
SURF-AND-TURF BURGER

I prepared this ultrasophisticated burger for an appearance on *Live with Regis and Kelly*. **It was a huge hit.**

In a small, heavy saucepan over low heat, melt butter. Heat gently, so that most of the water in the butter evaporates and the milk solids sink to bottom. Skim any foam from the surface. Carefully pour off clarified butter and set aside. You should have approximately 3/4 cup clarified butter.

In a food processor, process cream cheese until smooth. Add lobster meat, chopped Brie, dill, lemon juice and salt and pepper to taste; process until mixed. Remove mixture from processor and shape into patties about 2 in wide and 1/2 in thick. Place on a waxed paper–lined tray and refrigerate, covered, until ready to use.

In a large bowl, combine sirloin, onion, garlic and mustard; season with Bonedust Seasoning and 1–2 tsp of Worcestershire sauce. Mix until well combined and shape into 12 patties, 3 to 4 in wide, pressing each patty firmly so it holds together. Place burgers on a waxed paper–lined tray and refrigerate, covered, for 30 minutes.

When patties are fully chilled, remove from refrigerator. Place 6 lobster patties on top of 6 sirloin patties. Top each lobster-sirloin stack with 1 of the remaining sirloin patties; using your hands, shape top and bottom sirloin patties together around lobster patty to completely enfold; press and crimp edges to form a tight seal. Transfer to a waxed paper–lined tray and freeze for 30 minutes before grilling.

Preheat grill to medium-high (about 400°F). In a small saucepan over low heat, stir together clarified butter, ketchup, herbs and remaining 2 tsp Worcestershire sauce; heat until warm. Remove from heat, cover and keep warm. Grill burgers for 4–6 minutes on one side. Turn over, baste with butter sauce and cook for 3–5 minutes more, or until beef burgers are just cooked and the lobster centers are warm and creamy.

Meanwhile, brush lobster claws with butter sauce and grill for 1–2 minutes, turning once, until lightly charred and heated through. Remove from grill and set aside.

When ready to serve, place buns on 6 plates. Separate buns and spread bottom half of each with mayonnaise and top with leaf lettuce, beef-lobster burger, lobster claw, onion slice and tomato slice. Cover with top half of each bun and serve.

1/2 lb butter
1/2 cup softened cream cheese
1 cup fresh or well-drained thawed frozen lobster meat
1/2 cup finely chopped Brie, chilled
2 tsp chopped fresh dill
1 tsp fresh lemon juice
Salt and freshly ground black pepper
1 1/2 lb ground sirloin
1 small onion, diced
2 cloves garlic, minced
1 tbsp Dijon mustard
2 tbsp Bonedust Seasoning (p. 22)
2 tsp + 2 tsp Worcestershire sauce
1/4 cup ketchup
1 tbsp chopped fresh herbs (p. 26)
6 lobster claws, removed from their shells
6 hamburger buns
1/4 cup mayonnaise
6 leaves leaf lettuce
1 small onion, thinly sliced
2 ripe tomatoes, thinly sliced

Serves 6

TEDDY'S GRILLED CHEESE BEEF BURGER WITH LUDICROUS BEER BUTTER BASTING SAUCE

Two grilled cheese sandwiches make for cheesy, gooey "buns" around this tasty burger.

Ludicrous Beer Butter Basting Sauce
1/2 cup melted unsalted butter
1 cup gourmet barbecue sauce
6 oz beer (about 1/2 bottle)
2 tbsp Better Butter Burger
Seasoning (p. 22)

Beef Burger
1 lb regular ground beef
1 small white onion, finely diced
1 jalapeño pepper, seeded and minced
3 cloves garlic, minced
1/4 cup beer
2 tbsp chopped flat-leaf parsley
1 tbsp Worcestershire sauce
1 tbsp Dijon mustard
2 tbsp Better Butter Burger
Seasoning (p. 22)
Salt and freshly ground black pepper
to taste

Grilled Cheese, Bacon and Onion Buns
1/2 cup softened unsalted butter
16 slices thick-sliced white or whole-wheat bread
8 slices processed cheese, thick grilled cheese style
1 red onion, sliced into 1/4-in rings and grilled
16 slices bacon, cooked crisp

Serves 4

To prepare the Ludicrous Beer Butter Basting Sauce: In a small bowl, combine melted butter, barbecue sauce, beer and Better Butter Burger Seasoning. Mix well and set aside for basting.

To prepare the Beef Burgers: In a large bowl, mix all ingredients. Form mixture into 4 large patties. Transfer patties to a large container; cover and refrigerate for 1 hour.

To prepare the Grilled Cheese, Bacon and Onion Buns: Butter 1 side of each slice of bread. Place slices on grill, buttered sides down. Add 1 slice of cheese in the center of each piece of bread. Garnish with a bit of grilled onion and 2 slices of cooked bacon. Top each garnished stack with a second slice of buttered bread, butter side up. Grill over medium heat until bread is golden and cheese has melted. Set aside.

Remove Beef Burgers from refrigerator and transfer to grill. Grill for 10–12 minutes, each side. When burgers are almost fully cooked, baste liberally with basting sauce.

To assemble, place 4 grilled cheese sandwiches on 4 plates and place 1 Beef Burger on top of each. Garnish with your favorite toppings and cover with another grilled cheese sandwich. Serve with lots of napkins, cold beer and extra Ludicrous Beer Butter Basting Sauce for dipping.

GREEK CHICKEN BURGER

These "Greek" chicken burgers are topped with feta cheese, tomatoes, cucumbers and avocado — they make for delicious though slightly messy eating.

In a large bowl, combine all ingredients except buns. Using your hands, thoroughly combine.

Divide chicken mixture equally into 4 portions. Form into balls, then gently press into patties, each about 1/2 in thick. Place on waxed paper–lined tray and refrigerate for at least 1 hour.

Spray cold grill with nonstick cooking spray and preheat to medium (about 350° F). Remove chicken burgers from fridge and place on preheated grill. Grill burgers until they are fully cooked and the juices run clear, about 6–8 minutes each side.

During the final few minutes of grilling, place buns or pitas on grill and grill-toast for 1–2 minutes, or until warmed through and lightly toasted. When fully cooked, remove burgers from grill and place on buns or in pitas. Serve with lettuce, tomatoes, cucumbers, avocado and crumbled feta cheese. Serve immediately.

2 lb ground chicken
2 tbsp chopped fresh mint
2 tbsp chopped fresh oregano
4 cloves garlic, minced
2 tsp finely grated lemon zest
1 tbsp fresh lemon juice
1 tbsp Better Butter Burger Seasoning (p. 22)
1 tbsp extra-virgin olive oil
4 buns or 2 large pitas

Serves 4

PORK 'N' GOAT-CHEESE BURGER

Cheesy and fantastic.

Place 1 lb ground pork in food processor. Process until meat is smooth in texture. Transfer meat from processor to a large mixing bowl and add remaining ground pork. Cover and refrigerate until needed. Finely crumble goat cheese into a small container. Cover and freeze for 15–20 minutes.

Preheat grill to medium-high (about 400°F). Skewer onion and red pepper, and brush with oil. Sprinkle with Bonedust Seasoning. Grill seasoned vegetable skewers for 5–6 minutes, each side, or until tender and lightly charred. Remove from grill and let cool slightly before removing vegetables. Dice vegetables and add to ground pork along with green onions and Better Butter Burger Seasoning; mix well until fully incorporated.

Reduce grill temperature to medium (about 350°F). Add frozen goat cheese to pork and mix together well. Divide cheese-and-pork mixture into 6 portions. Form into balls, then gently press into patties, each about 1/2 in thick. Grill on medium heat for 5–6 minutes, each side, basting with 1/4 cup Luther's Sheep Dip Marinade until meat is fully cooked and the cheese is melted and soft. Serve with remaining marinade for dipping.

Special equipment: 2 (10 in) bamboo skewers, soaked in water for at least 1 hour

1 lb + 1 lb lean ground pork
8 oz goat cheese
1 medium Vidalia onion, peeled and cut in chunks
1 medium red bell pepper, seeded and cut into chunks
2 tbsp olive oil
1 tbsp Bonedust Seasoning (p. 22)
4 green onions, sliced
1 tbsp Better Butter Burger Seasoning (p. 22)
1/2 cup Luther's Sheep Dip Marinade (p. 32)

Serves 6

MEATS

WHENEVER ANYONE ASKS me what my favorite food is, I usually respond with "all of it — except for blood sausage and Brussels sprouts." But what I love most is meat. Big, juicy steaks cut extra thick and heavily marbled with fat. And there is simply no better way to cook meat than on the grill. Grilling allows meat to sear on the outside while the inside stays juicy and tender. I believe that barbecue is the purest form of cooking, dating back to when fire first met food with the caveman **Q**-dude doing the cooking! It is primal, and truly offers your food the best flavors. The char, the smoke and the fire all blend with the meat to give it the succulence, tenderness and full flavor that you and your meat deserve.

I'm also into wild game, like venison in a smoky, savory chocolate sauce, or grilled rare ostrich. And I like rotisserie of pork loin, where the meat is juicy and the fat rolls off your chin. Meat and fire baby, pure and simple.

ON STEAKS

A BIG, JUICY STEAK is my favorite food — and, for me, the best of the best is the rib steak. Bone in or boneless, it has the most flavor. My next favorite cut is the striploin: I usually order it about 1 1/2 to 2 inches thick, 12 to 16 ounces each. Seasoned with salt, pepper and garlic and cooked blue-rare, about 90 seconds per side, it's delicious!

MY RULES FOR BUYING AND COOKING GREAT STEAKS

RULE NO. 1 Buy the best-quality steak you can afford. Not all top cuts (for example, rib eye and striploin) are tender. There are many grades of meat. In the U.S., depending on the type of meat, you have USDA Prime, Choice, Select and Standard, down through Cutter and Canner. In Canada, meats are graded as A, AA, AAA, with A being basic quality and AAA being the best. Keep in mind that usually the more expensive the cut of meat is, the better its quality is likely to be.

There are other cuts to look for, too: CAB (Certified Angus Beef) is expensive but delicious. USDA Choice is reasonably priced, and will often be very tasty. Then, of course, there is Prime, which is the best quality you can get. For the super-rich, there's Japanese Kobe beef, loaded with marbling and extremely expensive. But, again — if you have the means — I highly recommend it.

What makes a great steak? Simply put, marbling. The more "marbled" a steak is, the better it's going to taste. Which brings me to Rule No. 2...

RULE NO. 2 Fat = Flavor. The more fat there is inside, the more flavorful and tender your steak will be.

RULE NO. 3 Find yourself a good butcher. I like my steaks cut about 1 1/2 to 2 inches thick and about 12 to 16 ounces each, depending on the cut. A thicker steak cooks more evenly, and there's far less chance of it drying out on the grill. Keeping the juices in your steak, by letting the cooked meat rest for about 5 minutes once it's off the grill, will also yield better flavor.

HOW TO GRILL THE PERFECT STEAK

If you've spent serious dough on some great steaks, you won't need to tenderize them, only marinate them, if you want to add flavor. Personally, I like to take a big-ass rib steak or porterhouse and marinate it for 2 hours in Guinness or Mill Street Brewery Coffee Porter or Steam Whistle Pilsner — all of them work great.

Season your steaks with lots of coarsely ground sea salt, black pepper and garlic. For cooking a great steak, I prefer to use charcoal, since it gives the best flavor. Whatever you use, make sure it's hot — 600°F-plus, if you can. Once you start cooking the steaks, remember: High heat, lid open; be patient; never leave your grill; don't poke, cut or stick your steaks; and have a beer.

STEAK CUTS

TENDERLOIN

Of all the cuts, tenderloin is the most tender. Tenderloin comes from the short loin of beef; it lies between the rib and the sirloin and never really does anything but just sit there being tender. Tenderloin may be cooked whole or cut into wonderfully tender steaks. Be careful not to overcook this cut: It doesn't have a lot of fat, so it tends to dry out the more it cooks. Quite often, restaurants wrap tenderloin with a strip or two of bacon, to keep it moist and succulent.

STRIPLOIN

The striploin steak is one of the most popular cuts of beef. It comes from the top loin muscle in the short loin of beef. It is best grilled to medium-rare and is often served with a peppercorn sauce. This steak is known by many names, the most popular being New York strip steak and Kansas City steak. A bone-in striploin steak is known as a shell steak. My favorite way to eat a New York striploin is blue-rare, nicely seasoned and brought to room temperature.

RIB-EYE STEAK

My favorite, this steak is cut from between the rib and chuck sections. The bone-in rib steak is also known as cowboy steak. Rib steak is an extremely tender cut of beef and it's heavily marbled with fat, giving it maximum flavor. It's best to grill this steak to medium-rare, which allows the internal fat to melt and bring out the natural juices and flavor. I remember having a rib steak at the Chicago Chop House: It was so good that I woke up in the middle of a delicious steak dream just drooling about it. It rocked! Thank God for the leftover piece I'd saved in my hotel room mini bar.

T-BONE STEAK

This steak is named after the shape of the bone in it, a T that separates the striploin from the small tenderloin. Cut from the center of the short loin, this is a large steak that's often shared; but if you're truly hungry, it is a real meal for one. I like to serve T-bones with lots of sautéed onions and mushrooms, topped with crumbled blue cheese.

PORTERHOUSE STEAK

A porterhouse steak is cut from the large end of the short loin and has the same T-shaped bone as the T-bone. It has a larger tenderloin portion and is truly a meal for two; it's sometimes called the king of steaks. Porterhouses are often cut into 2-in-thick portions, weighing approximately 36 ounces. Rub these steaks with garlic, black pepper and fresh rosemary, and grill them over medium-high heat.

SIRLOIN STEAK

Cut from the area between the short loin and round, the sirloin has three main muscles. Sirloin steaks are quite flavorful, but they require marinating to make them a little more tender. A teriyaki marinade is the most popular marinade to use on sirloin. This cut gives you the best of both worlds — the strip and the tenderloin. Delicious! A steak for one, or more if ya feel like sharing.

FLANK STEAK

The flank steak comes from the lower hind region of beef. It is a tougher cut of steak and requires marinating to make it tender. As it doesn't have a lot of internal fat, be careful not to overcook it. Marinated in an Asian marinade, this steak will have great flavor: It is best served thinly sliced, and is a great steak for a salad or steak sandwich.

SKIRT STEAK

Skirt steak is the diaphragm muscle cut from the flank steak. It's a tough piece of meat that needs to be well trimmed of fat and sinew and marinated for a long period of time — I'd say 24 to 48 hours — to tenderize it. I tenderize this cut with either a meat mallet or a needler, an instrument that has 48 little stainless steel blades. When pushed into a piece of meat, these blades cut through flesh and membrane to make everything tender. You can find a needler at most restaurant supply stores.

HANGER STEAK

The hanger steak hangs between the rib cage and loin cage. Hanger steaks have a little stronger flavor than regular steaks and need to be very fresh. Ask your butcher for this tender cut of beef, which isn't usually found in grocery stores. Marinate it with stronger-flavored herbs and spices and lots of garlic. It is best cooked rare-to-medium and sliced thinly.

COOKING STEAK: HOW DO YOU LIKE YOURS DONE?

★ Blue-rare: A blue-rare steak is quickly charred on the outside and barely cooked on the inside. For best results, bring the steak to room temperature before cooking.
★ Rare: A rare steak has a cool red center.
★ Medium-rare: A medium-rare steak has a warm red center.
★ Medium: A medium steak has a pink center, and the juices will run clear.
★ Medium-well: A medium-well steak has a hot pink center, and the juices are clear.
★ Well-done: A well-done steak is gray throughout, without any trace of pink. The juices run clear.
★ Super well-done: This steak is weighted with a brick until heavily charred on the outside. It's gray inside and no juices remain.

How to Test for Doneness for the Perfect Steak
The best way to test for "doneness" in a steak is to use a meat thermometer.

Blue-rare	130°F
Rare	130° to 140°F
Medium-rare	140° to 145°F
Medium	145° to 150°F
Medium-well	150° to 160°F
Well-done	160° to 170°F
Super well-done	170°F plus

The next best method to test for doneness is the hand touch method. Relax one hand and touch the soft, fleshy part at the base of your thumb with your other hand. This soft texture is similar to the texture of a blue-rare to rare steak. Now touch your thumb and forefinger together and again touch the base of your thumb. This texture is similar to a medium-rare steak. Next, touch your thumb to your middle finger. This firmer texture is similar to the texture of a medium steak. Next, touch your thumb to your fourth finger. The semi-firm texture at the base of your thumb is similar to a medium-well steak. Lastly, touch your thumb to your pinky finger. The very firm texture at the base of your thumb is similar to a well-done steak.

This method of testing for a steak is relatively easy, and you will never find yourself looking for a thermometer while grilling.

One last note: Never cut into a steak to test for doneness. Cutting allows all the natural juices to escape, leaving you with a dry and tasteless piece of meat.

WORKIN' MAN'S PORTERHOUSE WITH BLUE COLLAR BUTTER

Blue cheese, beer and a big, juicy porterhouse steak: the perfect meal after a hard day's work.

Blue Collar Butter

1 cup softened butter
1/4 cup crumbled blue cheese
2 tbsp chopped flat-leaf parsley
1/2 tsp cracked black peppercorns
2 tbsp red chili peppers, seeded
and minced
3 cloves garlic, minced
Salt and freshly ground black pepper

Beer-Lime Marinade

1 (8 oz) bottle beer
Juice of 1 lime
3 tbsp vegetable oil
3 cloves garlic, minced
1 tbsp coarsely ground black pepper

2 (36 oz) porterhouse steaks
2 tbsp extra-virgin olive oil
4 tbsp Amazing Steak Spice (p. 23)

Serves 2

To prepare the Blue Collar Butter: In a food processor, process all the ingredients for Blue Collar Butter. Transfer to an airtight container, cover, and freeze until needed. You will have more Blue Collar Butter than required for this recipe — keep it in the freezer and use on grilled meat or vegetables.

To prepare the Beer-Lime Marinade: In a large, rectangular glass baking dish, combine all marinade ingredients; mix well. Place steaks in marinade, ensuring meat is completely covered. Cover and refrigerate for 2 hours.

When steaks are fully marinated, preheat grill to medium-high (about 400°F). Remove meat from dish and discard marinade. Remove Blue Collar Butter from freezer and set aside. Rub marinated steaks with olive oil and Amazing Steak Spice, firmly pressing so that seasoning adheres to meat. Grill steaks for 8–10 minutes, each side, for medium-rare doneness. Transfer steaks from grill to plates and let sit for 3 minutes. Top each with a large dollop of Blue Collar Butter and serve immediately with beer.

BROWN SUGAR AND BOURBON SIRLOIN STEAKS

Bourbon and brown sugar are a great mix with steaks. Serve this with Roasted Smashed Sweet Potatoes (see p. 213).

1/3 cup + 1/4 cup bourbon whiskey
1/4 cup + 1/4 cup brown sugar,
firmly packed
3 tbsp kosher salt
1/2 cup chopped fresh thyme
1 tsp Bonedust Seasoning (p. 22)
6 boneless beef sirloin steaks,
cut 1 in thick

Serves 6

In a large bowl, combine 2 1/2 cups water, 1/3 cup bourbon, 1/4 cup brown sugar, salt, thyme and Bonedust Seasoning. Stir until sugar is dissolved. Place steaks in a large resealable plastic bag. Pour enough bourbon–brown sugar mixture over steaks to ensure that meat is covered. Seal bag and marinate, refrigerated, for 6–8 hours, turning bag occasionally.

In a small bowl, combine remaining 1/4 cup bourbon and 1/4 cup brown sugar; mix well. Cover with plastic wrap and set aside until needed.

When steaks are fully marinated, preheat grill to medium (about 350°F). Remove steaks from bag and discard marinade. Rinse steaks and pat dry with paper towels. Grill to desired doneness, turning once halfway through the grilling. Remove from grill and set aside for 2–3 minutes before slicing. To serve, transfer steak slices to a platter and drizzle with reserved bourbon–brown sugar mixture.

Workin' Man's Porterhouse on the toolbox-grill

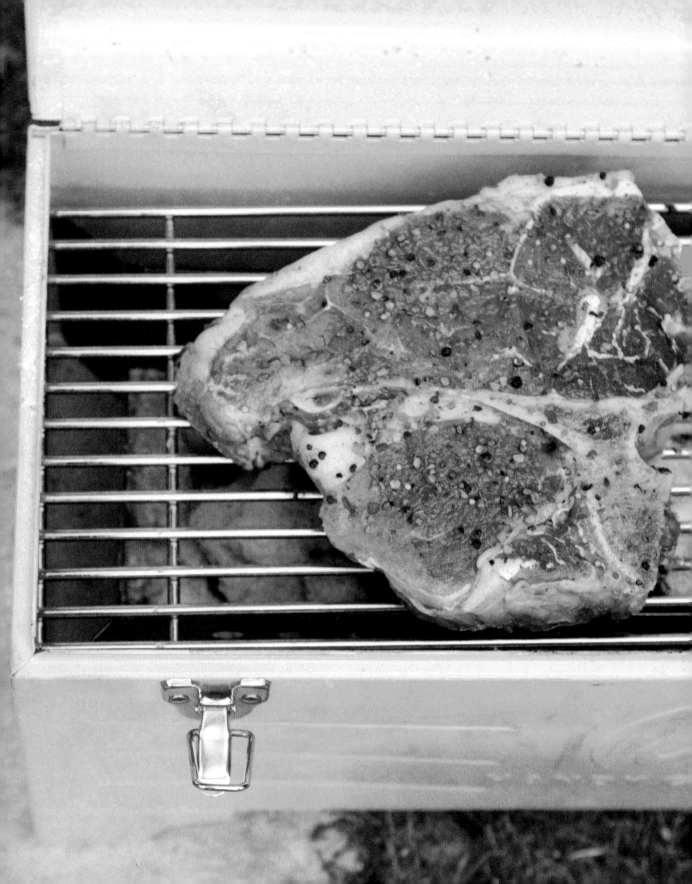

BIG, JUICY RIB STEAK

1 tbsp coarsely ground black pepper

3 cloves garlic, minced

1 tsp olive oil

1 (16 oz) boneless rib steak, cut a minimum of 1 1/2 in thick, at room temperature

2 tbsp melted butter

1 tbsp really good balsamic vinegar

1 tbsp mixed chopped fresh herbs

1 1/2 tsp coarse sea salt (like fleur de sel) or Smoked Salt Steak Rub (p. 28)

Serves 1

A big, juicy rib steak, heavily marbled and weighing in at about 16 oz or more, is a thing of beauty.

Fire up your grill to high, about 600°F or more. (I prefer to cook this steak over lump charcoal on either my Big Green Egg grill or my Primo grill. Charcoal gives this steak the best flavor. With lump charcoal the grill temperature can be about 750°F.) While the grill heats up, combine the black pepper, garlic and oil in a small bowl. Rub the steak all over with the pepper-garlic mixture, pressing firmly so that the mixture adheres to the meat. Set aside.

In another bowl, combine melted butter, vinegar and herbs. Set aside and keep warm. Season the steak with coarse salt and place on the grill at a 45° angle; grill for 2–3 minutes to sear. Turn steak another 45° and cook for another 2–5 minutes. Flip steak over and baste with butter-balsamic-herb mixture. Continue to grill for 2–5 minutes more on a 45° angle. Turn steak 45° and cook for another 2–5 minutes. Flip steak again. (Steak should now have that fancy steakhouse-chef-diamond-grill-mark pattern.) Remove from grill and set aside for 5 minutes. Carve and serve immediately.

BACON-WRAPPED BEEF TENDERLOIN CHURRASCO

1 lb sliced bacon (about 16 slices)

2 lb beef tenderloin

2 tbsp extra-virgin olive oil

1/4 cup Smoked Salt Steak Rub (p. 28)

1/2 cup gourmet barbecue sauce

Serves 4 to 6

Churrasco is Brazilian barbecue, a technique perfected over centuries by the gauchos, who cooked tenderloin skewered on metal spits over coals in a pit dug in the ground.

Preheat charcoal grill to medium heat (about 350°F), following the manufacturer's instructions.

Place bacon in a foil pan or baking sheet and set on grill. Cook for 5–6 minutes, until much of the fat is rendered and bacon is half cooked but not yet crisp. Remove bacon from grill, drain on paper towels and let cool.

Cut beef tenderloin into equal-sized 2-oz pieces. In a large bowl, toss tenderloin pieces in olive oil and Smoked Salt Steak Rub, pressing firmly so that spices adhere to meat. Carefully wrap one piece of bacon around each piece of seasoned tenderloin. Thread bacon-wrapped beef onto metal skewers so that skewer pierces and secures bacon ends.

Place beef skewers onto charcoal grill and cook, turning occasionally, for 6–8 minutes for medium-rare, basting with barbecue sauce during the last 2 minutes of grilling time. (Bacon should be lightly charred and crisp.) Remove skewers from grill and carefully slide beef pieces onto a large platter. Serve immediately with extra barbecue sauce for dipping.

T-BONE WITH BIG YELLA GRAVY

Serve with lots of bread to sop up this delicious gravy.

4 (20 oz) T-bone steaks (1 1/2 to 2 in thick)
1 cup Big Yella Mustard Marinade (p. 33)
Kosher salt
Cracked black peppercorns

Big Yella Gravy
3 tbsp + 1 tbsp cold unsalted butter
2 Vidalia onions, diced
2 cloves garlic, minced
3 tbsp all-purpose flour
1 cup Smoked Beef Stock (p. 261)
3/4 cup Big Yella Mustard Marinade (reserved from steaks)
Salt and freshly ground black pepper

Serves 4

Place T-bone steaks in a large resealable plastic bag. Pour enough Big Yella Mustard Marinade into bag to cover. Seal and marinate in the refrigerator for 2 hours or overnight, turning occasionally. When fully marinated, remove from bag, reserving marinade, and season with kosher salt and cracked peppercorns to taste, pressing firmly so that seasoning adheres to meat.

To prepare the Big Yella Gravy: In a medium saucepan over medium-high heat, melt 3 tbsp butter. Add onion and garlic and sauté for 3–4 minutes. Add flour, stirring constantly for 4–5 minutes, until flour is golden brown. Pour in Smoked Beef Stock, and whisk until smooth. Continue whisking and add reserved Big Yella Mustard Marinade; bring to a boil. Reduce heat to medium and simmer for 10–12 minutes, stirring occasionally, until liquid thickens; season with salt and pepper to taste. Remove from heat and whisk in remaining 1 tbsp of butter. Set aside over low heat to keep warm.

Preheat grill to medium-high (about 400ºF). Place marinated T-bone steaks on grill and cook for 6–8 minutes each side for medium-rare doneness. Remove steaks from grill and set aside for 3–4 minutes before serving. Serve with warm Big Yella Gravy poured over top.

TANGY PAPAYA-MARINATED FLANK STEAK

Enzymes in the papaya help to tenderize flank steak, as well as making it taste amazing!

1 (2 lb) flank steak
1 medium ripe papaya, peeled and cut into chunks
1 medium Spanish onion, peeled and sliced
2 green onions, thinly sliced
1 tbsp hot mustard powder
1 tbsp peeled and grated fresh ginger
3 tbsp olive oil
1 tsp chopped fresh coriander
Salt and freshly ground pepper

Serves 4 to 6

Rinse steak and pat dry with paper towels. Cut several 1/4-in-deep incisions in a diamond pattern, about 1/2 in apart, on both sides of the flank steak and set aside.

In a food processor, combine papaya, onion, green onion, mustard powder and ginger and process briefly. Pour in olive oil and continue processing until puréed. Add coriander and season with salt and pepper; pulse to incorporate. Put scored steak in a large resealable plastic bag and pour papaya–marinade over. Seal bag and marinate steak for 8–12 hours.

Once steak is fully marinated, preheat grill to medium-high (about 400ºF). Remove steak from bag, discarding marinade, and season with salt and pepper to taste. Grill steak 3–4 minutes each side for medium-rare. Remove steak and set aside for 2–3 minutes before thinly slicing across the grain. Serve immediately.

JAPANESE COWBOY STEAKS

Wasabi and balsamic vinegar may seem like a surprising combination, but the tangy, spicy flavors work perfectly on a well-marbled, juicy steak.

Preheat grill to medium-high (about 400°F). Season steaks, on all sides, with Amazing Steak Spice, firmly pressing so that spices adhere to meat. Grill steaks, basting with Wasabi Balsamic Glazing Sauce during the last half of grilling time, for 8–12 minutes each side for medium-rare doneness. Remove steaks from heat and set aside for 2–3 minutes before thinly slicing on the bias. Transfer the slices to 4 plates and serve with pickled ginger and spicy wasabi paste.

2 (24 oz) cowboy steaks (bone-in rib eye, about 2 in thick), at room temperature
4 tbsp Amazing Steak Spice (p. 23)
1 cup Wasabi Balsamic Glazing Sauce (p. 254)

Serves 4

BEER-LIME MARINATED SKIRT STEAK

Beer and lime juice are great tenderizers and give this steak a lot of flavor. Serve with flour tortillas and all the fixin's, and you've got killer fajitas!

In a glass dish large enough to hold the steak, whisk together beer, lime juice, Bonedust Seasoning, garlic, Worcestershire sauce, soy sauce, olive oil, serrano peppers and coriander. Place steak in the beer–lime juice mixture, turning to coat. Marinate, covered with plastic wrap and refrigerated, for 24–48 hours. The longer, the better.

When skirt steak is fully marinated, preheat grill to high (about 500°F). Remove steak from dish, discarding marinade, and grill for 1–2 minutes each side for rare to medium-rare doneness. (Be careful not to overgrill — the meat is thin and it dries out quickly.) Squeeze lime juice over steaks. Remove from grill and thinly slice across the grain. To make fajitas, serve with warm flour tortillas, salsa, guacamole, sour cream, shredded Jack cheese and assorted grilled peppers, onions and tomatoes.

2 (8 oz) bottles beer
1/2 cup fresh lime juice
4 tbsp Bonedust Seasoning (p. 22)
8 cloves garlic, minced
1/4 cup Worcestershire sauce
2 tbsp soy sauce
2 tbsp extra-virgin olive oil
4 serrano peppers, seeded and minced
1/2 bunch chopped fresh coriander
2 lb skirt steak, trimmed
2 limes, halved

Serves 4 to 6

BBQ COCA-COLA BEEF BRISKET

Coca-Cola does a great job of tenderizing brisket.

Special equipment: Smoker
Hickory wood chunks (amount
depends on the size of your smoker),
soaked in water for 1 hour

1 (10 to 12 lb) beef brisket
2 qt Coca-Cola
1/3 cup Amazing Steak Spice (p. 23)

Serves 8 to 12

Rinse brisket and pat dry with paper towels. Place brisket in a large, clean plastic container. Pour over enough Coca-Cola to ensure brisket is covered. Seal and refrigerate for 48 hours. When brisket is fully brined, prepare smoker according to manufacturer's instructions, to a temperature of 180°F to 220°F.

Remove brisket from container, discarding cola, and rub with Amazing Steak Spice, pressing firmly so that spices adhere to meat. Place in smoker, fat side up, and smoke for 6–8 hours while monitoring temperature and smoke levels. Adjust vents and add wood chips and charcoal as necessary.

After about 8 hours of smoking, remove brisket. Wrap in double layer of aluminum foil; return foil-wrapped brisket to smoker and continue to smoke for another 4–6 hours. Remove brisket from smoker and set aside, unopened, for 30 minutes.

After 30 minutes, unwrap brisket. Serve thinly sliced or shredded, with your favorite barbecue sauce. Any leftover brisket may be wrapped tightly in plastic wrap and frozen for up to 1 month.

BOB'S-KE-BOBS

My friend Bob Bryan at McCain Foods grills these skewers of pork loin and vegetables, which are always a big hit.

Special equipment: 12 (10 in) bamboo
skewers, soaked in water for 1 hour

2 lb pork loin, cut into 1-in cubes
1 cup Grill-Roasted Garlic
Marinade (p. 35)
1 green zucchini, cut into 1-in chunks
1 yellow zucchini, cut into
1-in chunks
3 peppers, cut into 1-in chunks
8 button mushrooms
2 Spanish onions, peeled and cut into
1-in chunks
12 cherry tomatoes
2 tbsp + 1 tbsp Bonedust
Seasoning (p. 22)
1 cup gourmet barbecue sauce

Serves 4 to 6

Thread pork cubes onto skewers and place into a large resealable bag in a baking dish. Pour in enough Grill-Roasted Garlic Marinade to cover skewered pork. Seal bag and refrigerate, in dish, for 1 hour.

Meanwhile, thread green zucchini onto other skewers, leaving a small gap between each piece. Repeat with remaining vegetables, skewering each vegetable onto separate skewers. Spray skewered vegetables with nonstick cooking spray and season with 2 tbsp Bonedust Seasoning.

Preheat grill to medium-high (about 400°F). Remove pork skewers from bag, discarding marinade, and season with 1 tbsp of Bonedust Seasoning. Grill pork skewers for 2–3 minutes. Add vegetable skewers and grill, along with pork skewers, for 6–8 minutes or until vegetables are lightly charred and tender, and pork is cooked through. Baste with barbecue sauce during the final few minutes of grilling. Remove vegetable and pork skewers from grill and set aside to cool slightly. Remove meat and vegetables from skewers and place in a large bowl. Toss with extra barbecue sauce, if desired, and serve immediately with rice.

PLANKED BEEF TENDERLOIN WITH SMOKY MASHED POTATOES

Special equipment: 1 untreated cedar plank (at least 12 x 10 x 1 in), soaked in water for 1 hour

Smoky Mashed Potatoes
4 large Yukon Gold potatoes, peeled and quartered
1/4 cup table cream
1 tbsp softened butter
Salt and freshly ground black pepper

2 (8 oz) beef tenderloin steaks
2 tbsp Amazing Steak Spice (p. 23)
1 (8 oz) wheel Brie or Cambozola cheese, sliced in half horizontally
Bonedust Seasoning (p. 22)

Serves 2

This recipe was given to me by David Coulson, one of my friends at Napoleon Gourmet Grills. He suggests making the potatoes the day before and refrigerating overnight.

To prepare the Smoky Mashed Potatoes: In a large pot of boiling salted water, cook potatoes until tender, about 15–20 minutes. Drain well and let dry, 10–15 minutes. In a small saucepan over low heat, combine cream and butter, stirring to incorporate; warm slightly. Return potatoes to pot and mash together with cream-butter mixture, making sure not to overmash: There should be lumps in the mashed potatoes. Season with salt and pepper and set aside to cool before refrigerating, covered, overnight.

When ready to prepare beef, preheat grill to high (about 500° to 550°F). Season tenderloin steaks with Amazing Steak Spice, pressing firmly so that seasoning adheres to meat. Sear steaks on 1 side for 2–3 minutes. Transfer steaks to a presoaked cedar plank and plank-roast each steak with chilled mashed potatoes. Reduce grill temperature to medium-high (about 400°F) and plank-roast steaks over indirect heat for 20 minutes with grill lid closed.

Increase grill temperature to high (about 500°F). Remove planked steaks from grill and top each with a wheel of cheese. Sprinkle with Bonedust Seasoning and return to grill. Roast over direct heat for 5–10 minutes, or until cheese has melted and potatoes are golden brown and crisp. Using tongs and oven mitts, remove smoking planks from grill and place on another, unused, plank or heat-resistant platter. Serve immediately.

PLANKED HERBED BEER MEATLOAF

This is the best meatloaf you've ever tasted.

In a large bowl, thoroughly combine ground sirloin, ground pork, 1/4 cup barbecue sauce, onion, mustard, garlic, green onion, herbs and 4 oz of beer. Season with salt and pepper to taste. Pack meatloaf mixture onto center of a presoaked cedar plank, forming an oval shape and leaving a 2-in border around the edge. Starting at the bottom of the meatloaf, stretch one slice of bacon around one side of the meatloaf and press lightly to adhere. Repeat on other side of meatloaf, forming a border around the bottom, leaving no meat exposed between the bacon and the plank. Stretch one piece of bacon lengthwise on the top of the meatloaf and repeat with remaining bacon slices, overlapping slightly, until all bacon is used and no meatloaf is left exposed. Sprinkle with Bonedust Seasoning. Cover and refrigerate bacon-wrapped meatloaf for 1 hour to set.

Remove one grate from grill and position foil pan in center of grill to catch any drippings. Fill foil pan with 1/2 in of water and replace grill grate. Preheat grill to medium-high (about 400°F). In a saucepan over high heat, combine 4 oz of beer and 1 cup barbecue sauce and bring to a boil. Reduce heat to medium and simmer for 3–4 minutes, or until mixture has thickened and reduced by half. Remove from heat and set aside for basting.

Transfer planked meatloaf from fridge to grill, overtop the foil pan. Close grill lid. When plank begins to crackle and smoke, reduce heat to medium (about 350°F). Plank-bake bacon-wrapped meatloaf for 35–45 minutes, keeping lid closed but checking at least 2–3 times to make sure that plank has not ignited. When a thermometer inserted into center of meatloaf reads 165°F, baste meatloaf with barbecue sauce–beer mixture. Close lid and let sauce caramelize for 3–5 minutes. Using tongs and oven mitts, remove smoking plank from grill and set aside for 3 minutes on metal baking sheet. To serve, slice planked meatloaf into 2-in slices and serve with extra barbecue sauce on the side for dipping.

Note: To remove foil drip pan from grill, allow grill to cool, remove grate and then carefully lift out drip pan. Discard drippings and pan, and replace grate in grill.

Special equipment: 1 untreated cedar plank (at least 12 x 10 x 1 in), soaked in water for 1 hour

1/2 lb ground sirloin
1/2 lb ground pork
1/4 cup + 1 cup gourmet barbecue sauce
1 Spanish onion, minced
3 tbsp Dijon mustard
2 cloves garlic, minced
2 green onions, chopped
2 tbsp chopped fresh herbs (p. 26)
4 oz + 4 oz beer
Salt and freshly ground black pepper
1 lb bacon (about 16 slices)
2 tbsp Bonedust Seasoning (p. 22)

Serves 8

BEEF TENDERLOIN INJECTED WITH COGNAC BUTTER

Grilling tenderloin whole, instead of cut into smaller steaks, helps keep this lean cut nice and juicy. For extra decadence, I've also injected it with cognac butter.

In a small bowl, whisk together 1/2 cup melted butter, 1/4 cup cognac and 1 tbsp thyme. Continue whisking until well combined; set aside.

Place tenderloin on a flat surface and pat dry with paper towels. Fill a Cajun injector with butter-and-cognac mixture and inject in several places. Cover with plastic wrap and store in the refrigerator for at least 2 hours.

When meat is marinated, preheat grill to medium-high (about 400°F). Remove tenderloin from wrap and rub with olive oil and Smoked Salt Steak Rub, pressing firmly so that seasoning adheres well to the meat. Set aside at room temperature.

Meanwhile, heat 1 tbsp butter in a sauté pan over medium-high. Add sliced shallots and cook for 3–4 minutes or until just tender. Add oyster mushrooms to pan and cook for 2–3 minutes more. Add 2 tbsp cognac, and with a spatula or wooden spoon deglaze by scraping up the browned bits from bottom of pan. Remove from heat and stir in remaining 2 tbsp butter and 2 tbsp thyme. Season mixture with salt and pepper to taste and set aside, keeping warm.

Place tenderloin on grill and cook for 6–8 minutes, each side, for medium-rare. Remove from grill and set aside for 3–5 minutes. If you like, you can inject the cooked tenderloin with some of the sauce from the mushrooms and shallots. Once the meat has rested, slice and serve topped with shallot–oyster mushroom mixture.

Special equipment: Cajun injector

1/2 cup + 1 tbsp + 2 tbsp melted unsalted butter
1/4 cup + 2 tbsp cognac
1 tbsp + 2 tbsp chopped fresh thyme
1 (2 to 4 lb) tenderloin
2 tbsp olive oil
1/4 cup Smoked Salt Steak Rub (p. 28)
6 shallots, peeled and thinly sliced
1 lb oyster mushrooms
Salt and freshly ground black pepper

Serves 6 to 8

SLOW-SMOKED PULLED PORK

This recipe serves many hungry people, and will probably still leave you with leftovers.

Special equipment: Smoker
2 cups apple-wood chunks, soaked in water for 1 hour

1 cup brown sugar, firmly packed
1/2 cup chili pepper
1/2 cup kosher salt
2 tbsp onion powder
2 tbsp garlic powder
2 tbsp freshly ground black pepper
2 tbsp mustard powder
2 tbsp chili powder
2 cups unsweetened apple juice
6 to 7 lb pork shoulder,
at room temperature
2 cups gourmet barbecue sauce

Serves 8 to 12

In a medium bowl, combine brown sugar, chili pepper, kosher salt, onion powder, garlic powder, black pepper, mustard powder and chili powder. Mix well and set aside. Fill a spray bottle with apple juice and set aside.

Preheat smoker, following manufacturer's instructions, to a temperature of 200° to 220°F, adding more charcoal, as needed, and soaked apple-wood chunks. Rub pork shoulder liberally with brown sugar–spice mixture, pressing firmly so that spices adhere to meat. Place seasoned pork shoulder in smoker. Smoke pork shoulder for 1 hour, carefully monitoring smoker temperature and smoke levels, adding more wood chunks and charcoal as necessary and opening vents as needed. After 1 hour, open smoker and spray pork shoulder with apple juice. Close and smoke pork shoulder for another 7–8 hours, spraying pork with apple juice every hour and monitoring temperature and smoke levels.

After 8 hours, insert thermometer into thickest part of meat to test for doneness. Pork should reach an internal temperature of 165°F when fully cooked. Remove smoked pork shoulder from smoker and wrap tightly in aluminum foil, ensuring pork is well sealed in the foil to retain moisture. Set aside for 30 minutes.

When pork has cooled, remove from foil and, wearing rubber gloves, hand-shred pork into a large foil pan. Mix shredded smoked pork with barbecue sauce and serve immediately on soft kaiser buns with T-Bone's Diablo Slaw (p. 72).

JUST PEACHY PORK TENDERLOIN

While visiting my best friend, Wally, I picked up some juicy local peaches at a roadside stand. After a hard day of golf, I made us this sweet-and-spicy pork tenderloin.

Dice half the peaches into 2-in segments. Place in a food processor and add peach juice, olive oil, vinegar, garlic and ginger. Pulse ingredients until smooth. Add fresh herbs and salt and pepper to taste. Pulse one final time to combine. Transfer peach marinade to a large resealable plastic bag containing pork tenderloin. Seal bag and marinate in refrigerator for 1 hour.

Preheat grill to medium-high (about 400°F). Season remaining peaches with 1 tbsp Indonesian Cinnamon Rub. Place peaches on preheated, seasoned grill and cook for 4–5 minutes, turning once, until lightly charred and tender. Remove from grill, and dice into 1/2-in segments. Set aside.

Remove pork from bag and pour marinade into a medium saucepan. Add honey and grilled, diced peaches. Transfer saucepan onto preheated grill and bring marinade to a boil. Reduce heat to medium and allow to simmer for 5–10 minutes, or until liquid is reduced by half and sauce is slightly sticky. Remove from grill and set aside for basting.

Season pork tenderloin with remaining 2 tbsp Indonesian Cinnamon Rub on all sides. Place tenderloin on preheated grill and cook for 4–5 minutes. Baste with reduced peach marinade and turn over. Cook for an additional 4–5 minutes, basting continually during the final minute of cooking time. Remove from grill and set aside for 2–3 minutes before carving into 1-in-thick medallions. Serve drizzled with extra sauce.

6 fresh peaches, pitted, peeled and cut in half
1/4 cup peach juice
3 tbsp extra-virgin olive oil
2 tbsp white balsamic vinegar
2 cloves minced fresh garlic
1 tbsp peeled and grated fresh ginger
3 tbsp chopped fresh coriander
2 tbsp chopped flat-leaf parsley
Kosher salt
Coarsely ground black pepper
2 (1 to 1 1/2 lb) pork tenderloins
1 tbsp + 2 tbsp Indonesian Cinnamon Rub (p. 24)
3 tbsp honey

Serves 4 to 6

SPINNING OUT OF CONTROL: USING YOUR ROTISSERIE

For some reason, the rotisserie — basically, a big rotating rod of skewered meat over the grill — is considered by many to be the most intimidating feature of a barbecue. Yet, in actual fact, it's one of the easiest ways to cook. Simply stated, rotisserie grilling is low-and-slow cooking and it's great for any large cut of meat that requires an extra-long cooking time, such as a roast or pork loin.

When you're ready to rotisserie-grill a cut of meat, all you do is gently push the rotisserie rod through the meat until the tines on one end have penetrated the meat. Then, lift the skewered meat and secure both fork ends on either side of the rotisserie. A counter-weight will ensure that the meat is properly balanced and that it turns smoothly. It's a good idea to have a water-filled tray on the grill to add moisture, so that the meat doesn't dry out.

Keep the main burners off and use only the rotisserie flames at the back of the grill. Turn the heat down to low and let the cooking begin. A good rule of thumb is 20–30 minutes of cooking time per pound. Basting of rotisseried meat should always be done in the last quarter of cooking time, and if you want, add wood chips as a flavoring agent. For safety, make sure that you always wear well-insulated cooking mitts.

With the lid closed and the rotisserie on, your grill becomes a convection oven that will produce a fabulous, evenly roasted piece of meat every time. Keep it low and slow, baste frequently and let the juiciness begin.

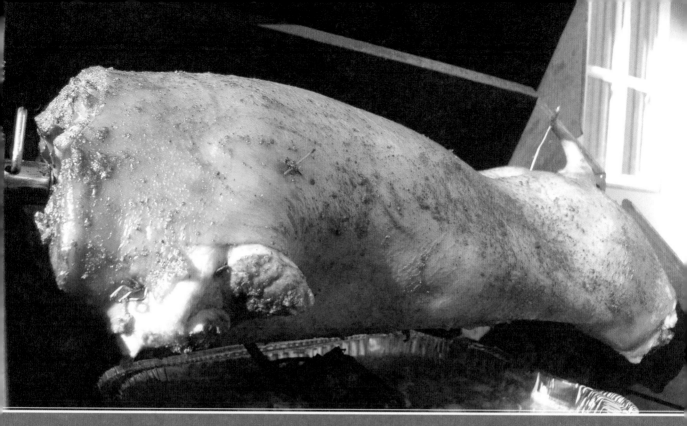

★ *LOW AND SLOW IS THE KEY TO GREAT ROTISSERIE.*

JAMAICAN JERK-RUBBED PORK TENDERLOIN WITH MAPLE JERK BBQ SAUCE

In the mountains outside of Kingston, Jamaica, my friend Lafonda made this dish — spicy, tangy, with lots of fresh herbs. She rocks. Here's my version.

To prepare the Jamaican Jerk Paste: In a food processor or blender, purée the habanero peppers, green onions and 1/4 cup water. Add coriander, parsley and garlic; process until smooth. Pour in olive oil and lemon juice, and season with allspice, salt, cloves, cumin and black pepper. Process until thoroughly combined. Transfer to a container and refrigerate, covered, until needed. Jerk paste will keep up to 2 weeks in the refrigerator.

Place pork loin in a deep roasting pan. In a medium bowl, whisk together jerk paste, beer, sugar and salt. Pour over pork loin and marinate, covered and refrigerated, for 24 hours.

To prepare the Maple Jerk BBQ Sauce: In a large bowl, whisk together barbecue sauce, maple syrup, F@$#'n Jerk Rub and beer. Transfer to an airtight container and refrigerate, covered, until ready to use.

When pork loin is fully marinated, preheat grill to high (about 500°F). Remove loin from roasting pan and discard marinade. Skewer pork with rotisserie rod and secure with rotisserie spikes. Place pork on the rotisserie, season with salt and close lid. Sear meat for 15 minutes before reducing heat to medium-low. Continue roasting, basting frequently with Maple Jerk BBQ Sauce, for 1 to 1 1/2 hours, or until a meat thermometer inserted into the loin reads 150°F. Remove pork from the rotisserie and carefully remove the rotisserie rod. Let pork loin sit for 10 minutes before basting with sauce once again. Cut loin into 1-in-thick slices and serve with remaining sauce.

Jamaican Jerk Paste

4 habanero or Scotch bonnet peppers
6 green onions, coarsely chopped
1 cup fresh coriander
1 cup flat-leaf parsley
6 cloves garlic
1/4 cup extra-virgin olive oil
1/4 cup fresh lemon juice
2 tbsp ground allspice
2 tsp salt
1 tsp ground cloves
1 tsp ground cumin
1 tsp freshly ground black pepper

1 boneless pork loin (4 to 5 lb, and 12 to 18 in long)
2 cups beer
1/2 cup sugar
1/4 cup salt

Maple Jerk BBQ Sauce

2 1/2 cups gourmet barbecue sauce
1/2 cup maple syrup
1/4 cup F@$#'n Jerk Rub (p. 28)
1/2 cup beer

Serves 8

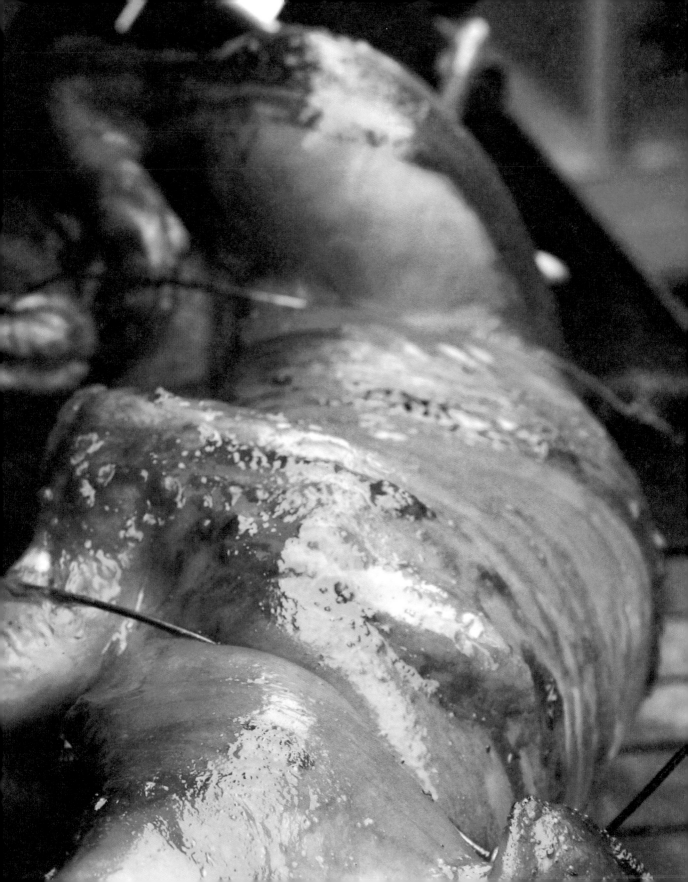

DOUBLE-THICK PORK CHOPS

Ask your butcher to cut a boneless loin chop at least 2 to 3 inches thick. I first had this in Lynchburg, Tennessee, with a little Jack Daniel's, of course!

In a small saucepan over low heat, combine fat, 4 oz Jack Daniel's and 1 tsp Bonedust Seasoning. Using a Cajun injector, inject each chop in the center with one-quarter of the mixture. Rub chops with 4 tbsp of Bonedust Seasoning, pressing firmly so that seasoning adheres to meat. Set aside.

In another small saucepan, melt butter over medium-high heat. Add garlic and onion and sauté for 2–3 minutes. Add brown sugar and stir in honey, remaining Jack Daniel's, vinegar, ketchup and soy sauce; continue stirring and bring to a boil. Reduce heat to low and simmer for 10 minutes, stirring occasionally. Remove from heat and set aside.

Preheat grill to high (about 500°F). Grill chops for 1–2 minutes, each side, to sear. Reduce heat to medium (about 300°F) and close lid. Slow-roast for 12–15 minutes, basting occasionally with Jack Daniel's–brown sugar sauce, until just cooked through and hot. Remove from grill and chow down.

Special equipment: Cajun injector

4 tbsp bacon fat or melted butter
4 oz + 1/4 cup Jack Daniel's whiskey
1 tsp + 4 tbsp Bonedust Seasoning (p. 22)
4 (8 oz) boneless pork loin chops (about 3 in thick)
2 tbsp softened butter
3 cloves garlic, minced
1/4 cup onion, diced
1/2 cup brown sugar, firmly packed
1/4 cup honey
2 tbsp malt vinegar
1/4 cup ketchup
2 tbsp soy sauce
Salt

Serves 4

SUCKLING ROAST PIG WITH APPLE BASTING SAUCE

For this recipe, you'll need 1 rotisserie rod, rotisserie tines, a rotisserie motor, 10 to 12 feet of steel wire (not aluminum wire), 1 meat thermometer — and a nice, juicy porker.

To prepare the Apple Basting Sauce: In a large bowl, combine applesauce, apple juice, honey, vinegar, lemon juice, coriander, nutmeg, cayenne pepper, kosher salt and ground black pepper. Whisk in melted butter and set aside. (You should have about 5 cups for basting.)

Preheat grill to high (about 500° to 550°F). Thoroughly rinse suckling pig under cold running water, then pat dry. Skewer pig with rotisserie rod and secure with rotisserie spikes. Wrap pig with wire to secure. Roast pig for 20 minutes before reducing heat to 250° or 300°F. Continue to roast, basting liberally and frequently with sauce, until fully cooked and an internal thermometer inserted into thickest part of meat reads 180°F, about 3–4 hours.

Apple Basting Sauce
1 cup applesauce
3 cups apple juice
1/2 cup honey
2 tbsp apple cider vinegar
Fresh lemon juice
1/4 cup chopped fresh coriander
Dash of nutmeg
Pinch of cayenne pepper
1 tbsp kosher salt
2 tsp freshly ground black pepper
1/4 cup melted butter or liquefied bacon fat

1 (20 to 23 lb) suckling pig
Sea salt

Serves 20

VEAL BREAST WITH CHEESY POLENTA AND TRIPLE-SMOKED BACON STUFFING

Cheesy Polenta and Triple-Smoked Bacon Stuffing

1 tbsp salt

2 cups cornmeal

1/4 cup Jack Daniel's whiskey

1/4 cup + 3 tbsp softened unsalted butter

1/2 cup + 1/2 cup freshly grated Parmesan cheese

Salt and freshly ground black pepper

2 medium Spanish onions, sliced into rings

1 lb Triple-Smoked Bacon (p. 238)

2 tbsp Bonedust Seasoning (p. 22)

2 tbsp Grill-Roasted Garlic (p. 219)

1 cup cheddar cheese

2 green onions, thinly sliced

2 tbsp chopped fresh thyme

2 tbsp chopped flat-leaf parsley

2 cups Smoked Chicken Stock (p. 261)

Salt and coarsely ground black pepper

Reserved veal bones removed from breast

1 (2 to 3 lb) boneless veal breast, with pocket for stuffing

2 tbsp Bonedust Seasoning (p. 22)

2 carrots, peeled and chopped

2 white onions, cut in half

2 cloves garlic, crushed

1/2 cup white wine

1 1/2 cups Smoked Chicken Stock (p. 261)

Serves 6 to 8

Make friends with a butcher. Ask the butcher for a nice veal breast and then ask him to remove the bones and save them for you. Finally, ask the butcher to cut a pocket into the center of the breast for this amazing cheesy stuffing.

To prepare the Cheesy Polenta and Triple-Smoked Bacon Stuffing: Spray a baking sheet with nonstick cooking spray and set aside.

In a medium saucepan, over high heat, bring 6 cups water and salt to a boil. Reduce heat to medium and slowly add cornmeal, stirring constantly for about 5 minutes. Add Jack Daniel's, 1/4 cup butter and 1/2 cup Parmesan cheese, and season with salt and pepper to taste. Remove polenta from heat and spread in an even layer on greased pan. Place in refrigerator for about 20 minutes to set.

While polenta is chilling, preheat grill to medium (about 350°F). Spray onion and slices of bacon with nonstick cooking spray and season with Bonedust Seasoning. Grill seasoned onion and bacon slices for 5–6 minutes, until lightly charred and tender. Remove from grill and let cool slightly.

Remove polenta from fridge and carefully invert onto clean cutting board. Cut chilled polenta into 4 x 2-in slices and spray with nonstick cooking spray. Grill polenta slices for 3–4 minutes each side, or until lightly charred.

Dice grilled bacon and onion and place in a large mixing bowl. Remove polenta slices from grill and dice into 1-in chunks; add to bacon–onion mixture in bowl. Toss in Grill-Roasted Garlic, cheddar cheese, 3 tbsp butter, green onion, thyme and parsley; mix well. Stir in Smoked Chicken Stock and season with salt and pepper to taste.

Spray cast-iron pan with nonstick cooking spray and turn polenta stuffing mixture into pan. Top with remaining 1/2 cup Parmesan cheese and cover with aluminum foil. Place pan in grill and grill-bake with lid closed 20–30 minutes, or until heated through. Remove foil and grill for an additional 10–15 minutes, with grill lid closed, until cheese is golden brown and bubbling. Carefully remove Cheesy Polenta and Triple-Smoked Bacon Stuffing from grill and set aside until ready to use.

Preheat grill to medium (about 350°F). Line the bottom of a large roasting pan with reserved veal bones. Spoon stuffing into pocket of veal breast. Secure opening with skewers and rub stuffed veal breast with Bonedust Seasoning, pressing firmly so that spices adhere to meat.

Place stuffed, seasoned veal breast onto bones in roasting pan. Scatter carrot, onion and garlic around meat. Pour white wine and Smoked Chicken Stock over veal and vegetables. Cover pan with aluminum foil and transfer to grill. Grill-roast, with lid closed, for 2 1/2–3 hours. Remove foil and baste with juices from pan. Close grill lid and continue to grill-roast, uncovered, for another 30 minutes, basting occasionally with pan juices, until top of veal breast is golden brown and an internal temperature of 160°F is reached. Carefully remove roasting pan from grill and transfer stuffed veal breast to a clean cutting board; let sit for 10–15 minutes before carving. Remove skewers and cut into 6 or 8 large slices. Serve immediately with the roasted vegetables.

GRILLED ASIAN-STYLE LAMB CHOPS

These succulent lamb chops have a spicy and delicious Asian-inspired marinade.

Preheat grill to high (about 500°F). In a medium bowl, combine all ingredients except lamb and steak spice. Mix well and set aside.

Season lamb chops with Amazing Steak Spice, pressing firmly so that spices adhere to meat. Transfer to a shallow glass baking dish and pour half the marinade over seasoned lamb. Set aside to marinate for 15 minutes.

Remove lamb from marinade and grill with lid open for 6–7 minutes or until medium-rare, turning once and basting frequently with remaining marinade. Remove chops from grill, garnish with more fresh herbs and serve.

4 cloves garlic, minced
2 red chili peppers, seeded and chopped
1 green onion, finely chopped
1/2 cup mixed chopped fresh herbs (coriander, dill, mint)
3 tbsp extra-virgin olive oil
1/4 cup soy sauce
1/4 cup Thai sweet chili sauce
1/4 cup rice vinegar
2 lamb racks, cut into 1 1/2- to 2-in- thick chops
2 tbsp Amazing Steak Spice (p. 23)

Serves 4

LAMB LOINS WITH LIME SOUR CREAM DUNK

Pinch saffron threads

1/4 cup cracked black peppercorns

3 tbsp smoked paprika

1 tbsp toasted and ground
cumin seeds

1 tbsp chopped fresh coriander

2 tbsp kosher salt

2 tbsp extra-virgin olive oil

4 (8 to 12 oz) boneless lamb loins

Lime Sour Cream Dunk

1 1/2 cups sour cream

1 tsp toasted and ground cumin seeds

Juice of 1 lime

1/2 tsp grated lime zest

2 tbsp chopped fresh coriander

Salt and freshly ground black pepper

Serves 4 to 6

Lime Sour Cream Dunk might sound strange, but it rocks on this grilled lamb.

In a small bowl, cover saffron threads with 3 tbsp hot water and let steep. In another bowl, combine cracked peppercorns, paprika, cumin, coriander, salt and olive oil. Add saffron threads and water to bowl; mix well to form a paste. Rub paste on lamb loins, ensuring that meat is thoroughly coated. Transfer rubbed loins to container; cover and refrigerate for 1 hour.

To prepare the Lime Sour Cream Dunk: In a small bowl, combine sour cream, cumin, lime juice and zest and coriander; season with salt and pepper to taste. Cover with plastic wrap and refrigerate until needed.

Preheat grill to medium-high (about 400°F). Remove lamb loins from refrigerator and bring to room temperature before transferring to grill. Grill lamb loins, turning once, for 10–12 minutes for medium-rare. Remove lamb loins from grill and set aside for 3–5 minutes before slicing into 2-oz chunks. Serve with Lime Sour Cream Dunk for dipping.

VENISON CHOPS WITH SAVORY SMOKED CHOCOLATE SAUCE

2 Frenched venison racks
(each with 8 ribs)

1/4 cup Bonedust Seasoning (p. 22)

2 tbsp softened butter

2 cloves garlic, minced

1 shallot, finely chopped

2 poblano peppers, roasted, peeled, seeded and cut into 1-in strips

1 cup heavy cream

1/4 cup cognac

1 cup coarsely chopped bittersweet Smoked Chocolate (p. 228)

1 tbsp chopped fresh savory

Salt and freshly ground black pepper

Serves 8

This spicy, savory sauce is great with venison.

Rub the venison with Bonedust Seasoning, pressing firmly so that seasoning adheres to meat; set aside.

Melt butter in a small saucepan over medium-high heat. Add garlic and shallot and sauté 1–2 minutes, or until tender. Add the poblano peppers, cream and cognac, and bring to a boil. Reduce heat to low and, stirring constantly, add the chocolate a little at a time until melted. Simmer gently for about 5 minutes, or until liquid thickens. Stir in savory, and salt and pepper to taste. Remove sauce from heat and keep warm.

Preheat grill to medium-high (about 400°F). Grill venison racks for 7–10 minutes, each side, for medium-rare. Remove racks from grill and set aside for 5 minutes before cutting. Once cooled, slice each rack into 4 thick chops and transfer to plates. Spoon sauce over each chop and serve.

Venison chops get the King of the Q stamp

BUTTER-BASTED CORNMEAL-CRUSTED RACK OF LAMB

The crunchy cornmeal crust makes this rack of lamb taste especially tender. This recipe calls for "Frenched" lamb racks, which simply means that the meat is scraped from the ends of the bones.

Butter Baste

1/2 lb unsalted butter

1 jalapeño pepper, grilled, seeded and minced

2 cloves garlic, minced

1 tbsp chopped fresh coriander

Salt and freshly ground black pepper

Cornmeal Crust

1/4 cup cornmeal

1/2 cup freshly grated Parmesan cheese

2 tbsp chopped fresh coriander

Kosher salt to taste

Cracked black peppercorns to taste

2 (1 1/2 lb) Frenched lamb racks

1/2 cup Bonedust Burn BBQ Paste (p. 29)

Serves 4 to 6

To prepare the Butter Baste: In a small saucepan over medium heat, melt butter. Add all remaining baste ingredients and mix well. Remove from heat and set aside for basting.

To prepare the Cornmeal Crust: In a small bowl, combine all ingredients for Cornmeal Crust.

Preheat grill to medium-high (about 400°F) and season a griddle pan with nonstick cooking spray. Rub meat portion of lamb racks on all sides with Bonedust Burn BBQ Paste, pressing firmly so that spices adhere to meat. Coat seasoned meat portion of lamb racks with Cornmeal Crust, pressing gently but firmly so that it adheres. Transfer crusted lamb racks onto preheated griddle pan and sear for 2–3 minutes per side. Move lamb to top rack of grill. Reduce heat to medium (about 350°F) and close grill lid. Grill-roast for 12–15 minutes, basting with reserved Butter Baste during the last few minutes of grilling. Remove lamb racks from grill and baste once more. Set aside racks for 5 minutes before slicing between each bone. Serve drizzled with remaining Butter Baste.

GRILLED OSTRICH

Ask your local butcher where to find ostrich. Unlike chicken, ostrich is deep red in color and should be cooked medium-rare.

1 (1 1/2 to 2 lb) ostrich loin
1 cup Cabernet Marinade (p. 32)
2 tbsp Amazing Steak Spice (p. 23)

Serves 6 to 8

Rinse ostrich loin under cold water and pat dry. Place loin in a large resealable plastic bag. Pour Cabernet Marinade into bag, turning loin to coat on all sides. Marinate, sealed and refrigerated, for at least 1 hour.

Preheat grill to medium-high (about 400°F). Remove ostrich loin from marinade, discarding any remaining liquid. Rub ostrich with Amazing Steak Spice, pressing firmly so that spices adhere to loin. Place seasoned loin onto grill and grill for 5–6 minutes, each side, for medium-rare. Remove from grill and set aside for 1–2 minutes before slicing. Slice grilled loin across the grain into 1/2-in slices and arrange on a platter. Serve immediately.

RIBS

I LOVE RIBS — baby backs, St. Louis ribs, rib tips, tails and country-style ribs. Bone-sucking, tender, meaty, fall-off-the-bone — ribs are, in fact, my life. I have "cooked" millions of pounds of ribs as head of product development for one of the largest ribs producers in North America. In that role, I develop recipes for a variety of clients, resulting in about 1 to 1 1/2 million pounds of cooked ribs a month.

Ribs are the ultimate summer food. Although that doesn't mean I don't cook them in winter, they really seem to shine when eaten outside, with a big group of friends getting sticky! I often allow one or even two racks per person, but if you are not being a global glutton, half a rack will do. Have wet naps, napkins and lots of soapy water on hand to clean up with. I like to use cloth napkins, which I moisten and keep warm on the grill wrapped in some tinfoil — gets the grease and sticky off your fingers really well. Have fun and let the juices run down your chin.

A NOTE ON TYPES OF RIBS AND COOKING METHODS

BABY BACK RIBS are the ultimate rib. Cut from the loin, they're much leaner than spareribs and tend to have a higher meat-to-bone ratio. When prepared properly, these ribs provide the best eating.

Whether the ribs are fresh or frozen, look for ribs that have more loin meat attached. A baby back rib should weigh between 1 1/4 and 2 pounds. Baby back ribs are more expensive than spareribs, but they're the best quality. As the saying goes, you get what you pay for.

PORK SPARERIBS

Spareribs are cut from the side, or underbelly, of the pig. These ribs, weighing between 2 1/2 and 3 1/2 pounds, are quite meaty, but they're also fattier than baby back ribs. Spareribs are usually sold with the soft bone brisket attached — tough cartilage that is best trimmed off and used in soup stocks. Ask your butcher to remove the brisket for you. The term "St. Louis rib" indicates that the soft bone brisket has been removed, which produces a rib that is more uniform in size and easier to cook and eat.

COUNTRY-STYLE PORK RIBS

Country-style pork ribs, which come from the rib end of the pork loin, are extremely meaty. Priced lower than baby back ribs and spareribs, country-style ribs require a little longer cooking time to ensure tenderness but are well worth the wait.

PORK BACK RIB TAIL PIECES

When the butcher prepares pork baby back ribs, the small "tail" piece must be removed from the end of the rib. Tail pieces are approximately 6 to 8 inches long and have small, flat bones. They are to pork what the wing is to chicken — a great snack food. Rib tail pieces are not always available and are best ordered through your butcher. Allow at least 4 to 6 pieces per person.

PORK SHOULDER

A whole pork shoulder consists of the blade bone, shank and foreleg and weighs approximately 15 to 20 pounds. This is a lot of meat, and unless you are feeding a crowd of people and have a lot of time on your hands, I don't recommend purchasing a whole shoulder. You can find smaller cuts from the shoulder at your local butcher shop or grocery store. The picnic roast (a.k.a. shoulder roast or Boston butt) is a smaller cut (approximately 5 to 7 pounds) and easier to prepare. The best method for preparation is to slowly smoke the shoulder pieces over low heat: Low and slow makes for succulent and tender.

BEEF RIBS

These are enormous ribs that are cut from the loin. Because most grocery stores don't sell beef ribs, it's best to order from your butcher. "Monster Bones" or "Dinosaur Ribs," as they are frequently referred to on menus, are succulent and meaty. The best way to eat these is with your hands, so have a lot of napkins handy.

BEEF SHORT RIBS

This inexpensive cut of meat is readily available in grocery stores. Cut from the belly plate or the chuck areas of a steer, short ribs are composed of layers of meat, fat and flat rib bones. (The fat cap of a short rib should be trimmed before cooking.) These ribs are quite chunky and take a fair amount of time to cook. You may also purchase what are called Maui or Miami ribs. These ribs are cut approximately 1/2 inch thick across the short ribs and have 4 or 5 bones in each. Once marinated, they grill quickly.

LAMB RIBS

Lamb ribs are popular in South Africa, Australia and the South Pacific — much more so than in North America. Smaller than pork ribs, lamb ribs weigh in at just around a pound and have a thick fat cap that should be removed before cooking. There's not a lot of meat on lamb ribs, so allow 2 racks per person. If you are a lover of lamb, then these ribs will really make you smile.

COOKING METHODS

BOILING

Some chefs say never to boil ribs. I believe that you can, and boiling does tenderize the ribs, but if you do, you have to flavor the water with apple cider, pineapple juice, beer, ginger ale or stock, since boiling tends to remove flavor from the meat. It's not my favorite method, and when I do boil it's only pork spareribs, never beef or lamb ribs.

Cooking Time: Cooking liquid temperature, 210°F.

Allow approximately 30 minutes per pound.

2 to 3 pounds spareribs — 90 minutes

1 to 2 pounds back ribs — 60 minutes

STEAMING

When it comes to tender pork ribs, my friend Dave Nichol swears by steaming. I agree with him: Steaming ribs allows the meat to tenderize without losing flavor. A large steamer pot will do the job. Flavor the steaming liquid with garlic, onions and assorted herbs and spices before steaming ribs. Never steam beef ribs.

Cooking Time: Bring cooking liquid to a boil. Place steamer insert in pot and add ribs. Allow approximately 30 minutes per pound.

2 to 3 pounds spareribs — 90 minutes

1 to 2 pounds back ribs — 60 minutes

1 pound lamb ribs — 45 minutes

OVEN ROASTING

Oven roasting is a great way to cook ribs. This method suits all types of ribs — pork, beef and lamb. When preparing ribs for roasting, always rub with a flavored barbecue seasoning (see Rubs, Pastes and Marinades, p. 20). Preheat your oven to 350°F and place seasoned ribs on a wire rack in a roasting pan.

Cooking Time: Preheated 350°F oven.

2 to 3 pounds spareribs or beef ribs — 75 to 90 minutes

1 to 2 pounds back ribs or country-style ribs — 60 to 75 minutes

1 pound lamb ribs — 45 to 60 minutes

GRILLING

Grilling ribs requires low heat, much patience and strong desire: The results are worth it. The temperature of your grill should remain at around 325°F. Since cooking on a grill involves dry heat, you need to have some moisture to keep the ribs from drying out. Place a small pan of water in the bottom of the grill among the coals or on top of the grill bars. Marinate your ribs for 4 to 6 hours before rubbing with your favorite barbecue seasoning. Place ribs directly on the grill, meat side up, close the lid and cook until meat is tender. Near the end of the grilling time, brush with more of the sauce.

Cooking Time: Preheated 325°F grill.

2 to 3 pounds spareribs or beef ribs — 90 minutes

1 to 2 pounds back ribs or country-style ribs — 75 minutes

1 pound lamb ribs — 60 minutes

SMOKING

Smoking ribs — or real barbecue — is as much an art form as it is a method of cooking. Various styles of smokers are available for backyard use. Whatever kind you use, three basic principles apply: the same three principles as for grilling ribs, but with a few modifications. Low heat is a must — around 200° to 225°F. You must have patience (smoking can take anywhere from 3 to 7 hours, depending on the size and cut of your meat). And you must truly desire smoked ribs. So sit back, relax, crack a cold one and tend to your ribs.

Before you begin smoking, prepare your ribs: It's best to marinate them for 4 to 6 hours, or overnight, and then rub them with your favorite spice rub.

To begin, heat a small amount of charcoal to between 200° and 225°F. (For best results, use a charcoal smoker. You can smoke on a gas grill, but true lovers of barbecue smoke only over coals with flavored wood chips.) Presoak smoking chips in water for at least 1 hour before adding to hot coals — do note that you will need to replenish chips every so often during the smoking. Try a variety of flavored smoking chips — hickory and mesquite are the most popular, but cherry, apple and maple chips offer great flavor as well. When in the South, I use pecan wood: It adds a sweet, nutty flavor to the ribs.

Once the coals are hot, place a pan of hot water in the bottom of the smoker. Set the grill over the hot coals and place ribs, meat side up, on the grill. Close smoker lid and smoke; every hour, check and add additional coals and smoking chips as needed to maintain the temperature around 200° to 225°F.

Cooking Time: Preheated 200° to 225°F smoker.

Soaked smoking chips.

2 to 3 pounds pork spareribs or beef ribs — 3 to 4 hours

6 to 8 pounds pork picnic or pork butt roast — 5 to 6 hours

1 to 2 pounds pork back ribs or country-style ribs — 3 hours

BRAISING: My Favorite Cooking Method

I started out like many, boiling and steaming, but I was never satisfied with the results. I sensed the ultimate rib was still out there. Then I met a rib cooker by the name of Jerry Gibson. Jerry's ribs were incredible. Nirvana was at hand. Jerry's secret for great-tasting ribs is braising — a combination of roasting and steaming in the oven.

Preheat oven to 325°F. Rub ribs with your favorite BBQ seasoning. Place ribs, meat side down and overlapping, in a roasting pan. Add 1 to 2 cups of liquid (juice, beer or water) and place 3 to 4 slices of lemon on the back of each rack of ribs. Cover and braise until fully cooked and the bones can be pulled cleanly from the meat.

Cooking Time: Preheated 325°F oven.

2 to 3 pounds pork spareribs, beef ribs or beef short ribs — 2 to 3 hours

1 to 2 pounds pork back ribs or country-style ribs — 2 to 2 1/2 hours

1 pound lamb ribs — 1 1/2 hours

SMOKIN' BEER-BASTED RIBS, A.K.A. WHAT-I-DO-AT-HOME RIBS

You'll need at least 6 hours to smoke these tasty rubbed and pilsner-basted ribs. My preferred brand of pilsner is Steam Whistle Pilsner, and as for what barbecue sauce to use, I can't help but favor my King of the Q Smokin' Beer BBQ Sauce or my King of the Q Outstanding Gourmet-Style BBQ Sauce, cause both are "da bomb."

Special equipment: Smoker

4 (2 1/2 lb) racks St. Louis ribs
8 tbsp Competition Rib Rub (p. 25)
1 (12 oz) bottle pilsner
1/2 cup melted bacon fat
1 cup gourmet barbecue sauce

Serves 4 to 8

Remove membrane from St. Louis ribs. Rub with Competition Rib Rub, pressing firmly so that seasoning adheres to meat. Allow ribs to dry marinate for 1 hour, covered and refrigerated.

Meanwhile, in a medium saucepan, bring pilsner to a boil. Reduce heat to medium and simmer until liquid reduces by half, about 10–15 minutes. Remove from heat and stir in bacon fat and barbecue sauce; set aside.

Set up smoker by following manufacturer's instructions. The temperature should be between 180° and 220°F. Remove ribs from refrigerator and transfer to smoker. If you have a rib rack, place ribs on rack in smoker (a rib rack allows more ribs on a shelf and a more even smoke distribution). Smoke ribs for 2–3 hours, rotating ribs as necessary and adding more coals and hickory wood chunks as required.

When ribs are fully smoked, transfer to a tray and baste both sides with bacon fat–barbecue sauce mixture. Wrap ribs in a double layer of heavy-duty aluminum foil. Return to smoker and smoke for 3 more hours, or until ribs are juicy and tender. Remove ribs from smoker. Unwrap and wiggle a rib bone to test for tenderness.

Preheat grill to medium-high (about 400°F). Grill ribs for 8–10 minutes each side, basting with bacon fat–barbecue sauce mixture until lightly charred and hot. Remove from grill and baste with remaining sauce. Cut ribs into 3 or 4 sections, dig in and get sticky.

APPLE JACK BASTED BACK RIBS

Some might think this recipe should serve eight people, instead of four, but I believe in one rack of ribs per person because it's all about a whole lot of grillin', glazin', dippin' and lickin'.

4 racks pork back ribs, about 1 1/2 lb each
3 tbsp Indonesian Cinnamon Rub (p. 24)
1 small onion, sliced
1 cinnamon stick
1 (2 in) knob fresh ginger, sliced
1 cup apple cider
1/4 cup Jack Daniel's whiskey

Apple Jack Basting Sauce
1/2 cup packed brown sugar
1/2 cup apple butter
1/4 cup Jack Daniel's whiskey
3 tbsp apple cider

Serves 4

Remove membrane from back of ribs or, using a sharp knife, score the membrane on the backside of the ribs in a diamond or criss-cross pattern.

Rub ribs on all sides with Indonesian Cinnamon Rub, pressing firmly so that seasoning adheres to meat; set aside. (Note that the ribs may be rubbed and stored, covered, in the refrigerator up to 24 hours in advance.)

Preheat oven to 325°F. In a roasting pan, scatter the onion, cinnamon stick and ginger. Add apple cider and Jack Daniel's. Place the ribs, meat side down, in roasting pan. Cover pan with lid or aluminum foil. Braise ribs in oven for 2–2 1/2 hours, or until tender and the bone pulls cleanly from the meat. Remove from oven and let cool slightly.

To prepare the Apple Jack Basting Sauce: In a medium bowl, combine all basting sauce ingredients. Mix well and set aside.

Heat grill to medium-high (about 400°F). Grill ribs for 5–6 minutes, each side, until lightly charred, crispy and heated through. During the last 5 minutes of grilling, baste ribs liberally on both sides with Apple Jack Basting Sauce. When done, remove ribs from grill, glaze with remaining sauce, and serve immediately.

MAMAJUANA SMOKED RIBS WITH A BBQ PRALINE CRUST

Special equipment: Smoker
Pecan wood chips, soaked in bourbon for 20 minutes

BBQ Pralines

1 1/2 cups coarsely chopped raw cashews
1 tbsp Bonedust Seasoning (p. 22)
2 tbsp + 1 tbsp rum
1/4 cup heavy cream
1/4 cup unsalted butter
1 cup + 2 tbsp brown sugar, firmly packed
1 1/2 tsp vanilla extract

Ribs

4 racks pork back ribs (approx. 1 lb each)
6 to 8 tbsp Cochin Curry Masala Seasoning (p. 24)

Mamajuana Basting Sauce

1/2 cup brown sugar, firmly packed
1/2 cup passion fruit jam
1/4 cup dark rum
3 tbsp freshly squeezed orange juice
1/2 cup gourmet barbecue sauce

Serves 4

Inspired by a Dominican Republic drink known as Mamajuana (also described as Dominican Viagra!), these ribs go through a two-stage cooking process. First a slow braise to tenderize the ribs, then grilling and basting for that char flavor and crispy goodness.

To prepare the BBQ Pralines: Toast cashews over medium-high heat in a frying pan for 4–5 minutes, turning frequently for even toasting. Sprinkle Bonedust Seasoning over nuts and lightly shake pan to evenly coat. Add 2 tbsp of rum, 1 tbsp at a time, while continuing to gently shake pan over heat. Allow alcohol to cook off. Remove from heat and set aside to cool.

In a small, heavy saucepan over high heat, add cream, butter, brown sugar, vanilla and remaining tbsp of rum. Stir well and bring to a boil. Once boiling, do not stir; continue boiling for 5–10 minutes or until a candy thermometer inserted into mixture reads between 235° and 240°F. Remove from heat and immediately add toasted cashews to saucepan; toss with a wooden spoon to thoroughly coat. Spoon cashews onto a foil-lined tray and store in freezer until needed.

To prepare the Ribs: Remove membrane from back of ribs or, using a sharp knife, score the membrane on the backside of the ribs in a diamond or criss-cross pattern — scored lines should be 1 in apart. Rub ribs with Cochin Curry Masala Seasoning, pressing firmly so that spices adhere to meat; set aside. (Note that the ribs may be rubbed and stored, covered, in the refrigerator up to 24 hours in advance.)

Prepare your smoker according to manufacturer's instructions, to a temperature of 225°F. Place ribs in smoker and add soaked wood chips to coals. Close lid and smoke ribs for 2 hours, maintaining a constant temperature between 180° and 220°F. Replenish coals, water and wood chips as needed. After 2 hours, remove ribs from smoker. Wrap ribs in a double layer of heavy-duty aluminum foil and return to smoker. Smoke ribs for another 3–4 hours, or until meat is tender and ribs wiggle a little when pulled.

To prepare the Mamajuana Basting Sauce: In a medium bowl, combine all basting sauce ingredients. Mix well and set aside.

Heat grill to medium-high (about 400°F). Grill ribs for 5–6 minutes, each side, or until crispy and heated through, basting liberally with sauce during the last 5 minutes of grilling. Remove ribs from grill and glaze with remaining basting sauce. Layer BBQ Pralines on a clean, flat surface and place ribs, meat side down, on the nuts, creating a BBQ Praline crust. Serve immediately.

BBQ RIBS IN HONEY BROWN LAGER SAUCE

2 (12 oz) bottles honey brown lager
3 tbsp coarse salt
3 tbsp packed brown sugar
3 tbsp Bonedust Seasoning
(p. 22)
4 lb pork spareribs or loin back ribs

Honey Brown Lager Sauce
1/2 cup honey
1/2 cup ketchup
1/4 cup brown sugar, firmly packed
1/4 cup honey brown lager
2 tsp Bonedust Seasoning (p. 22)

Serves 4

Allow yourself a bit of time for this rib recipe: It requires 6 hours to brine the ribs and another 1 1/2 hours to grill, but trust me, it's all worth it!

In a large bowl, combine lager, salt, brown sugar and Bonedust Seasoning. Stir until salt, sugar and seasoning are dissolved; set aside.

Cut ribs into 2 portions and place in a large resealable plastic bag. Pour brine over ribs and seal bag. Place in a shallow dish and refrigerate for at least 6 hours, flipping the sealed bag every few hours.

To prepare the Honey Brown Lager Sauce: In a medium bowl, combine honey, ketchup, sugar, lager and Bonedust Seasoning. Mix well and set aside.

When ribs are fully marinated, preheat grill to medium (about 350°F). Remove ribs from bag and discard brine. Pat ribs dry with paper towels. Place ribs, bone side down, on grill rack over a drip pan. Close lid and grill for 1 1/2–1 3/4 hours, or until meat is tender and ribs wiggle a little when pulled. During the last 5 minutes of grilling time, brush ribs with Honey Brown Lager Sauce. When done, remove ribs from grill and serve with extra sauce for dipping.

MAPLE SYRUP MARINATED BONELESS PORK RIBS WITH JIM BEAM BBQ SAUCE

These are authentic country-style ribs. If you don't have any Jim Beam, substitute your favorite bourbon.

To prepare the Jim Beam BBQ Sauce: Sauté onion and garlic in vegetable oil over medium heat for 2–3 minutes. Add brown sugar and stir until dissolved. Stir in soy sauce, Worcestershire sauce, molasses and black pepper; keep stirring and bring to a boil. In a small bowl, combine 1 cup water and cornstarch until fully incorporated. Add to boiling mixture, stirring rapidly. Reduce heat to low and simmer for 1 minute, or until liquid has thickened. Remove from heat and add Jim Beam. Set aside for basting.

To prepare the Maple Syrup Marinade: In a small bowl, combine all marinade ingredients. Mix well and set aside.

On a clean work surface, rub ribs with Bonedust Seasoning, pressing firmly so that spices adhere to meat. Transfer to a glass dish large enough to hold the ribs and pour in marinade, turning to thoroughly coat. Cover and refrigerate for 30 minutes, or for as long as 4 hours.

Heat grill to medium-high (about 400°F). Remove ribs from marinade and grill for 8–10 minutes, each side, or until fully cooked — a thermometer inserted into the thickest part of the meat should read a minimum of 170°F. During the last 5 minutes of grilling, brush ribs on both sides with reserved Jim Beam BBQ Sauce until ribs are sticky and lightly charred.

Jim Beam BBQ Sauce
1 cup finely diced onion
1 tbsp chopped fresh garlic
1 tbsp vegetable oil
1 cup brown sugar, firmly packed
2 tbsp dark soy sauce
1 tbsp Worcestershire sauce
2 tbsp molasses
1/2 tsp freshly ground black pepper
2 tsp cornstarch
2 oz Jim Beam bourbon whiskey

Maple Syrup Marinade
4 cloves garlic, chopped
2 jalapeños, seeded and chopped
2 oz Jim Beam bourbon whiskey
2 tbsp extra-virgin olive oil
1 green onion, finely chopped
2 tbsp maple syrup

4 pieces boneless country-style pork ribs, cut 1- to 2-in thick
3 tbsp Bonedust Seasoning (p. 22)

Serves 4

BISON RIBS WITH WASABI BALSAMIC GLAZE

Bison is very lean and will cook faster than you think.

Preheat oven to 250°F. Rub ribs with Amazing Steak Spice and curry paste, pressing so that spices adhere to meat. Spread seasoned bison ribs evenly in a large roasting pan. Pour in beer and 1 cup water; sprinkle garlic, onion and chili peppers over top of ribs. Braise bison ribs for 4 hours, or until meat pulls away easily from the bone. Remove ribs from oven and cool.

Heat grill to medium-high (about 400°F). Grill ribs for 5–6 minutes, each side, basting liberally with Wasabi Balsamic Glazing Sauce during the last few minutes of grilling. Remove ribs from grill and serve immediately.

1 rack bison ribs (approx 6 to 8 lb)
2 tbsp Amazing Steak Spice (p. 23)
4 tbsp curry paste
1 (12 oz) bottle beer
3 cloves garlic, minced
1 small onion, chopped
6 green chili peppers, chopped
1 1/2 cups Wasabi Balsamic Glazing Sauce (p. 254)

Serves 4

BBQ Ribs in Honey Brown Lager Sauce

BALSAMIC GLAZED SAUSAGE-AND-PEPPER STUFFED RIBS

2 racks pork spareribs
(2 to 3 lb each)
2 tbsp Mediterranean-Style
Rub (p. 23)
1 lemon, thinly sliced
2 cups apple juice
1 loaf olive baguette (about 22 slices)
2 cloves garlic, minced
1 onion, diced
2 stalks celery, diced
6 slices bacon, cooked crisp
and chopped
1 lb cooked Italian sausage meat
1/4 cup chopped sun-dried tomatoes
in oil
1/4 cup sliced green olives
1 long green chili pepper, diced
1/4 cup mixed chopped fresh
herbs (p. 26)
1/4 cup melted butter
Salt and freshly ground black pepper
Vegetable oil

Balsamic BBQ Glaze

1 cup balsamic vinegar
1/4 cup honey
1/4 cup mixed chopped fresh
herbs (p. 26)

Serves 4

The secret to these perfect grill-roasted stuffed ribs is to use indirect heat.

Preheat oven to 325°F. Using a sharp knife, score the membrane on the backside of the ribs in a diamond or criss-cross pattern. Rub with Mediterranean-Style Rub, pressing firmly so that seasoning adheres to meat. Place ribs, meat side down, in a roasting pan. Top each rib with 3–4 slices of lemon. Pour apple juice into pan and cover with lid or foil. Transfer roasting pan to oven and braise ribs for 2–2 1/2 hours, or until meat is tender and ribs wiggle slightly when pulled. When ribs are fully braised, remove roasting pan from oven and set aside.

Meanwhile, cut baguette into 1/2-in cubes. Spread bread cubes on a baking sheet and transfer to 200°F oven; bake for 30 minutes, or until bread has dried. In a large bowl, combine the dried bread cubes, garlic, onion, celery, bacon, Italian sausage, sun-dried tomatoes, olives, chili pepper and fresh herbs. Add 1/2 cup boiling water and the melted butter, stirring to fully mix: The stuffing should hold together but should still be moist. Season with salt and pepper to taste.

Place 1 rack of ribs, curved side up, on a work surface. Stuff the curved side of the rack with all the stuffing, pressing it firmly to form a log along the inside of the rack. Place the other rack, curved side down, on top of the stuffing, pressing firmly. Tie the ribs together several times with string, at 2-in intervals. Brush with a little vegetable oil.

To prepare the Balsamic BBQ Glaze: In a small bowl, combine balsamic vinegar, honey and fresh herbs. Set aside for basting.

Heat grill to medium (about 350°F). Place stuffed ribs on grill, away from direct heat. Close lid and grill for 10–15 minutes, each side, or until ribs are lightly charred and stuffing is heated through. Baste stuffed ribs with Balsamic BBQ Glaze during the last half of grilling time, so that the outside is sticky and lightly charred. Remove ribs from grill and let stand for 5 minutes. Cut between every second bone and serve.

RIB TIPS WITH SOUTHERN COMFORT BASTING SAUCE

4 racks pork sparerib tips, cut into 1 1/2- to 2-in chunks (about 5 to 6 lb of rib tips)
1/4 cup Sweet Rib Rub (p. 25)
1 can cream soda (clear cream soda, not the pink kind)

Southern Comfort Basting Sauce
1/2 cup peach preserves
1/4 cup honey
1/4 cup Southern Comfort
1/2 cup gourmet barbecue sauce
1 tsp hot pepper sauce
1 tsp fresh lemon juice

Serves 8

The rib tip is the soft breastbone of the sparerib. When cooked properly, rib tips are tender and chin-drippin' good.

Preheat oven to 325°F. In a small bowl, toss rib tips with Sweet Rib Rub to coat evenly; transfer to roasting pan. Pour in 1 can of cream soda and 2 cups water. Cover and braise rib tips for 2 1/2–3 hours, or until tender.

To prepare the Southern Comfort Basting Sauce: In a medium-sized, heavy saucepan, combine all basting sauce ingredients. Mix well and set aside.

Preheat grill to medium-high (about 400°F). Remove rib tips from oven and transfer to a bowl, discarding cream soda braising liquid. Grill ribs for 10 minutes, turning frequently and basting during the last half of grilling time. Remove rib tips from grill and transfer to a large bowl. Add remaining basting sauce and toss rib tips to fully coat. Serve immediately and make sure to have lots of napkins handy.

HONEY-ROASTED GARLIC SPARERIB TIPS

Tender braised ribs basted with a sweet and tangy sauce, then tossed with honey-roasted peanuts? Make lots!

Season sparerib tips with Competition Rib Rub, pressing firmly so that spices adhere to ribs. Transfer to a container, cover, and refrigerate overnight.

    Preheat grill to medium (about 350°F). Place a small pan of water on top of grill or among coals. Place rib tips on grill, close lid and cook for approximately 1 1/2 hours, or until meat is tender.

To prepare the Honey-Roasted Garlic Sauce: In a medium saucepan over medium-high heat, combine all sauce ingredients. Reduce heat to low and simmer for 5 minutes. Remove from heat; set aside.

    When rib tips are almost cooked, baste liberally with sauce on all sides. Close lid and allow sauce to caramelize for 3–4 minutes. Remove ribs from grill and cool slightly before cutting. Transfer to a large bowl and add remaining sauce and honey-roasted peanuts; toss and serve immediately.

4 lb pork sparerib tips
4 tbsp Competition Rib Rub (p. 25)

Honey-Roasted Garlic Sauce
1 cup honey
1/2 cup apple juice
1/4 cup soy sauce
1/4 cup apple cider vinegar
1/4 cup Grill-Roasted Garlic (p. 219)
Salt and freshly ground black pepper to taste

1 cup ground honey-roasted peanuts

Serves 4 to 6

TEQUILA AND HONEY-COFFEE LAMB RIBS

Tequila, honey and coffee give these ribs a sweet, roasted flavor — they are succulent and delicious.

Preheat oven to 325°F. Rub lamb ribs with Margarita Paste, pressing firmly so that paste adheres to meat.

To prepare the Braising Liquid: In a large roasting pan, combine 1/2 cup coffee liqueur, tequila, lime juice, 2 cups water, garlic, onion, thyme, coriander and Espresso Blast Paste. Place a meat rack in the pan. Place seasoned lamb on the meat rack in roasting pan. Cover and bake for 2 1/2–3 hours, or until tender. The meat should pull easily from the bone.

To prepare the Honey-Coffee BBQ Baste: In a small saucepan over medium heat, combine soy sauce, honey, coffee liqueur, chopped thyme and garlic. Bring to a boil, remove from heat and add butter. Set aside.

    Heat grill to medium-high (about 400°F). Grill lamb ribs for 6–8 minutes each side, basting with Honey-Coffee BBQ Baste until ribs are lightly charred and sticky. Remove ribs from grill and serve immediately.

4 racks lamb ribs (12 to 16 oz each)
6 to 8 tbsp Margarita Paste (p. 30)

Braising Liquid
1/2 cup coffee liqueur
1/2 cup tequila
3 tbsp fresh lime juice
1 head garlic, smashed and peeled
1 medium onion, chopped
6 sprigs thyme
6 sprigs coriander
3 tbsp Espresso Blast Paste (p. 30)

Honey-Coffee BBQ Baste
1 tbsp soy sauce
1/2 cup honey
1/4 cup coffee liqueur
1 tbsp chopped fresh thyme
2 cloves garlic, minced
2 tbsp cold butter

Serves 4

Rib tips on the grill, and plated

WINTER GRILLING AND SMOKING

When it comes to cold weather, I much prefer to stay indoors, but I still love to fire up the grill and have a feast. So I have developed some tips for grilling in the great outdoors.

1. The most important rule when it comes to winter grilling is: Never, ever bring your grill indoors to cook. You will die. Gas and charcoal grills produce carbon monoxide — if you die, you can't eat. Got it? Good.

2. Bundle yourself up in your warmest clothes. But don't overdo it: You still need to be able to move around. Keep a path shoveled to the grill or smoker. Brush any snow off your grill, and remove the cover. (You better have a cover, since it will help your grill last longer.)

3. Give some thought to your fuel. Natural gas is the easiest to use and provides a constant fuel source. Charcoal is a bit more involved. Once it gets hot, you have to monitor it and add more fuel when necessary. Propane is the hardest to work with when you're winter grilling — the colder it gets, the more sluggishly propane flows. As the propane tank empties, it slows down even more. I recommend keeping your propane tank full, and having a spare on hand. When not using, store tanks in the garage in a well-ventilated area. This will keep the fuel a bit warmer, which should make the task easier.

4. Once you fire up the grill, keep the lid closed as much as possible to keep the heat in. Every time you open that lid, you lose heat.

5. Only grill easy stuff in winter: Burgers, steaks, chops and chicken breasts are good choices. You want food that won't take too long to cook. That said, the rotisserie works great, too!

YOU BETTER HAVE A GRILL COVER. IT WILL HELP YOUR GRILL LAST LONGER.

BEEF RIBS WITH BEEFY ONION BBQ GLAZE

Rich and fatty, beef ribs are truly decadent. These are to die for, tossed in a dark steakhouse-style glaze. You will need a big roasting pan, to accommodate both racks. You may have to cut the racks into smaller pieces.

2 racks meaty beef ribs (each about 3 lb)

4 tbsp liquid concentrated beef stock (such as Bovril)

6 tbsp + 2 tbsp Smoked Salt Steak Rub (p. 28)

2 medium green onions, thinly sliced

4 cloves garlic, minced

2 tbsp mixed chopped fresh herbs (p. 26)

2 (12 oz) bottles Guinness or other dark beer

1/2 cup HP or A1 steak sauce

1/4 cup brown sugar, firmly packed

1 cup crumbled blue cheese

2 tbsp chopped flat-leaf parsley

Serves 4 to 6

Preheat oven to 325°F. Brush beef ribs on all sides with concentrated beef stock. Rub beef ribs with 6 tbsp Smoked Salt Steak Rub, pressing firmly so that seasoning adheres to meat. Place ribs in a large roasting pan.

In a small bowl, mix together the remaining 2 tbsp Smoked Salt Steak Rub, onion, garlic, remaining concentrated beef stock and fresh herbs. Spread onion mixture over beef ribs. Pour in 4 cups of beer and drink any leftover beer, if you like. Cover and place in oven on bottom rack. Steam-braise ribs for 3–4 hours, until the meat has pulled back along the rib bones and is tender.

Remove from oven, uncover and let cool in pan. Remove ribs from pan, wrap and refrigerate until needed. Transfer onion liquid and bits from the pan into a medium pot and bring to a boil over medium-high heat. Reduce heat to low and simmer for 10–15 minutes. Skim off any excess fat in the pot. Add steak sauce and brown sugar. Using a hand blender, purée mixture in pot until smooth; set aside for basting.

Preheat grill to medium-high (about 400°F). Grill ribs for 8–10 minutes, each side, basting with puréed sauce until lightly crisp, charred and heated through. Baste with extra sauce and cut ribs in between every second bone. Toss cut ribs in a large bowl with remaining sauce, crumbled blue cheese and parsley, and serve.

Mi Pho-Glazed Hawaiian Beef Short Rib Strips on the grill

MI PHO–GLAZED HAWAIIAN BEEF SHORT RIB STRIPS

"Maui" ribs are beef short ribs cut across the bone, 1/2 inch thick, 1 1/2 inches wide and 5 rib bones across. I'm not sure what this has to do with Hawaii...but ask your butcher to cut these ribs 1 inch thick instead, for extra meatiness. Salty, spicy Mi Pho #1 Marinade is perfect for the quick grilling of these ribs.

Place ribs in a resealable bag. Pour in Mi Pho #1 Marinade, close, seal and shake to coat. Store in refrigerator and marinate for 24 hours or overnight.
To prepare the Mi Pho Glazing Sauce: In a medium bowl, combine all glazing sauce ingredients. Mix well, cover and refrigerate until needed.

When ribs are fully marinated, preheat grill to high (about 500° to 550°F). Remove ribs from marinade, and grill for 2–3 minutes, each side, basting liberally with Mi Pho Glazing Sauce. Remove ribs from grill and serve immediately with a big bowl of steamed rice and lots of condiments.

4 lb beef short ribs, cut across the bones, 1 in thick
1 cup Mi Pho #1 Marinade (p. 31)

Mi Pho Glazing Sauce
1/2 cup Mi Pho #1 Marinade (p. 31)
1/4 cup hoisin sauce
1/4 cup honey
2 tbsp red wine vinegar

Serves 4 to 6

BIRDS

BIRDS — the different types of chicken, from finger-lickin' wings to the whole thing, as well as other birds such as duck, quail, Cornish hens and even turkey — have to be among the most popular items to grill because it's so easy to get good results. There are only two simple rules to follow: When cooking, make sure chicken and turkey are always well-done (chicken must be cooked to a minimum internal temperature of 170°F); and when cooking a boneless, skinless chicken breast, direct heat over medium-high works best. For everything else, I recommend low and slow, whether grilling wings or smoking whole birds — low and slow gives ya juicy birds.

Of course, my favorite way to cook birds is beer-can style. And I'm also a big fan of smoked duck and stuffed turkey, as well as small, succulent, quick-cooking quail.

SPATCHCOCK CHICKEN WITH TANGERINE CHIPOTLE BASTE

A "spatchcock" chicken has been split along the backbone and pressed flat — it's a great way to grill a whole bird.

1 cup + 1/4 cup freshly squeezed tangerine juice
1/2 cup mixed chopped fresh herbs (p. 26)
2 tbsp extra-virgin olive oil
2 tbsp peeled and grated fresh ginger
2 tbsp lemongrass, minced
3 tbsp rice vinegar
1 tbsp kosher salt
1 tsp coarsely ground black pepper
1 tsp cayenne pepper
2 (3 lb) whole chickens
1/2 cup honey
2 tbsp soy sauce
2 tsp puréed chipotle pepper in adobo sauce

Serves 4

In a medium bowl, combine 1 cup tangerine juice, herbs, oil, ginger, lemongrass, rice vinegar, salt, pepper and cayenne pepper. Mix well and set aside.

Using kitchen or poultry shears, cut both sides of backbone, the entire length of one of the chickens; remove and discard bone. If desired, use shears to cut out rib bones, as well. Turn, breast side up, and press firmly to flatten. Repeat with other chicken. Transfer birds to a large glass baking dish and pour marinade over chicken, turning to coat. Cover and marinate, refrigerated, for 4–6 hours, or overnight.

When chicken is fully marinated, preheat grill to medium-high (about 400°F). In a bowl, whisk together remaining tangerine juice, honey, soy sauce and chipotle purée until smooth. Set aside glaze for basting. Remove chicken from refrigerator, discarding marinade, and place birds directly on grill. Grill chicken for 12–15 minutes each side. About halfway through grilling time, brush chicken liberally with glaze. Continue to grill until glaze caramelizes; turn and repeat on other side. Check the meat for doneness by piercing thighs with a skewer; if juices run clear, the meat is fully cooked. Brush any remaining glaze over chicken and transfer to a clean cutting board: Let sit for 5 minutes. Slice each chicken in half and serve with wet naps and extra sticky glaze for drizzling.

MARGARITA CHICKEN LEGS

These delicious, limey chicken legs are great served with Salsa Verde (p. 256).

Special equipment: Cajun injector

6 chicken legs, with skin on
3 oz tequila
1/2 cup Margarita Paste (p. 30)
1/4 cup vegetable oil
Salt and freshly ground black pepper

Serves 6

Rinse chicken legs under cold water and pat dry with paper towels. Using a Cajun injector, inject chicken legs with tequila, about 1/2 oz per chicken leg. Using a small sharp knife, make 1/2-in-deep slashes into injected chicken. Rub Margarita Paste all over, working it into slashes. Cover, refrigerate and marinate chicken for 4–6 hours, or overnight.

When chicken is fully marinated, preheat grill to medium-high (about 400°F). Grill for 2–4 minutes, each side, or until golden brown. Reduce heat to low (about 250°F); close grill lid and grill-bake chicken legs for 20 minutes, or until fully cooked and skin is lightly charred and crisp. Remove and serve immediately with margaritas and Salsa Verde (p. 256).

CHICKEN GRILLSICLES WITH RUM BUTTER SAUCE

I first made these in the Dominican Republic, and now they are a signature dish at my restaurant, Teddy's Island BBQ. Remember those Popsicles rolled in nuts that you had when you were a kid? These are chicken "Grillsicles" rolled in nuts.

Cut chicken into large chunks, about 2 in each. Liberally coat with Bonedust Seasoning. Skewer seasoned chicken, packing meat firmly together on each skewer. (Make 'em big, about 8 oz of chicken per person.)

To prepare the Rum Butter Sauce: In a small saucepan over medium heat, combine all sauce ingredients. Heat gently, whisking to combine. Remove from heat and set aside.

Preheat grill to medium-high (about 400°F). Brush chicken lightly with vegetable oil. Place chicken skewers on grill and, turning occasionally, sear chicken on all sides, about 4–5 minutes. Reduce heat to medium-low, close grill lid and indirectly grill-roast for 18–22 minutes, or until fully cooked and the internal temperature has reached 170°F. Baste with Rum Butter Sauce during last 6 minutes of grilling time, until the skewered chicken is very sticky. Line a flat work surface with aluminum foil. Cover foil with an even layer of crushed cashew nuts. Give chicken a final baste, remove from grill and roll skewers in the nuts to form a crust. Serve immediately.

Special equipment: 4 large sugar-cane skewers or bamboo skewers or wooden chopsticks

1 lb boneless, skinless chicken breasts (about 4 breasts)
1 lb boneless, skinless chicken thighs or legs (about 4 to 6 thighs)
4 tbsp Bonedust Seasoning (p. 22)

Rum Butter Sauce
1/2 cup softened butter
2 tbsp peeled and grated fresh ginger
1 tbsp chopped fresh garlic
1/2 cup peach jam
1/2 cup honey
1 tbsp soy sauce
3 oz dark rum
2 green onions, finely chopped

3 tbsp vegetable oil
2 cups crushed nuts (cashews or peanuts or both)

Serves 4

THE BEER-CAN TECHNIQUE

My favorite way to cook most birds is beer-can style. As the liquid boils, it creates steam and keeps the bird moist from the inside out. Meanwhile, it's roasted crisp from the outside in — just the way birds ought to be!

And don't worry. As tasty as they are, these recipes won't get you drunk — all the alcohol is burned off in cooking, leaving only flavor! Here are a couple of tips on the beer-can technique:

★ Make sure to use metal cans only, not glass, which can explode from the heat of the grill. Tallboy cans work best for larger birds. If you're concerned about paint from the can transferring to your food, just wrap the can in tinfoil.

★ Open the can, and take a couple of sips. You want to give the steam a bit of room to form.

★ The technique works just as well with any canned liquid — try ginger ale, iced tea or a can filled with fruit juice. Whatever liquid you use, either discard after cooking or reduce it in a saucepan for a delicious sauce.

★ If your grill doesn't have a lid, just use your oven. Set your oven to 350°F and roast for approximately 20 minutes per pound.

★ Make sure not to bang or bump your grill while cooking.

★ There are all kinds of beer-can-chicken-holders you can buy that provide extra stabilizing support. Some are even designed with a tray you can fill with your favorite liquid.

★ Use barbecue gloves or oven mitts to remove can from chicken, once it's cooked.

Enjoy!

THIS IS ONE OF THE ALL-TIME BEST METHODS FOR COOKING A WHOLE BIRD ON A GRILL OR IN THE OVEN.

BEER-CAN CHICKEN WITH MY SOON-TO-BE-FAMOUS WHITE TRASH BBQ SAUCE

Special equipment: 4 foil pie plates
Cajun injector

White Trash BBQ Sauce

1 cup ranch dressing
1 cup mayonnaise
1/2 cup whipping cream
2 tbsp fresh lemon juice
1/4 cup mixed chopped fresh herbs (p. 26)
1 tbsp Worcestershire sauce
2 tsp hot pepper sauce
1 tsp salt
3 cloves garlic, minced
1/2 cup freshly grated Parmesan cheese

Butter Sauce Injection

1/2 cup softened butter
1/4 cup hot pepper sauce
2 tbsp fresh lemon juice
1 oz Jack Daniel's whiskey

2 (3 to 4 lb) whole chickens
1/2 cup Bonedust Seasoning (p. 22)
2 cans lager or ale

Serves 4

When I grill beer-can chicken, I use tallboy-size beer cans. Always take a few sips of beer before inserting a can into the cavity of the chicken. There should be room at the top, when the steaming begins. I first made this recipe in my Sticky Fingers and Tenderloins cookbook. It just rocks.

To prepare the White Trash BBQ Sauce: In a medium saucepan, combine all sauce ingredients. Over medium heat, bring mixture to a boil, stirring constantly. Adjust seasoning as necessary and keep warm over minimum heat.

To prepare the Butter Sauce Injection: In a small saucepan over medium heat, melt butter. Stir in remaining Butter Sauce ingredients. Continue stirring until fully combined. Remove from heat and set aside.

Preheat grill to medium-high (about 400°F). Wash chickens, inside and out, with cold water and pat dry with paper towels. Rub with Bonedust Seasoning, firmly pressing so that spices adhere to birds, inside and out. Open beer cans. Take a few sips from each beer can. Put 1 pie plate inside another. Set 1 beer can on each of the doubled-up pie plates. Place a chicken over the top of each beer can and push down so that the can is well inside and the bird is standing upright.

Using a Cajun injector, inject the Butter Sauce mixture into the chicken (breast and legs). Place the injected beer-can chickens on their pie plates on the grill. Close lid and grill-roast for 50–60 minutes, or until fully cooked and golden brown, occasionally basting with the juices that have collected in the pie plates. (To check for doneness, insert a meat thermometer into the thigh. Temperature should be a minimum of 160°F). Remove chickens from grill and serve with White Trash BBQ Sauce, Cedar-Planked Mashed Potatoes (p. 213) and the juices that have collected in the pie plates.

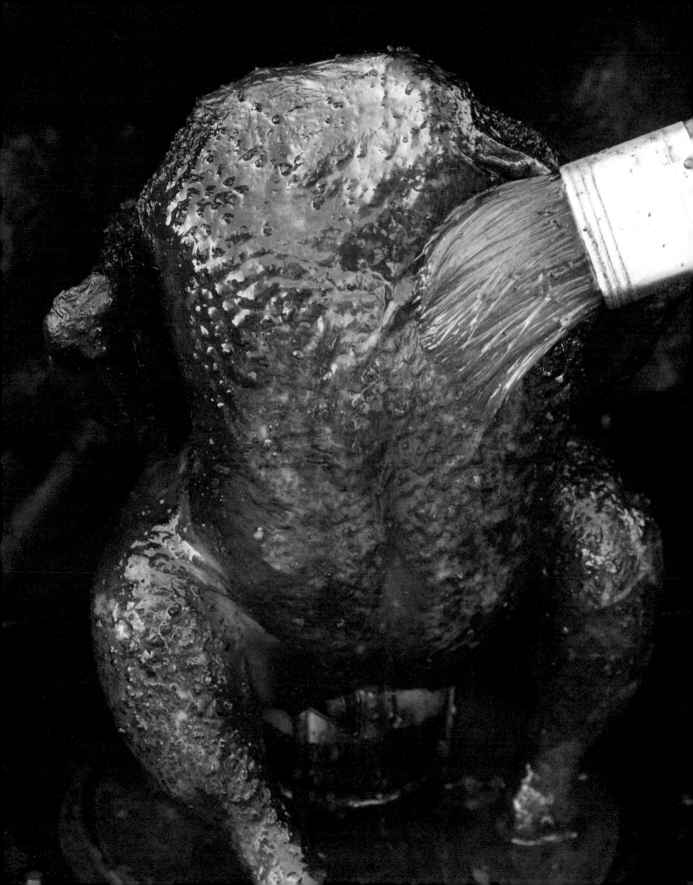

CHICKEN BREASTS STUFFED WITH SPINACH AND CRAB

Stuffing chicken breasts can be a bit tricky. Be patient, and use your knife to slowly carve out the space you need.

1 to 2 tbsp softened butter
1 small onion, finely diced
8 (6 oz) boneless chicken breasts, with skin on
1/4 cup Bonedust Seasoning (p. 22)
Salt and freshly ground black pepper
1 cup blanched spinach, squeezed to remove excess water
1/2 cup crabmeat
1/2 cup softened cream cheese
2 tbsp freshly grated Parmesan cheese
1 tbsp chopped fresh herbs (p. 26)
1 tbsp red wine vinegar
1 tsp coarsely ground black pepper
2 green onions, finely chopped
1 tsp crushed red pepper flakes
Pinch of ground nutmeg
Salt

Serves 8

In a skillet, melt butter over medium heat. Add onion and sauté for 2–3 minutes, or until tender. Remove from heat and chill in refrigerator.

Preheat grill to medium-high (about 400°F). Place chicken breasts on a waxed paper–lined cutting board, skin side down, and remove chicken tenderloins. Lightly pound tenderloins flat and set aside. Using a sharp knife, cut a pocket about 1 in deep from the top of the breast to the bottom. With your fingers, push around inside the pocket to enlarge it. Season chicken inside and out with Bonedust Seasoning and salt and pepper to taste; set aside.

Meanwhile, in a large bowl, mix together spinach, reserved chilled sautéed onion, crabmeat, softened cream cheese, Parmesan cheese, herbs, vinegar, pepper, green onion and red pepper flakes; season with nutmeg and salt to taste. Divide the stuffing into 8 equal portions and shape each portion into a firmly packed oval. Place 1 stuffing portion in each chicken cavity. Place 1 flattened tenderloin over each cavity and tuck the tenderloin into the opening, firmly pressing the edges to make a tight seal. Grill chicken, skin side down, for 6–8 minutes, or until lightly charred. Turn stuffed breasts and grill for another 6–8 minutes, or until breasts are fully cooked on both sides and the stuffing is hot. Remove from grill and allow chicken to rest 2–3 minutes, so that stuffing can set. Slice each breast in half and serve immediately.

WEST INDIAN CURRY CHICKEN THIGHS

This curry can be as spicy, or not, as you like. Simply adjust the amount of chili peppers to your taste.

Preheat grill to medium-high (about 400°F). Rub chicken thighs with Cochin Curry Masala Seasoning, pressing firmly so that spices adhere to meat; season with salt and pepper to taste. Grill for 8–10 minutes, each side.

Meanwhile, in a sauté pan, add oil, chili peppers, onion, carrot, pumpkin, cubanelle pepper, yucca, okra, green beans and garlic. Sauté, stirring occasionally, for 10 minutes or until heated and vegetables are lightly browned. Remove from heat and set aside.

Remove thighs from grill and place in a foil pan. Cover with sautéed vegetables and pour Smoked Chicken Stock and orange juice over all. Transfer foil pan to grill and continue grilling for 30–45 minutes, or until chicken is fully cooked and vegetables are soft and tender. Remove from heat; serve vegetables and chicken thighs over steamed rice.

12 chicken thighs, skin on
1/4 cup Cochin Curry Masala Seasoning (p. 24)
Salt and freshly ground black pepper
2 to 3 tbsp vegetable oil
4 red hot chili peppers, minced
1 large onion, diced
2 medium carrots, diced
2 cups peeled and diced fresh pumpkin
2 cubanelle peppers, diced
1 yucca or potato, peeled and diced
1 cup okra
2 cups green beans
4 cloves garlic, minced
2 cups Smoked Chicken Stock (p. 261)
1/2 cup freshly squeezed orange juice

Serves 6

BONELESS HALF CHICKEN WITH SWEET-AND-SOUR BBQ SAUCE

Ask your butcher to debone the chicken for you. Serve this yummy chicken with BBQ Fried Rice (p. 209).

Season chicken with Cochin Curry Masala Seasoning, rubbing the seasoning under the skin. Transfer seasoned chicken halves to a container, cover and refrigerate for 4–6 hours.

To prepare the Sweet-and-Sour BBQ Sauce: In a small saucepan, whisk together honey, ketchup, mango chutney, lemon juice, herbs, olive oil, Worcestershire sauce, garlic and hot sauce to taste. Over medium heat, whisking occasionally, bring sauce to a boil. Reduce heat to low and simmer for 10 minutes, whisking occasionally. Remove from heat, add coriander and season with salt and pepper to taste. Set aside to cool.

When ready to prepare chicken, preheat grill to medium-high (about 400°F). Grill chicken, skin side down, for 6–8 minutes. Turn and baste the skin liberally with Sweet-and-Sour BBQ Sauce. Grill for another 6–8 minutes, turning and basting the meat side. Remove chicken from the grill and serve with remaining sauce for dipping.

4 boneless half chickens, with skin on
2 tbsp Cochin Curry Masala Seasoning (p. 24)

Sweet-and-Sour BBQ Sauce
1 cup honey
1/2 cup ketchup
1/2 cup mango chutney
1/4 cup fresh lemon juice
2 tbsp chopped fresh herbs (p. 26)
2 tbsp extra-virgin olive oil
1 tsp Worcestershire sauce
4 cloves garlic, minced
Hot pepper sauce
Handful chopped fresh coriander
Salt and freshly ground black pepper

Serves 4

CORNISH HENS WITH RED BULL ROCKET BBQ SAUCE

Special equipment: 4 foil pie plates

Red Bull Rocket BBQ Sauce
1 (8 oz) can Red Bull energy drink
3 oz Jägermeister liqueur
1 cup gourmet barbecue sauce
1/2 cup chopped fresh coriander

4 Cornish game hens
2 tbsp Bonedust Seasoning (p. 22)
4 (8 oz) cans Red Bull energy drink

Serves 4

Red Bull is an energy drink that "gives you wings," which is just what Cornish hen needs!

To prepare the Red Bull Rocket BBQ Sauce: In a small pot over medium heat, bring 1 can of Red Bull to a low boil. Reduce heat and simmer for 20 minutes or until liquid is reduced by half. Remove from heat and add Jägermeister and barbecue sauce. Stir to combine, add coriander and set aside for basting.

Preheat grill to medium-high (about 400° to 450°F). Remove top grill rack, if necessary, to make room for hens. Rinse Cornish hens under cold running water and pat dry. Season, inside and out, with Bonedust Seasoning, firmly pressing so that spices adhere to meat. Open 4 cans of Red Bull energy drink and take several sips from each. Holding one bird steady over opened can, push upward so that more than half the can is in the cavity and the hen is standing upright. Repeat with the remaining 3 hens. Stand each hen on a pie plate positioned on a metal drip pan. Transfer pan to grill. Close lid and roast hens for 30–45 minutes, or until fully cooked and golden brown, basting liberally with sauce during the last half of grilling time. (To check for doneness insert a meat thermometer into the thigh. It should read 170° to 180°F.) Remove from grill and serve with extra sauce for dipping.

QUAIL IN JÄGER BOMB SAUCE

Special equipment: 16 metal skewers or bamboo skewers soaked in water for 1 hour

8 fresh quails
2 tbsp Bonedust Seasoning (p. 22)

Jäger Bomb Sauce
1 (8 oz) can Red Bull energy drink
1/2 cup honey
Splash of hot pepper sauce
2 oz Jägermeister liqueur
1/2 cup gourmet barbecue sauce
2 tbsp melted butter

Serves 4

This recipe was inspired by Jägermeister, an herbal liqueur.

Using kitchen or poultry shears, cut both sides of backbone the entire length of each quail. Remove and discard bones. Turn breast side up and press firmly to flatten. Place flattened quails, skin side down, on a smooth work surface. Skewer each quail, making an X pattern, by running two skewers crosswise from leg to breast. Rub quails with Bonedust Seasoning, firmly pressing so that spices adhere to skin.

To prepare the Jäger Bomb Sauce: In a medium bowl, combine all sauce ingredients; mix well and set aside for basting.

Preheat grill to high (about 500°F). Place quail on grill and grill for 5–6 minutes each side. Brush liberally with sauce during the second half of grilling time. Check that meat is cooked by piercing thighs with a skewer; if juices run clear, meat is fully cooked. Baste quail with any remaining sauce and transfer from grill to a platter. Let sit for 5 minutes before serving.

Quail in Jäger Bomb Sauce

BACON-WRAPPED DRUMSTICKS

12 chicken drumsticks
1/4 cup Bonedust Burn BBQ
Paste (p. 29)
12 slices bacon
4 cloves garlic, minced
1/2 cup brown sugar, firmly packed
1/4 cup corn syrup
2 tbsp white wine vinegar
1 tbsp chopped fresh herbs (p. 26)
1/4 cup Dijon mustard
2 tbsp grainy mustard
Salt and freshly ground black pepper

Serves 6

These are perfect to take on picnics. Bring them along with Sweet-and-Sour Slaw, crusty bread and a few cans of beer.

Lightly score the chicken legs in 2 or 3 places on both sides. Rub legs liberally with Bonedust Burn BBQ Paste, pressing the seasoning into the scored meat. Cover and refrigerate for 4–6 hours, or overnight. When fully marinated, remove chicken and wrap a slice of bacon around each drumstick, securing in place with a toothpick. In a medium bowl, whisk together all remaining ingredients and set aside.

Preheat grill to medium (about 350°F). Place bacon-wrapped drumsticks in a grill basket. Grill drumsticks, basting liberally with sauce, until chicken is fully cooked and the bacon is crisp, about 10–12 minutes each side. (If bacon flares up, move chicken to the side of the grill and cook over indirect heat.) When cooked, remove from grill basket to a large bowl. Pour on remaining sauce and toss to fully coat. Serve immediately, or refrigerate for eating later.

WHITE TRASH CHICKEN CHILI

4 (6 to 8 oz) boneless, skinless
chicken breasts
2 tbsp Bonedust Seasoning (p. 22)
2 tbsp + 2 tbsp vegetable oil
1 large white onion, diced
3 cloves garlic, minced
2 stalks celery, diced
1 1/2 cups diced celery root
4 large jalapeño peppers,
seeded and diced
2 lb ground chicken
2 (14 oz) cans baked beans
1 (14 oz) can white kidney beans
4 cups Smoked Chicken Stock (p. 261)
1/2 cup whipping cream
Hot pepper sauce
Salt and freshly ground black pepper
1/2 cup ranch dressing
1/4 cup sour cream
1 cup shredded white cheddar cheese
Mixed chopped fresh herbs (p. 26)

Serves 8

All the white stuff in this chili — ranch dressing, whipping cream, sour cream — makes it so trashy delicious.

Preheat grill to medium-high (about 400°F). Rub chicken breasts with Bonedust Seasoning, gently pressing so that spices adhere to meat. Grill seasoned chicken breasts for 6–8 minutes, each side, or until fully cooked. Remove from grill, cool slightly, and dice into 1/2-in pieces. Set aside.

In a large crockpot or Dutch oven over medium-high heat, warm 2 tbsp of oil. Add onion, garlic, celery, celery root and jalapeño peppers. Sauté for 4–5 minutes, or until tender. Transfer to a bowl and set aside.

Add 2 tbsp more oil to the pot and fry ground chicken, in batches, until fully cooked. Be careful not to overcrowd the pot. Drain any excess fat from pan. Return cooked ground chicken to pot. Add baked beans, sautéed onion mixture and drained kidney beans, stirring to incorporate. Stir Smoked Chicken Stock and cream into the pot and bring to a boil. Cover, reduce heat to low and simmer for 20–30 minutes. Add diced grilled chicken to pot and season with hot sauce, salt and pepper to taste. Stir in ranch dressing and sour cream and serve garnished with white cheddar cheese and fresh herbs.

SMOKED BROWN SUGAR BUTTER CHICKEN HALVES

Brown sugar and my Indonesian Cinnamon Rub make this chicken sticky and sweet.

Using kitchen or poultry shears, cut along both sides of backbone, the entire length of each chicken. Remove and discard bones. Using a sharp knife, cut through breastbone to completely separate each chicken into halves. Rub with Indonesian Cinnamon Rub, pressing seasoning into skin and meat.

In a medium bowl, combine brown sugar, schnapps, butter, Parmesan cheese, herbs and garlic. Mix well. Lift skin from flesh and rub butter mixture under the skin, and all over the outside of each bird.

Prepare your smoker, according to manufacturer's instructions, to a temperature of 225°F. Add hickory smoking chips. Place chicken, skin side up, on smoking rack and close the lid. Smoke chicken halves for 4–6 hours, or until a meat thermometer, inserted into the thickest part of the meat, reads 180°F. Replenish smoking chips, coals and water as required.

Preheat grill to medium (about 350°F). Transfer smoked chicken halves to grill, bone side down. Close lid and grill-roast, basting with maple syrup, for 5–10 minutes or until the skin is crisp and chickens are hot. Remove from grill to a platter; season with salt and pepper to taste and serve.

Special equipment: Smoker
Hickory smoking chips or chunks, soaked in water

2 (3 to 4 lb) chickens
1/2 cup Indonesian Cinnamon Rub (p. 24)
1/4 cup brown sugar
2 oz cinnamon schnapps
1/4 cup softened butter
1/4 cup freshly grated Parmesan cheese
1/2 cup chopped fresh herbs (p. 26)
4 cloves garlic, minced
1/2 cup maple syrup
Salt and freshly ground black pepper

Serves 4

CARLOS TOSCA'S CUBAN CHICKEN MOJO

My good friend and ex–Toronto Blue Jays manager Carlos Tosca loves this Cuban marinade — he says it reminds him of food back home. The guava gives a great island flavor to this BBQ sauce.

2 cups Mojo Marinade (p. 35)
1 whole chicken, cut into 8 pieces
1 cup Guava BBQ Sauce (p. 255)

Serves 4

Divide Mojo Marinade and set aside half for basting. In a large stainless steel or glass bowl, pour remaining marinade over chicken. Marinate chicken, covered and refrigerated, for 4–6 hours or overnight.

When chicken is fully marinated, preheat grill to medium-high (about 400°F). Remove chicken from refrigerator and discard marinade. Grill for 8–10 minutes, each side, or until fully cooked. Baste with reserved Mojo Marinade, halfway through the grilling time. Remove chicken from heat and serve immediately with Guava BBQ Sauce.

GRILLED TURKEY STEAKS WITH APRICOT MUSTARD SAUCE

8 (6 oz) turkey steaks (each about
1 in thick)
1 1/2 cups Big Yella Mustard
Marinade (p. 33)

Apricot Mustard Sauce
3/4 cup apricot jam
1 tbsp fresh lemon juice
1 tbsp white balsamic vinegar
1 tbsp grain mustard
2 tbsp honey
1 tbsp soy sauce
1 tbsp chopped fresh coriander
Salt and freshly ground black pepper

Serves 8

These delicious turkey steaks are great served with Grill-Roasted Cauliflower (see p. 219).

Spread turkey steaks in a glass dish large enough to hold all 8 in one layer. Pour Big Yella Mustard Marinade over them, turning to coat both sides. Cover with plastic wrap and marinate in the refrigerator for 4 hours.

To prepare the Apricot Mustard Sauce: In a small saucepan over medium heat, combine all sauce ingredients. Cook for 3–5 minutes, stirring until smooth. Transfer to a bowl and set aside, keeping warm.

Preheat grill to medium-high (about 400°F). Grill turkey for 4–5 minutes each side, or until fully cooked. Serve immediately with Apricot Mustard Sauce.

CHERRY WOOD SMOKED TURKEY DRUMSTICKS

Special equipment: Smoker
Cherry wood chunks, soaked in water
for 1 hour

4 turkey drumsticks, with skin on
2 cups Luther's Sheep Dip
Marinade (p. 32)
6 tbsp Bonedust Seasoning (p. 22)

Serves 4

These smoked turkey drumsticks are even more flavorful when presoaked cherry wood chips are added to the coals.

Rinse turkey drumsticks and pat dry. Place in a large glass dish and pour Luther's Sheep Dip Marinade over top, turning to coat both sides. Cover and marinate in the refrigerator for up to 24 hours.

When turkey is fully marinated, prepare your smoker, according to manufacturer's instructions, to a temperature of 180° to 220°F. Add presoaked cherry wood chunks to coals. Remove drumsticks from refrigerator and discard marinade. Pat dry with paper towels. Detach skin from top of each drumstick and peel down the leg, from the wide end to the knuckle. Using half the Bonedust Seasoning, season flesh. Roll skin back up to cover and season with remaining Bonedust Seasoning, pressing so that the spices adhere to the skin. Smoke for 4 hours, adding more presoaked cherry wood chunks and coals as needed.

After 4 hours, wrap each turkey drumstick in aluminum foil and continue to smoke for another 1–2 hours, or until fully cooked to an internal temperature of 180°F. Remove from smoker and let sit for several minutes before unwrapping foil. Serve immediately.

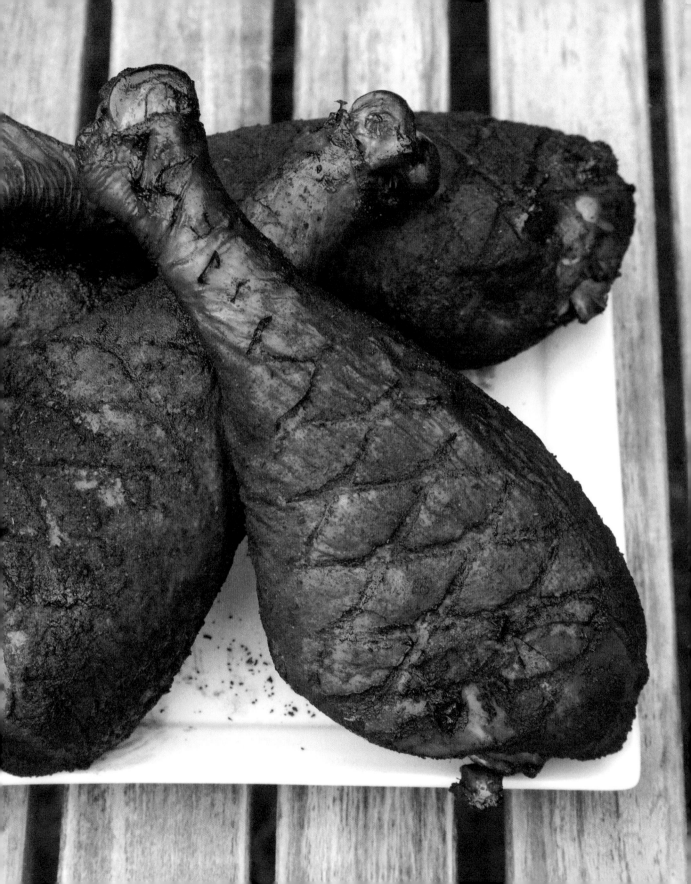

RUM TURKEY STUFFED WITH PULLED PORK AND BAGELS

I met Craig at the buskers' festival in Halifax. He told me of a turkey he'd barbecued for Thanksgiving — it was stuffed with sausage meat and cubed bagels. Here's my version of Craig's recipe.

1 (12 to 15 lb) turkey

2 cups kosher salt

8 "everything" bagels ("everything" means sesame seeds, poppy seeds, garlic flakes and onion flakes), cut into 1-in cubes

1 large onion, diced

1 lb ground sausage meat

2 cups Slow-Smoked Pulled Pork (p. 128)

1/2 cup gourmet barbecue sauce

3 stalks celery, chopped

1/2 cup melted butter

Salt and freshly ground black pepper

1 cup melted butter

1/2 cup sultana raisins

4 tbsp Bonedust Seasoning (p. 22)

1/2 cup melted butter

1 cup dark rum

Serves 12

Rinse turkey under cold running water. Place the neck in the body cavity and transfer turkey to a large bucket. In another large bucket, combine 4 quarts water and kosher salt, stirring until salt is dissolved. Pour brine liquid over turkey. (Add more water if necessary to completely cover the turkey, adding 1 tbsp of salt for every additional cup of water.) Brine the turkey, covered and refrigerated, for 24 hours.

Once bird is fully brined, remove turkey from bucket, and remove the neck from inside turkey cavity; set neck aside. Rinse turkey under cold water to remove any excess brine and pat dry with paper towels; set aside.

In a large bowl combine cubed bagels, onion, sausage meat, pulled pork, barbecue sauce, celery and melted butter. Mix well and season with salt and pepper to taste. Add raisins and mix well. Stuff the turkey, packing firmly but being careful not to overstuff (reserve some stuffing for the neck cavity). Once stuffed, close the cavity by stretching excess skin across opening and securing with thin metal skewers. Press the drumsticks to the body and tie together with kitchen string. Fill the neck cavity with remaining stuffing; pull excess skin over the stuffing and secure with thin metal skewers.

Set up grill for indirect cooking at 425°F. Season the outside of turkey and turkey neck with Bonedust Seasoning. Place on grill grate, away from heat source. Grill-roast turkey for 30 minutes, basting occasionally with the melted butter mixed with the rum, before reducing heat to 325°F. Cover loosely with a tent of aluminum foil and grill for 20 minutes per pound or until fully cooked. An internal thermometer inserted into the thickest part of the meat and stuffing should read 180°F. Remove turkey from grill, reposition foil tent over top and let sit for 20 minutes. Remove stuffing, transfer to bowl and keep warm. Carve turkey and serve with warm stuffing.

ASIAN BBQ SMOKED DUCK

1/2 cup dark soy sauce
1/2 cup shao hsing wine
1 (4 to 5 lb) duck
1/2 cup + 3 tbsp Indonesian
Cinnamon Rub (p. 24)
1 cinnamon stick
2 star anise

Serves 6 to 8

This duck is marinated in a delicious Asian wine and rubbed with aromatic Southeast Asian spices. Shao hsing wine, a Chinese rice wine, can be found in Asian and specialty food markets. You'll need at least 12 hours — but preferably 24 — to fully marinate the duck.

In a large bowl, combine soy sauce, shao hsing wine and 2 cups water. Mix well and set aside.

Clean duck by removing gizzard, heart and other organs from the interior. Discard other organs, but, if you like, do reserve duck liver to make pâté. Rinse duck, inside and out, with cold running water; drain and pat dry. Place duck, breast side down, on a cutting board. Using kitchen shears, remove backbone by cutting down either side of the spine. Remove ribs with kitchen shears, being careful not to cut through the skin. Rub duck inside and out with 1/2 cup Indonesian Cinnamon Rub, firmly pressing so that the seasoning adheres to the meat. Place duck, breast side down, in a deep glass baking dish and pour soy mixture overtop, ensuring duck is completely covered. Add cinnamon stick and star anise to the dish. Cover and refrigerate for 12–24 hours.

Once duck is fully marinated, prepare smoker according to manufacturer's instructions, to 200°F. Remove duck from refrigerator and discard marinade. Rub duck, inside and out, with remaining 3 tbsp of Indonesian Cinnamon Rub, firmly pressing so that spices adhere well to meat. Place duck in smoker and smoke for 4–5 hours, or until an internal temperature of 170°F is reached. When done, remove from smoker, slice and serve immediately.

SEAFOOD

WHETHER OVER GAS or charcoal, the best way to cook fish is on the grill. My favorite method of grilling seafood is planking — grilling fish on cedar planks set directly on the grill. It's fast and results in the most flavorful fish. From salmon to shrimp and more, I'll plank whatever I can and whatever works. But other rustic methods of grilling fish work well, too. Wrapping fish tightly in banana leaves or aluminum foil keeps it moist and delicious. And grilling mussels on a bed of presoaked pine needles makes for a fast and delicious dinner.

When grilling tuna or swordfish, I like to keep it basic — using a kettle grill with lump charcoal. Once, while filming my television show in the Dominican Republic, I stuck my Apollo charcoal grill in the ocean and stood knee-deep in the pristine sea to grill a delicious and very rare tuna. (Always make sure your tuna is just lightly seared and oh-so-rare when grilled... It's the tastiest.) The perfect way to grill fish!

LEARN TO SPANK
THE PLANK

Planking goes way back — it's an ancient method of cooking that traces its roots to the Haida people on Canada's west coast. It's fast and easy and it adds a delicious sweet, smoky flavor to food.

There are a variety of woods to plank on: Apple, cherry and maple wood planks all impart wonderful flavors to food. My favorite wood for planking is western red cedar: It produces sweet-tasting and flavorful food.

Always presoak your plank prior to grilling. For added flavor, you can also soak the plank in juice or even beer, but never soak in straight alcohol.

Place your plank directly on a grill preheated to 500° to 600°F and close the lid. Grill the plank for 2–3 minutes, or until it begins to crackle and smoke. Be prepared for the amount of smoke that is generated — it's what imparts the flavor, but it takes some getting used to.

When you hear the crackling or see smoke escaping from the barbecue, carefully open the lid and place whatever you're grilling on the heated plank. Close the lid and let the cooking begin. Check every 4–5 minutes to make certain the plank isn't on fire. If there is a fire, use a spray bottle of water to put out the flames, and reduce the heat to medium-low.

When the food is cooked, carefully remove the plank from the grill, place on a serving platter and enjoy.

Opening spread: Bacon-Wrapped Scallops (p. 201)

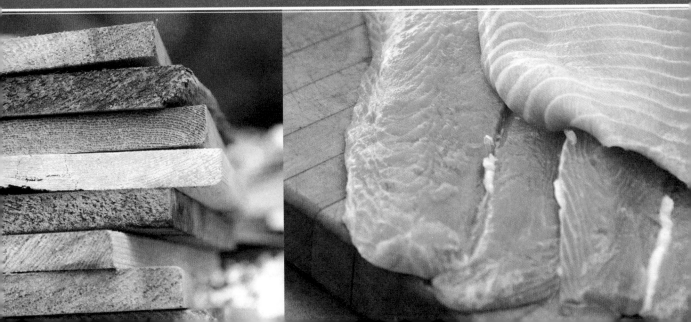

PLANKING IS THE ESSENCE OF COOKING AT ITS MOST PRIMAL, *USING NATURAL ELEMENTS TO CREATE FOOD IMBUED WITH FLAVOR, TOUCHED BY FIRE AND LICKED WITH SMOKE.*

PLANKED MONKFISH WITH CHILI-SPICED CRAWFISH CRUST

Monkfish is a rich, meaty fish that gets a Cajun treatment in this delicious, spicy dish.

Preheat grill to high (400° to 500°F). Season tomatoes, onion and red pepper with 1 tbsp olive oil and 1 tbsp Bayou Bite Cajun Seasoning. Fire-roast for 8–10 minutes, turning frequently, until lightly charred and blistered. Remove from grill and cool slightly.

Peel charred skin from tomatoes and pepper. Coarsely chop tomatoes, onions and pepper. In a bowl, combine chopped tomato, onion and pepper, crawfish, garlic, red chili pepper, coriander, vinegar and remaining tbsp of oil; season with salt and pepper to taste and set aside.

Preheat grill to very high (approximately 550° to 600°F). Season monkfish chops with remaining 2 tbsp Bayou Bite Cajun Seasoning, gently pressing so that spices adhere to fish. Wrap each monkfish chop in 2 slices of prosciutto and secure with a toothpick.

Place prosciutto-wrapped monkfish chops on plank, evenly spaced. Spoon equal amounts of crawfish-crust mixture on top of each monkfish chop, piling it up and pressing down gently to settle the crust. Place plank on the grill and close lid. Plank-bake monkfish chops for 15–18 minutes, or until cooked through. Using a pair of tongs and barbecue gloves, remove the smoking plank from grill and place on top of another plank or on a heat-resistant surface. Using a vegetable peeler, shave thin slices of Parmesan cheese and garnish monkfish with the cheese before serving.

Special equipment: 1 untreated cedar plank (at least 12 x 10 x 1 in), soaked in water at least 1 hour

2 plum tomatoes, halved lengthwise
1 small Vidalia onion, quartered
1 large red bell pepper, halved and seeded
1 tbsp + 1 tbsp extra-virgin olive oil
1 tbsp + 2 tbsp Bayou Bite Cajun Seasoning (p. 23)
1 cup crawfish tail meat, or baby shrimp
2 cloves garlic, minced
2 red chili peppers, minced
1 tbsp chopped fresh coriander
1 tbsp white balsamic vinegar
Kosher salt
Cracked black peppercorns
4 (10 to 12 oz) monkfish chops
8 slices prosciutto
1/2 cup shaved Parmesan cheese

Serves 4

Cautionary Notes on Using Planks:

Please use care, and follow these tips when planking.

★ Use untreated western red cedar planks (or another type of suitable wood). Do not use a plank more than once.
★ Always presoak your planks in water at least 1 hour before using.
★ Have a spray bottle of water and a fire extinguisher at the ready, as backup.
★ Never leave the grill when planking.
★ If planks should ignite, reduce burner temperature and open lid. Using spray bottle, douse flames, close lid and continue planking.
★ Be aware of wind direction when planking. Never open your grill lid to the wind, and stand with your back to the wind to avoid getting smoke in your eyes.
★ Allow planks to cool completely before discarding. I use cold water to cool the planks after cooking and before discarding.

LOBSTER-STUFFED CEDAR-PLANKED RAINBOW TROUT

Lobster meat goes well with the delicate flavor of trout.

Special equipment: 1 untreated cedar plank (at least 12 x 10 x 1 in), soaked in water for 1 hour

2 slices bacon, finely diced
1/4 cup shallots, finely diced
2 green onions, chopped
2 cloves garlic, minced
1 tsp chopped fresh thyme
1 presteamed lobster tail, meat coarsely chopped
3 to 4 tbsp Riesling wine
1/4 cup butter
Salt and cracked black peppercorns
1 corn muffin, crumbled
3 small trout, backbones and heads removed
1 clove garlic, minced
1/2 tsp salt
1/2 tsp cracked black peppercorns

Serves 2

In a sauté pan over medium-high heat, cook bacon for 3–4 minutes, or until lightly browned. Add shallots and cook for 2 minutes more. Add green onion, garlic, thyme and lobster meat, and continue sautéing for 3–4 minutes, or until vegetables soften and the lobster is heated through. Add Riesling and deglaze pan by scraping up browned bits from the bottom; add butter. Season with salt and cracked peppercorns to taste. Turn off heat, stir in crumbled muffin and set aside, keeping warm.

Preheat grill to high (about 500° to 550°F). Being careful not to overseason, rub the inside of trout with minced garlic, salt and pepper. Spread 2 tbsp of lobster stuffing along inside and fold the trout closed. Carefully place the stuffed and seasoned trout onto a presoaked plank and transfer plank directly to the grill. Close the lid and plank-bake trout for 20–25 minutes, or until fish is golden brown and firm to the touch and flakes easily with a fork. Using a pair of tongs and barbecue gloves, remove smoking plank from grill and place onto another plank or a heat-resistant surface. Separate trout from the plank by running a knife or spatula between the two. Spoon remaining lobster stuffing overtop and serve immediately.

ULTIMATE PLANKED SALMON

This is my original planked salmon recipe, and the only recipe you need to use. It's perfect for first-time plankers.

Special equipment: 1 untreated cedar plank (at least 12 x 10 x 1 in), soaked in water for 1 hour

4 (6 oz) skinless salmon fillets
2 tbsp Bonedust Seasoning (p. 22)
1/2 cup chopped fresh dill
4 large shallots, diced
2 cloves garlic, minced
2 green onions, finely chopped
1 tsp grated lemon zest
1 tbsp extra-virgin olive oil
Salt and freshly ground black pepper
Juice of 1 lemon

Serves 4

Preheat grill to very high (about 550° to 600°F). Season salmon fillets with Bonedust Seasoning and set aside on a tray.

In a small bowl, mix together dill, shallots, garlic, green onion, lemon zest and olive oil; season with salt and pepper to taste. Evenly coat the top of the salmon fillets with the dill-and-shallot mixture. Place coated salmon on plank and place on grill. Close lid and plank-bake for 12–15 minutes or until salmon is cooked to medium. (There is no need to turn the salmon.) Before removing from the grill, squeeze lemon juice over planked salmon fillets. Using a pair of tongs and barbecue gloves, remove the plank from grill and place on top of another plank or on a heat-resistant surface and serve immediately.

PLANKED SHRIMP FUNDIDO

Fundido is like a Mexican fondue. Serve these plank-grilled cheesy hot shrimp in grill-toasted corn tortillas: Just dip, scoop, wrap and eat. Chihuahua brand cheese is my favorite for this recipe.

Preheat grill to medium-high (about 400°F). In a medium bowl, combine shrimp and 1 tbsp Bonedust Seasoning, tossing to coat shrimp well. Arrange shrimp in 4 piles, 2 shrimp to each pile, on presoaked plank; set aside.

Grill onion and jalapeño peppers for 8–10 minutes, turning, or until lightly charred. Remove from grill. Slice onion and chop jalapeños. Add to another bowl and season with remaining 1/2 tbsp of Bonedust Seasoning, mixing well to evenly coat vegetables.

Top each shrimp stack with grilled vegetable mixture and plank-grill for 12–15 minutes, or until shrimp are pink, opaque and just firm to the touch. Top grilled stacks with equal amounts of shredded cheese. Close grill lid and allow cheese to melt, about 2 minutes. Using a pair of tongs and barbecue gloves, remove smoking plank from grill and place on top of another plank or on a heat-resistant surface and serve.

Special equipment: 1 untreated cedar plank (at least 12 x 10 x 1 in), soaked in water for 1 hour

8 jumbo shrimp, shelled and deveined but with tail intact
1 tbsp + 1/2 tbsp Bonedust Seasoning (p. 22)
1 large onion, quartered
4 jalapeño peppers
2 cups shredded cheese (mozzarella, Mexican queso or pepper Jack)

Serves 4.

SWEET-AND-SAUCY SALMON

This simple sauce is perfect for grillin' and glazin'.

4 (8 oz) salmon fillets,
cut about 1 1/2 to 2 in thick
2 tbsp Amazing Steak Spice (p. 23)
2 tbsp butter
3 small shallots, diced
1 tbsp chopped fresh thyme
1/4 cup brown sugar, firmly packed
2 tbsp apple cider vinegar
2 tbsp bourbon
1 tbsp soy sauce
1/2 bottle gourmet barbecue sauce

Serves 4

Rub salmon filets with Amazing Steak Spice, gently pressing so that spices adhere to the steaks. Spray both sides of seasoned salmon steaks with nonstick vegetable oil cooking spray and set aside.

In a small saucepan, over medium heat, combine butter, shallots and thyme. Sweat for 3 minutes, stirring frequently. Add brown sugar, vinegar, bourbon, soy sauce and barbecue sauce. Bring to a low boil, stirring occasionally. Remove from heat and set aside for basting.

Preheat grill to medium high (about 400°F). Place the salmon on the grill and cook for 4–5 minutes, each side, basting liberally with barbecue sauce mixture during the last half of cooking time. Remove from heat, drizzle with extra sauce and serve.

SKATE WITH BALSAMIC SAUCE

When purchasing skate, avoid any that has a strong ammonia smell: It's just not fresh enough.

1 (1 1/2 to 2 lb) skinless skate wing
1 tsp Bonedust Seasoning (p. 22)

Balsamic Sauce
2 tbsp + 2 tbsp butter
1/4 cup diced shallots
1/4 cup capers, drained and squeezed to remove excess moisture
1 tsp grated lemon zest
1 tbsp fresh lemon juice
4 tbsp aged balsamic vinegar
Salt and freshly ground black pepper

Serves 2

Preheat grill to high (about 500°F). Rinse skate wing under cold water; pat dry. Season skate wing with Bonedust Seasoning, gently pressing so that spices adhere to the wing. Spray seasoned skate with nonstick cooking spray and place on a grill topper (these are perforated nonstick trays that fit on top of the grill grate to let you cook more delicate foods). Grill for 2–3 minutes each side. Reduce grill temperature directly below skate wing to low (about 250° to 300°F), close lid and cook for 8–10 minutes, or until flesh is tender and lifts away easily from cartilage.

To prepare the Balsamic Sauce: In a small saucepan over medium heat, melt 2 tbsp butter. Add shallots and capers and sauté for 2–3 minutes, or until tender and lightly colored. Add zest, lemon juice and vinegar and bring to a boil. Continue boiling for 1–2 minutes, or until liquid has reduced and thickened. Remove from heat and stir in remaining 2 tbsp butter; season with salt and pepper to taste. Set aside and keep warm.

Remove skate from grill. Cut the skate flesh from the wing by slicing from the thickest part of the fish to the tip of the wing. Arrange on a platter and serve drizzled with warm Balsamic Sauce.

HALIBUT WITH CHAMPAGNE AND GRAPES

This is a delicious, sophisticated dish that will impress your friends.

Thread as many grapes as you like onto 8 bamboo skewers and set aside.

Preheat grill to medium-high (about 400°F). Lightly brush halibut with 2 tbsp olive oil and season with Mediterranean-Style Rub, gently pressing so that spices adhere to the fish. Place seasoned halibut on grill, flesh side down, and grill for 3–4 minutes. Using a thin spatula, turn — don't flip — fillet to make criss-cross grill marks. Grill for another 1–2 minutes. Flip halibut over and close grill lid.

Meanwhile, in a sauté pan over medium heat, melt 1 tbsp butter. Add shallots and sweat until soft, about 2–3 minutes. Using a rubber spatula or a wooden spoon, deglaze pan with champagne by scraping up the browned bits on the bottom of the pan. Bring the champagne to a boil and continue boiling for 1–2 minutes, or until liquid is reduced by half. Add the thyme and 4 tbsp cold butter, stirring until butter is melted. Remove from heat and set aside, keeping warm.

Grill skewered grapes for 3–4 minutes, turning once. When skins of grapes are lightly charred, remove from heat and set aside.

Carefully remove halibut from grill, using a spatula, and leaving skin on grill. Transfer fish to a serving platter. Allow halibut skin to get crisp, about 1–2 minutes, before removing from grill and slicing into thin strips. Pour butter sauce over halibut and garnish with skewered grapes and crispy halibut skin strips. Serve immediately.

Special equipment: 8 bamboo skewers, soaked in cold water for 1 hour

1 bunch seedless green grapes
8 (8 oz) halibut fillets, with skin on
2 tbsp + 2 tbsp extra-virgin olive oil
4 tbsp Mediterranean-Style Rub (p. 23)
1 tbsp + 4 tbsp cold butter
4 shallots, thinly sliced
1/2 cup champagne
1 tsp chopped fresh thyme
Salt and freshly ground black pepper

Serves 8

SESAME GINGER KINGFISH IN BANANA LEAF BUNDLES

1 banana leaf
4 (8 oz) kingfish fillets
1/4 cup Sesame Ginger Paste (p. 30)
1 cup sticky rice, cooked as per package instructions, and chilled
2 tbsp Hot BBQ Fish Drizzle (p. 31)
1 mango, peeled, pitted and diced
4 sprigs Thai basil
1/2 cup soy sauce

Serves 4

Banana leaves can be bought in Asian or West Indian groceries. Cooking fish in banana leaves helps the spicy, tangy flavors to penetrate the fish.

Cut banana leaf into four 10 x 10-in squares and set aside.

Preheat grill to medium (about 350°F). Rub kingfish fillets with Ginger Sesame Paste, gently pressing so that sesame paste adheres to fish. Set aside.

Grill banana leaf, for 10 seconds each side, to lightly soften (leaf will turn a brighter green). Remove from grill. In the center of each grilled banana leaf square, place 1/4 cup rice, and flatten slightly to match shape of fish. Spoon 1/2 tbsp of Hot BBQ Fish Drizzle on rice. Place seasoned kingfish fillet onto rice and top with 2 tbsp diced mango. Carefully fold in sides of banana leaf to form a neat, square bundle. Secure with butcher's twine if necessary. Place kingfish bundles on grill and cook, with grill lid closed, for 8–10 minutes each side, or until fully cooked but still moist. Remove from grill.

To serve, place a bundle on each plate and carefully open to allow steam to escape. Drizzle a little extra Hot BBQ Fish Drizzle over fillets and garnish with Thai basil sprigs. Serve with soy sauce for dipping.

LIMONCELLO SWORDFISH WITH HERBED BUTTER BASTE

2 (8 oz) swordfish steaks, cut 1 to 1 1/2 in thick
1/2 cup Limoncello liqueur

Herbed Butter Baste
4 tbsp softened unsalted butter
1 tsp chopped lemon zest
1 tbsp fresh lemon juice
3 tbsp chopped fresh herbs (p. 26)
1 tsp cracked black peppercorns

4 tbsp Herbed Sea Salt Rub (p. 29)
2 tbsp extra-virgin olive oil

Serves 2

Limoncello is a sweet lemon-based liqueur from the south of Italy.

In a shallow glass baking dish, soak swordfish steaks in Limoncello liqueur for 15 minutes, turning once.

To prepare the Herbed Butter: In a small bowl, mix together butter, zest, lemon juice, chopped fresh herbs and cracked pepper. (Mixture should be soft but not liquid.) Set aside for basting.

Preheat grill to very high (500° to 600°F). Remove swordfish steaks from Limoncello marinade and season both sides with Herbed Sea Salt Rub, pressing firmly so that spices adhere to fish. Brush seasoned swordfish with olive oil and place on grill. Grill for 3–4 minutes, each side, until just cooked through, basting with reserved Herbed Butter Baste. Remove from grill.

To serve, top each swordfish steak with extra Herbed Butter Baste.

SPECK-WRAPPED SARDINES

12 fresh whole sardines, cleaned,
but with heads and tails attached
1 tbsp extra-virgin olive oil
2 tbsp coarse salt
1 tbsp cracked black peppercorns
12 thin slices speck or prosciutto or
serrano ham
4 cups Wasabi Balsamic Glazing
Sauce (p. 254)
1 lemon, cut into 6 wedges
1/4 cup Dijon mustard

Serves 6

**When preparing this recipe, avoid canned sardines. Buy
them fresh — about 6 inches in length. If you can't find
fresh sardines, then substitute with young herring or
sprat. Speck, similar to prosciutto, is a boned ham that is
salted, seasoned, cold smoked and then dry aged.**

Preheat grill to medium-high (about 400°F). Rinse sardines under cold water
and pat dry with paper towels. Place in a shallow dish and add oil; season with
salt and black pepper to taste. Tightly wrap 1 slice of speck around each
sardine, leaving head and tail exposed. Open fish grill basket and spray insides
with vegetable oil cooking spray. Place speck-wrapped sardines in basket and
secure to ensure fish won't move when basket is flipped. Place basket on grill
and cook for 3–4 minutes, each side, or until speck is crisp and golden brown.
Just before removing from grill, baste speck-wrapped sardines with Wasabi
Balsamic Sauce and cook for an additional 1 minute on each side. Transfer
basket and remove sardines from basket. Serve immediately with lemon
wedges, coarse salt, cracked peppercorns and Dijon mustard for dipping.

LEMONGRASS-SKEWERED TUNA WITH GUACAMOLE AND WASABI BUTTER — À LA BISH

Lemongrass-Skewered Tuna

2 (6 to 8 oz) tuna steaks, sushi grade, cut 1 1/2 to 2 in thick
2 tbsp Amazing Steak Spice (p. 23)
8 slices prosciutto
8 pieces lemongrass (6 to 8 in long), peeled and trimmed

Bish Guacamole

2 ripe avocados, peeled and diced
1 red onion, finely diced
1 cubanelle pepper, finely diced
3 tbsp finely diced pickled ginger
2 tbsp finely diced nori seaweed
Dash sesame oil
Squeeze fresh lime juice
Salt and freshly ground black pepper

Wasabi Butter

1 tbsp wasabi powder
1 tbsp cold water
1/4 cup softened butter
2 green onions, thinly sliced
Juice of 1/2 lime
Salt and freshly ground black pepper

Serves 4

While in Halifax, I had the pleasure of dining at Bish World Cuisine. Two words describe the experience: salaciously delicious. It is an experience not to be missed. Thanks to Chef Mark Giffin, here's my version of Bish fish.

To prepare the Lemongrass-Skewered Tuna: Cut tuna steaks into 2-in-square chunks. Season with Amazing Steak Spice, making sure that all sides are evenly coated, and gently pressing so that spices adhere to the tuna. Stack prosciutto slices on a flat surface and cut through layers lengthwise (after slicing, you should have 16 2 x 4-in strips). Place each strip of prosciutto onto a flat surface. Position 1 seasoned tuna cube at the end of each prosciutto strip and, starting with the tuna end, tightly roll so that the prosciutto forms a wrapper around 4 sides of the cube (2 sides are left exposed). Carefully skewer 2 pieces of prosciutto-wrapped tuna on each stalk of lemongrass. (Push lemongrass through center of tuna but do not pierce prosciutto.) Place tuna skewers in a shallow glass baking dish and refrigerate, covered, until ready to cook.

To prepare the Bish Guacamole: In a large bowl, combine avocado, red onion, cubanelle pepper, pickled ginger, nori seaweed, sesame oil and lime juice. Mix well and season with salt and pepper to taste. Cover with plastic wrap and refrigerate until needed.

To prepare the Wasabi Butter: In a small bowl, mix wasabi powder with water to form a thick paste. Mix in butter, green onion and lime juice; season with salt and pepper to taste and set aside.

Preheat grill to high (about 500° to 550°F). Place chilled tuna skewers on grill and sear for 1 minute each side, making sure all 4 sides of tuna are seared. Be careful not to overcook: Tuna centers should be rare. Remove skewers from grill and transfer to a large plate. Place a dollop of Wasabi Butter on each skewer and garnish with Bish Guacamole.

GRILL-STEAMED CLAMS

Make sure to use hard-shell clams for this recipe.

1/2 cup Bonedust Burn BBQ
Paste (p. 29)
Juice of 2 limes
2 to 3 lb large fresh (quahog or
hard-shell) clams, scrubbed
8 tbsp melted butter
Salt and freshly ground black pepper
Fresh lime juice

Serves 4

Preheat grill to high (about 500° to 550°F). In a large bowl, combine Bonedust Burn BBQ Paste, lime juice and clams. Toss to coat. Spoon clams onto grill. Close lid and grill-steam clams for 8–10 minutes, or until shells open. Discard any clams with unopened shells. Transfer steam-grilled clams to a large bowl and toss with melted butter; season with salt and pepper to taste. Add a squeeze of fresh lime and serve with fresh crusty bread for dipping.

MUSSELS IN ORANGE BUTTER SAUCE GRILLED WITH PINE NEEDLES

The pine needles, which cover the mussel shells during grilling, impart a sweet, woodsy flavor.

Special equipment: Pine needles

Orange Butter Sauce
Juice of 2 oranges
3 tbsp softened unsalted butter
1/4 cup chopped fresh herbs (p. 26)
1 tsp chopped red chili peppers
1 oz Cointreau

3 lb fresh mussels, cleaned
and debearded
1/4 cup Herbed Sea Salt Rub (p. 29)

Serves 4

To prepare the Orange Butter Sauce: In a medium saucepan over medium heat, warm the orange juice. Remove from heat, stir in butter, herbs, chili peppers and Cointreau. Set aside over low heat to keep warm.

Preheat grill to high (about 500° to 550°F). Season mussel shells with Herbed Sea Salt Rub and place directly on grill. Cover with pine needles, close lid and let mussels grill-steam for 4–5 minutes or until shells open. (Be careful and lean back when opening the lid; there will be a lot of smoke and ash.) Blow or fan off any remaining ash and discard any unopened mussels.

Transfer to a large bowl and pour warm Orange Butter Sauce over mussels. Serve immediately with grilled crusty bread.

BACON-WRAPPED SCALLOPS

Bacon gives a smoky flavor to scallops. Prepare these tasty morsels in advance for easy grillin' while entertaining (see photo on p. 182).

16 slices bacon
16 large sea scallops, trimmed (under 10-per-lb count)
2 tbsp Smoked Salt Steak Rub (p. 28)

**Serves 4 as a main course
or 8 as an appetizer**

Partially cook the bacon in a heavy skillet over medium-high heat, 3–4 minutes each side, to render most of the fat. Remove bacon from pan before it starts to brown and pat dry with paper towel; set aside.

Season scallops on all sides with Smoked Salt Steak Rub, gently pressing so that spices adhere to the scallops. Wrap each seasoned scallop in a slice of parcooked bacon and secure with a toothpick. Place on a waxed paper–lined tray and refrigerate, covered, for 30 minutes.

After 30 minutes, heat grill to medium-high (about 400°F). Grill scallops for 3–5 minutes each side, until they are lightly charred and bacon is crisp. Remove from grill and serve as an appetizer or main course.

LOBSTER HUMIDOR

I first made this dish while visiting the tobacco plantation and cigar-rolling facility where the premium Dominican cigar, La Flor Dominicana, is made. The decadent cigar inspired this twist on Lobster Thermidor.

3 (1 1/2 lb) whole Caribbean lobsters
2 tbsp + 2 tsp Bonedust Seasoning (p. 22)
2 tbsp melted butter
1 tbsp extra-virgin olive oil
1 cubanelle pepper, finely chopped
6 shiitake mushrooms, soaked in water, drained and sliced
1 small red onion, chopped
2 plum tomatoes, chopped
3 hot chili peppers, minced
3 cloves garlic, minced
2 tbsp chopped fresh thyme
1/4 cup Jack Daniel's whiskey
1/2 cup gourmet barbecue sauce
1 cup shredded Camembert cheese

Serves 6

Place lobsters on a clean, flat surface and cut down the middle lengthwise, so that each half has a part of the tail and head. Extract and discard "sac," bony bits and feathery gills from head. Coat lobster meat inside shell halves with nonstick cooking spray and season with 2 tbsp of Bonedust Seasoning.

Preheat grill to medium-high (about 400°F). Place lobster halves on grill, meat side down, and grill for 1–2 minutes or until shell begins to turn color. Turn lobsters shell side down, and brush lobster meat with butter.

Meanwhile, in a large skillet, heat olive oil over medium-high. Add cubanelle pepper, shiitake mushrooms, onion, tomatoes, chili peppers and garlic; season with 2 tsp of Bonedust Seasoning and fresh thyme and sauté for 2–3 minutes, or until tender. Drizzle vegetables with Jack Daniel's and flambé to burn off excess alcohol. Transfer and mound flambéed mixture onto the head end of each lobster half. Drizzle lobsters and vegetables, at shell end, with barbecue sauce and sprinkle with Camembert cheese (leave tail meat exposed and unadorned). Reduce heat to low, close lid and grill-bake for 6–8 minutes, or until lobsters are fully cooked and cheese is just melting. Remove from grill and serve immediately.

GRILLED SWEET PUSS OCTOPUS

On the eve of our wedding in the Turks and Caicos, Pamela and I were sitting on the dock at our rented villa. Up swam an octopus. Pamela was the first to see it, and said, "Catch that!" I ran for a net and placed it in front of the octopus. With a stick, I coaxed it into the net, grabbed it and wrestled it off my arms and into a pot. We ate it the night we were married. Sweet Puss Octopus, for my sweet.

To prepare octopus, turn body inside out. Remove and discard ink sac and eyes. Set the octopus aside. In a large stockpot, combine 6–8 cups cold water, coriander sprigs, lemon, onion, sliced garlic, Bonedust Seasoning, salt and sugar. Bring mixture to a boil over high heat. Add octopus and return to a boil. Reduce heat to medium, cover, and simmer for 45–60 minutes. Uncover. Remove from heat and let cool before refrigerating, covered, in cooking liquid overnight.

An hour before grilling time, remove octopus from refrigerator and discard liquid. Under running water, and using the back of a knife, remove the purple skin to expose the white flesh beneath. Season with minced garlic, chopped coriander, oregano, salt, pepper, lemon juice and olive oil. Marinate for 1 hour, turning once or twice.

When octopus is fully marinated, heat grill to medium-high (about 400°F). Grill for 2–3 minutes each side, basting with marinade, until heated through and lightly charred. Remove from grill and cut octopus in chunks. Season with a squeeze of fresh lemon juice and serve over baby greens.

1 (1 to 1 1/2 lb) octopus, eyes and ink sac removed
4 sprigs coriander
1 lemon, quartered
1 small onion, chopped
4 cloves garlic, sliced
1 tbsp Bonedust Seasoning (p. 22)
1 tbsp salt
1 tbsp sugar
4 cloves garlic, minced
1 tbsp chopped fresh coriander
1 tbsp chopped fresh oregano
Salt
1 tbsp coarsely ground black pepper
Juice of 1 lemon
2 tbsp extra-virgin olive oil

Serves 2 to 3

GRILLED CALAMARI WITH BALSAMIC BUTTER SAUCE

12 medium whole squid, fresh or frozen (thawed)
1 cup buttermilk
2 tbsp Bonedust Seasoning (p. 22)
1/4 cup extra-virgin olive oil
1/4 cup balsamic vinegar
4 cloves garlic, minced
2 tbsp chopped fresh basil

Balsamic Butter Sauce
5 tbsp softened unsalted butter
4 cloves garlic, minced
4 shallots, diced
2 tbsp capers, drained
1/2 cup balsamic vinegar
Salt and freshly ground black pepper

Serves 6

Balsamic Butter Sauce is the perfect accompaniment to this grilled squid dish.

Pull the mantle (body) from the tentacles of each of the squid. Remove and discard the hard transparent pen (backbone) and other inner matter. Rinse under cold water and peel off outer membrane.

Cut away eye section from tentacles and remove hard bone (beak) from center of tentacles. Rinse under cold water and pat dry. Using a sharp knife, score bodies every 1/2 inch, cutting about two-thirds of the way into the flesh. Place bodies and tentacles in a glass baking dish and cover with buttermilk, turning to coat. Marinate, covered and refrigerated, for 4 hours.

When it is fully marinated, remove squid and discard marinade; pat dry with paper towels. Season squid inside and out with Bonedust Seasoning. In a glass baking dish, whisk together oil, vinegar, garlic and basil. Add squid, turning to coat. Marinate for 20 minutes.

To prepare the Balsamic Butter Sauce: Melt 2 tbsp butter in a small saucepan over medium-high heat. Add garlic, shallots and capers and sauté for 2–3 minutes or until tender. Stir in vinegar and bring to a boil. Continue boiling for 2–3 minutes, or until liquid has reduced by half. Remove from heat and whisk in remaining 3 tbsp of butter, 1 tbsp at a time, until fully incorporated. Season with salt and pepper to taste and set aside in oven to keep warm.

Preheat grill to medium-high (about 450°F). Remove squid from marinade and drain well. Grill squid for 3–4 minutes, each side, until just cooked through. Transfer to a platter and pour Balsamic Butter Sauce over squid. Serve with a radicchio and endive salad.

SIDES

SOMETIMES THE SIDE dishes served in restaurants are better and more satisfying than the main courses. You know, a big bowl of creamed spinach or mashed potatoes or ooey gooey macaroni and cheese — and sometimes, if they're really good, even French fries.

Because these elements so often make the meal, I've devoted considerable energy and time to create tantalizing, thrilling, monster sides like Pulled Pork Baked Beans, Stuffed Big Mama Sicilian Eggplant, Dump Truck Taters and Butter-Injected Fully Loaded Baked Potatoes. But even the more sedate Fire-Roasted Beets and Grilled Rapini are enough to enhance and complete a planked salmon or rotisseried pork loin.

Whatever you do, have fun with these side dishes. Grill 'em up and fill that lovin' belly of yours. Remember: A sigh after a good meal is always a great sign.

BBQ FRIED RICE

Just about any grilled veggies and meats will work with this delicious rice — try peppers, zucchini, mushrooms or asparagus, and shredded chicken and pulled pork.

Heat your wok over high, until the pan is just smoking. Add oil to wok before adding onion and garlic. Sauté until onion has softened, about 1–2 minutes. Toss in shiitake mushrooms, sugar-snap peas and roasted corn; continue sautéing for 1 minute more. Add grilled vegetables, bacon and barbecued meat; mix well, before adding cooked rice. Pour in soy sauce, sambal oelek, rice wine vinegar and hoisin sauce, and mix together until ingredients are combined and coated with sauce. Cook for 3–4 minutes, or until most of the liquid is absorbed into the rice. Add a few drops of sesame oil and green onion, give rice one final toss and scoop into bowls. Serve immediately with a small amount of sambal oelek, if desired.

3 tbsp vegetable oil
1 medium white onion, sliced
1 tbsp chopped garlic
1/2 cup sliced shiitake mushrooms
1/2 cup sugar-snap peas
1/2 cup roasted corn kernels
1/2 cup finely chopped grilled vegetables
1/2 cup diced Triple-Smoked Bacon (p. 238)
1 lb barbecued meat
2 cups cooked white rice
1/4 cup soy sauce
2 tbsp sambal oelek chili sauce
3 tbsp rice wine vinegar
3 tbsp hoisin sauce
1 tsp sesame oil
4 green onions, sliced

Serves 8

STUFFED SICILIAN EGGPLANT

How do you get people to eat eggplant? Hollow it out and stuff it with tasty goodness!

Slice top off eggplant, about 1 inch below stem, and reserve. Cut a thin slice off bottom to allow eggplant to stand. Scoop out the eggplant, leaving a 1/2-in-thick rim to form a deep eggplant bowl. Dice the scooped-out eggplant.

In a large frying pan, heat 2 tbsp of olive oil. Sauté diced eggplant for 5–6 minutes. Remove from pan and put into a large bowl.

Preheat grill to medium-high (about 400ºF). In a large bowl, toss onion, mushrooms, bacon, tomatoes, pepper and zucchini with 2 tbsp olive oil and vinegar; season with salt and pepper to taste. Transfer vegetables to a grill pan and grill for 3–4 minutes, until lightly charred and tender. Remove from grill and let cool. Coarsely chop grilled vegetables and add to bowl with sautéed eggplant; mix well to combine. Add Parmesan, bread, garlic, fresh herbs and bocconcini cheese; season with salt and pepper to taste and mix well.

Stuff eggplant with vegetable mixture and top with eggplant lid. Reduce grill temperature to medium (about 350ºF). Place on cedar plank in center of grill rack. Plank-bake for 15–20 minutes, or until cheese in stuffing has melted.

Special equipment: 1 untreated cedar plank, soaked in cold water for 1 hour

1 (1 1/2 to 2 lb) eggplant
2 tbsp + 2 tbsp olive oil
1 large onion, quartered
1/2 lb oyster mushrooms
6 slices Triple-Smoked Bacon (p. 238)
2 plum tomatoes
1 red bell pepper
1 medium zucchini, thinly sliced lengthwise
2 tbsp balsamic vinegar
Salt and freshly ground black pepper
1/4 cup grated Parmesan cheese
2 cups cubed Italian crusty bread, toasted or day old
4 cloves garlic, minced
1/4 cup mixed chopped fresh herbs
8 balls bocconcini cheese, quartered
Salt and freshly ground black pepper

Serves 4 to 6

Previous spread: Pulled Pork in Baked Beans (p. 220).
Opposite: BBQ Fried Rice

POLENTA ON THE BOARD

Special equipment: 1 untreated cedar plank, soaked in cold water for 1 hour

4 ripe plum tomatoes, cut in half
1 large sweet onion, peeled and cut into 1/2-in rings
1 zucchini, thinly sliced lengthwise
1 tbsp extra-virgin olive oil
1 tbsp Bonedust Seasoning (p. 22)
1/2 cup Fire-Roasted Tomato Sauce (p. 250)
2 cups Smoked Chicken Stock (p. 261)
1 tsp salt
1 cup cornmeal
2 tbsp butter
1/2 cup grated Parmesan cheese
Salt and freshly ground black pepper
1 cup crumbled Gorgonzola cheese

Serves 4 to 6

Polenta is the ultimate comfort food, especially when smothered in veggies and lots of gooey cheese and planked to perfection.

Preheat grill to medium-high (about 400°F). Brush tomatoes, onion and zucchini with olive oil and sprinkle with Bonedust Seasoning. Grill vegetables for 4–5 minutes, turning once, until lightly charred and tender. Remove from grill and cool slightly.

Meanwhile, in a small saucepan, heat tomato sauce over medium heat for 3 minutes. Reduce heat to minimum and keep warm until needed.

In a large, heavy saucepan on high, bring the Smoked Chicken Stock to a boil and add salt. Reduce heat to medium-low and pour cornmeal in a steady stream, stirring with a wooden spoon. Stir for 15–20 minutes more, or until polenta is thick and smooth. Remove pot from heat and stir in the butter and 1/4 cup of the Parmesan cheese; season polenta with salt and pepper to taste. Let cool in the pot for 5 minutes.

Preheat grill to high. Spoon cooled polenta onto the cedar plank, piling it high and leaving a 1-in border around the edge of the plank. Make a small well in the center of the polenta and spoon tomato sauce into it. Arrange vegetables in tomato sauce and top with crumbled Gorgonzola cheese. Place plank on the center of the grill and close the lid. Bake for 10–15 minutes, or until polenta is lightly browned and cheese has melted.

Transfer plank to a heatproof platter and place in the center of the table; have your guests serve themselves.

ROASTED SMASHED SWEET POTATOES

For an ultra-decadent twist, microwave 1/2 cup of maple syrup on medium heat for 30–45 seconds; drizzle over sweet potatoes while still warm.

Preheat grill to medium (about 350°F). Place sweet potatoes on top rack of grill, close lid and roast for 45–60 minutes, or until flesh is soft all the way through when pierced with a fork. Remove sweet potatoes from grill and let cool slightly. Carefully remove skin, ensuring that no charred bits remain stuck to the sweet potatoes. Place potatoes in a large bowl and smash with a spoon until mixture resembles a chunky mash. Add butter, brown sugar and green onions; mix gently to combine. Season sweet potato mixture with salt and pepper to taste and serve immediately with extra butter and warm syrup for drizzling.

4 large sweet potatoes
1/4 lb softened unsalted butter
3 tbsp brown sugar
3 green onions, thinly sliced
Salt and freshly ground black pepper

Serves 6 to 8

CEDAR-PLANKED MASHED POTATOES

When mashing these cedar-planked Yukon Gold nuggets, go smooth or lumpy: These are your taters, so make 'em however you like.

Place potatoes in a large pot and cover with cold water. Add garlic, onion and salt and bring to a boil over high heat. Reduce heat to medium-low and simmer for 20–30 minutes, or until potatoes are fully cooked and tender.

Once cooked, drain potatoes and return pan to heat. Shake pan to remove excess moisture from potatoes, garlic and onion. Remove from heat. While still in the pot, mash together potatoes, garlic and onion. Stir in butter, cream and ranch dressing, and continue stirring until butter has melted. Let cool for 20 minutes before stirring in cheeses, parsley, salt and pepper; mix well. Transfer mash to a large bowl; cover and refrigerate for 24 hours.

When ready to grill, mound chilled mashed potatoes on plank. Firmly pat and smooth potato mound. Heat grill to medium-high (about 400°F); place plank on grill and close lid. Plank-bake for 20–25 minutes, or until mash is golden brown and crisp on the outside, and hot all the way through. Carefully remove plank from grill and transfer to a heat-resistant platter. Top with extra butter and serve.

Special equipment: 1 untreated cedar plank, soaked in water for 1 hour

2 lb Yukon Gold potatoes
4 cloves garlic, minced
1 small onion, sliced
1 tsp salt
6 tbsp softened unsalted butter
1/4 cup whipping cream
1/4 cup ranch dressing
1/2 cup grated white cheddar cheese
4 cheese strings,
cut into 1/2-in pieces
2 tbsp chopped flat-leaf parsley
Salt and freshly ground black pepper

Serves 8

DUMP TRUCK TATERS

I always serve these potatoes in the back of a toy dump truck with butter and sour cream on the side.

Place potatoes in a large pot. Add enough cold water to cover potatoes completely. Bring to a boil over high heat. Reduce heat to medium-low and simmer for 20–30 minutes, or until potatoes are fully cooked and tender. Drain well and let cool slightly.

Preheat grill to medium (about 350°F). In a small bowl, combine butter, Parmesan and parsley; season with salt and pepper to taste and set aside. Toss potatoes with olive oil and season with Amazing Steak Spice. Dump potatoes into a grill basket and grill for about 10–15 minutes, turning occasionally, or until lightly charred and cooked through. Transfer to the back of a toy dump truck, if you have one, and serve immediately.

2 lb mini potatoes, red or white
1/2 lb butter, softened
1/4 cup grated Parmesan cheese
1 tbsp chopped flat-leaf parsley
Salt and freshly ground black pepper
2 tbsp olive oil or vegetable oil
1 tbsp Amazing Steak Spice (p. 23)

Serves 6

BUTTER-INJECTED FULLY LOADED BAKED POTATOES

An injection of butter makes these the best baked potatoes you've ever tasted!

Preheat grill to medium-high (about 400°F). Scrub potatoes well and pat dry. In a large bowl, combine melted butter, salt and Bonedust Seasoning. Add potatoes and toss to evenly coat in spice mixture. Place potatoes on top rack of grill and grill-bake for 45–60 minutes, or until tender. Remove from grill and let cool for 5 minutes.

Fill a Cajun injector with melted butter. Inject grill-baked potatoes with butter in multiple spots. Cut a well, 3 in deep, in the top center of each potato, reserving top pieces. Fill each hollow with mozzarella cheese, sour cream, bacon and green onions; season with salt and pepper to taste. Serve immediately with your favorite barbecue sauce on the side.

Special equipment: Cajun injector

6 large baking potatoes
(8 to 12 oz each)
2 tbsp melted butter
1 tbsp kosher salt
1 tbsp Bonedust Seasoning (p. 22)
1/4 lb melted butter
1/4 cup shredded mozzarella cheese
1/4 cup sour cream
8 slices bacon, cooked and diced
2 green onions, chopped
Salt and freshly ground black pepper

Serves 6 to 8

GRILLED RAPINI

3 tbsp extra-virgin olive oil
2 tbsp balsamic vinegar
1 clove garlic, minced
Salt and coarsely ground
black pepper
1 bunch rapini, trimmed, washed
under cold water and drained
1 lemon, cut in half
1/4 cup grated Parmesan cheese

Serves 4 to 6

Serve this delicious grilled rapini (also known as broccoli rabe) with Skate with Balsamic Sauce (p. 190).

Preheat grill to medium-high (about 400°F). In a large bowl, whisk together olive oil, balsamic vinegar, garlic, salt and pepper. Add cleaned rapini and toss with olive oil–balsamic dressing. Using tongs, remove rapini from bowl and transfer to grill. Place rapini perpendicular to bars of grill, so it won't fall through gaps. Grill with lid open for 3–4 minutes. Carefully turn rapini and squeeze lemon juice directly onto greens. Close lid and allow rapini to cook for an additional 1–2 minutes. Remove rapini from grill and arrange on a serving platter. Season with salt and pepper to taste and sprinkle with Parmesan cheese before serving.

GRILLED OYSTER MUSHROOMS

1 lb oyster mushrooms
1/4 cup extra-virgin olive oil
2 tbsp soy sauce
2 tbsp balsamic vinegar
2 cloves garlic, minced
2 green onions, minced
Salt and freshly ground black pepper
1 tbsp chopped Thai basil

Serves 6

Use a grill basket to make sure you don't lose any of these little guys.

In a large bowl, soak mushrooms in warm water for 5 minutes. Meanwhile, in another bowl, whisk together olive oil, soy sauce, vinegar, garlic and green onion. Season marinade with salt and pepper to taste. Remove mushrooms from water and drain on paper towels. Add to bowl with marinade and toss to coat completely. Cover bowl with plastic wrap and marinate in refrigerator for 1 hour.

Preheat grill to medium-high (about 400°F). Remove mushrooms from marinade, reserving marinade for basting, and place on grill. Grill mushrooms for 3–5 minutes, each side, basting frequently with marinade until lightly charred. Transfer mushrooms to a serving platter, sprinkle with Thai basil and serve immediately.

CREAM CORN CASSEROLE

Serve this side with a heaping platter of your favorite ribs.

Pull back corn husks gently, remove silk and replace husks, twisting ends together, if necessary, to cover corn completely. Place corn in a large bucket. Pour beer and enough water in bucket to cover and marinate corn for 1 hour.

Preheat grill to medium-high (about 400°F). Grill corn in husks over direct heat for 20–25 minutes, or until husks are charred and corn is tender and lightly roasted. Cut kernels from fire-roasted ears of corn: You will need about 4–5 cups of corn kernels for this recipe.

In a large pot, melt butter over medium heat. Add onion and garlic and sauté for 2–3 minutes, or until onion is translucent. Stir in flour and cook until flour is golden brown. Add Smoked Chicken Stock 1/2 cup at a time, stirring constantly, and bring to a boil. Reduce heat to low and simmer for 15–20 minutes, stirring occasionally, until liquid is thick and smooth. Stir in cream, remove from heat and set aside.

In a large bowl, combine corn kernels, cream corn, Velveeta cheese and smoked chicken cream sauce; mix well. Stir in sage and season with salt and pepper to taste. Pour into a greased 8 x 12 x 12-in casserole dish and bake at 350°F for 30–40 minutes.

Top with breadcrumbs and Parmesan cheese and continue to bake for an additional 10–15 minutes, or until topping is golden brown and crisp. Serve immediately.

12 ears corn on the cob
1 bottle beer
3 tbsp butter
1 medium onion, diced
2 cloves garlic, minced
4 tbsp all-purpose flour
2 cups Smoked Chicken Stock (p. 261)
1/2 cup whipping cream
1 (14 oz) can cream corn
2 cups cubed Velveeta cheese
1 tbsp chopped fresh sage
Salt and freshly ground black pepper
1 cup fresh breadcrumbs
1/4 cup grated Parmesan cheese

Serves 8 to 10

FIRE-ROASTED BEETS

Unless you like the look of bright purple fingers, be sure to wear rubber gloves when preparing this recipe.

Preheat grill to medium-high (about 400°F). Place beets directly on top rack of grill. Close the lid and grill-roast beets for 30–40 minutes, turning occasionally, until tender and lightly charred. Remove beets from grill and let cool slightly. Using rubber gloves, peel skin off beets (skin should come away easily). Slice beets into 1/2-in rounds and arrange on a serving platter. Drizzle grill-roasted beet slices with a little olive oil and cider vinegar. Sprinkle with thyme and season with salt and pepper, to taste. Serve immediately.

4 medium beets
1 tbsp extra-virgin olive oil
2 tsp apple cider vinegar
1 tsp chopped fresh thyme
Coarse salt and cracked black pepper

Serves 4 to 6

GRILL-ROASTED CAULIFLOWER

Grill-roasting brings out all the natural sugars in cauliflower and makes it sweet and delicious.

In a large pot, bring 12 cups of water to a boil and then reduce heat to medium. Add Cochin Curry Masala Rub, green onions, coriander, garlic and ginger. Remove from heat and place cauliflower head in pot. Cover and marinate for 30 minutes.

Meanwhile, in a medium bowl, combine raisins, breadcrumbs, Parmesan cheese, coriander and butter; set aside.

Preheat grill to medium-high (about 400°F). When it is fully marinated, remove cauliflower from pot and place in the center of a double-layered 18 x 18-in square of heavy-duty aluminum foil. Top cauliflower with raisin-breadcrumb mixture, then bring corners of foil up to create a pouch. Crimp the corners to seal, and transfer pouch to grill. Roast foil-encased cauliflower for 20–30 minutes. Remove foil pouch from grill, open carefully to allow steam to escape, and serve.

1/4 cup Cochin Curry Masala Rub (p. 24)
2 green onions
2 tsp chopped fresh coriander
4 cloves garlic, minced
1 tsp grated fresh ginger
1 head cauliflower
1/2 cup golden raisins
1/2 cup fresh breadcrumbs
1/4 cup grated Parmesan cheese
2 tbsp chopped fresh coriander
3 tbsp melted butter

Serves 6 to 8

GRILL-ROASTED GARLIC

Serve as a spread for crusty French bread. If making ahead of time, place grilled garlic heads in a resealable plastic bag and store in refrigerator for up to 2 weeks, or in the freezer for up to 3 months.

Preheat grill to medium (about 325°F). With a sharp knife, cut the top off garlic heads, about one-quarter to one-third of the way down.

Place garlic heads in the center of a double-layered 12 x 12-in square of heavy-duty aluminum foil. Drizzle the heads with oil, then bring corners of foil up to create a pouch. Crimp the corners to seal and transfer pouch to grill. Roast foil-encased garlic heads for approximately 1 hour, or until tender.

Transfer foil pouch to tabletop, carefully unwrap to let steam escape and remove heads. Dig out the cloves with a small fork, or just squeeze the whole head until the cloves ooze out. Serve with slices of grilled bread.

4 heads garlic
1/4 cup extra-virgin olive oil

Makes 1/2 cup

PAMELA'S CORNBREAD

My wife Pamela's secret recipe.

1 cup all-purpose flour
3/4 cup cornmeal
1/4 cup sugar
1 tbsp baking powder
1 tsp salt
1 large egg
2/3 cup whole milk
1/3 cup softened unsalted butter
8 slices bacon, cooked and diced
1 small red onion, sautéed and sliced
1 cup shredded white cheddar cheese
Salt and freshly ground black pepper

Serves 10 to 12

Prepare grill for indirect grilling: Turn 1 side of grill to low and the other to high (about 500°F). In a large bowl, sift together flour, cornmeal, sugar, baking powder and salt. In a small bowl, and using a fork, beat together egg, milk and butter. Add bacon, onion and cheese and mix well to combine.

Slowly pour egg mixture into flour mixture and stir to form batter. Pour batter into a 10-in pan and spread evenly before transferring to grill side heated to low. Bake for 25–30 minutes, or until cornbread is golden brown and a toothpick inserted into center comes out clean. Cut into squares and serve with butter.

PULLED PORK BAKED BEANS

Cooked over an open fire pit — these baked beans are the real deal.

1 lb sliced bacon, in 1/2-in pieces
3 medium onions, diced
8 cloves garlic, minced
3 jalapeño peppers, seeded and diced
2 (14 oz) cans baked beans
1 (14 oz) can black-eyed peas
1 (14 oz) can red kidney beans
1 cup ketchup
1/2 cup brown sugar, firmly packed
1/2 cup prepared yellow mustard
1/4 cup malt vinegar
2 tbsp mustard powder
2 tbsp Worcestershire sauce
1 tbsp chopped fresh thyme
1 tsp freshly ground black pepper
1 tsp hot pepper sauce
1 lb Slow-Smoked Pulled Pork (p. 128)
2 smoked sausages, sliced
Salt
1/4 cup bourbon
1/2 cup beer
1/2 cup smoky barbecue sauce

Serves 8 to 10

In a large, heavy skillet, fry the bacon until just crisp. Remove bacon and drain on paper towels. Add onions, garlic and jalapeño peppers to skillet and sauté in reserved bacon fat for 4–5 minutes, or until soft. Transfer vegetables and crispy bacon to a Dutch oven on a grate over hot coals or hanging over a fire pit. Add the baked beans, black-eyed peas, red kidney beans, ketchup, brown sugar, prepared mustard, vinegar, mustard powder, Worcestershire sauce, thyme, pepper, hot sauce, pulled pork and sausages. Stir to combine and cover with lid. Using barbecue gloves, place a mound of hot coals on the lid. Cook for 20–30 minutes, stirring occasionally. Season to taste with salt; stir in bourbon, beer and barbecue sauce. Continue cooking for another 5 minutes, or until heated through. Serve immediately.

DESSERTS

GRILLING AND SMOKING desserts requires a bit of patience and a touch of luck, but once you get the hang of it, you'll be neglecting the kitchen and trading in your Easy-Bake Oven for a grill.

Grilling desserts can really lead to the most fabulous taste sensations, and in my opinion gas grills are the easiest to use when baking. With gas grills you can control the temperature, an important feature when grill-baking desserts such as Grilled Pineapple Rum Upside-Down Cake. For baking with charcoal, I recommend using the Primo grill or a Big Green Egg. These grills will allow you to control the temperature and still get that great smoky flavor.

Whether smoking or grilling, have a cocktail or two and be patient. Learn your grill and test everything. It'll be trial and error, but experimenting with dessert on either a grill or a smoker is a great opportunity for you to have fun and get sticky.

VANILLA WHISKEY CHERRIES

1 1/2 lb fresh cherries,
stems removed
1 cup sugar
1/2 cup vanilla schnapps
3/4 cup cherry whiskey
1 cup Jack Daniel's whiskey
1 cup rum
2 vanilla beans, halved

Makes approximately 2 quarts

These cherries need at least 30 days to drink in the whiskey and rum. Use, as desired, in drinks and desserts.

Rinse and drain cherries on paper towels. Place cherries in 2 sterilized quart jars. Cover cherries with sugar. Add vanilla schnapps, cherry whiskey, Jack Daniel's, rum and 2 vanilla bean halves to each jar. Seal jars and shake until sugar dissolves. Store in the refrigerator for 30 days.

GRILLED PINEAPPLE RUM UPSIDE-DOWN CAKE

1 fresh pineapple
1/2 cup spiced rum
(such as Captain Morgan)
1/4 cup + 1/4 cup unsalted butter
1/2 cup brown sugar, firmly packed
Maraschino cherries (optional)
1 1/3 cups sifted cake flour
2 tsp baking powder
1/4 tsp salt
3/4 cup sugar
1 large egg
1/2 cup whole milk
1 tsp pure vanilla extract

Makes 1 cake

Pineapple gets really sweet when grilled. This recipe, of course, has rum, which just makes it even better. Have a blast and enjoy it upside down.

Using a sharp knife, slice off top and bottom of pineapple. Slice rind away from the flesh. Cut out any "eyes" that remain from the rind. Cut pineapple into 1-in-thick rounds. Core each round. Place in a bowl, and add rum. Marinate pineapple for 2 hours.

Preheat grill to medium-high (about 400°F). Remove pineapple from rum. Drink rum. Grill pineapple for 2–3 minutes, each side, until lightly charred. Remove from grill and cool fully.

Preheat oven to 350°F. Over medium-low heat, melt 1/4 cup butter in a cast-iron pan. Add brown sugar and stir until dissolved. Remove pan from heat and arrange pineapple slices in sugar mixture. If you want, add maraschino cherries, placing 1 on each cored pineapple slice. Set aside.

In a medium bowl, combine cake flour, baking powder, salt and sugar. Sift together, 3 times, and set aside. Using a stand mixer, cream remaining 1/4 cup of butter. Add sifted ingredients, egg, milk and vanilla. If you have any leftover slices of grilled pineapple, coarsely chop and add to batter. Stir to mix well and then beat on high for 1–2 minutes. Pour batter over grilled pineapple in cast-iron pan. Transfer pan to oven and bake for 45–50 minutes, or until batter is cooked through. Remove pan from oven and let cool for 10 minutes. When cooled, invert pan over a plate and let stand, inverted, for 2 minutes. Carefully lift up pan to reveal upside-down cake. Serve with ice cream or whipped cream.

Previous spread: Maraschino cherries, ready for decorating Grilled Pineapple Rum Upside-Down Cake

GIMME S'MORE QUESADILLA

Drizzled with caramel and smoked chocolate sauce, these gooey treats inspire lotsa lovin'.

Preheat grill to high (about 500°F). Thread marshmallows onto bamboo skewers and spray with nonstick cooking spray. Grill skewered marshmallows, turning occasionally, until golden brown and warm, about 1–2 minutes.

Remove marshmallows from skewers and place in a bowl. Add Oreo pieces, Nutella and peanut butter. Using a spatula, mix until moist and sticky. Place 1 flour tortilla on a flat surface. Spoon 1/4 cup of the s'mores mixture onto right half of tortilla, leaving a small space around the edge of the tortilla. Fold over from left to right, forming a half-moon shape. Press down on tortilla, so that the filling sticks to the shell. Spray outside of quesadilla with nonstick cooking spray on both sides. Repeat with remaining flour tortillas. Cover with plastic wrap and refrigerate for up to 6 hours.

Preheat grill to medium (about 350°F). Grill quesadillas for 2–3 minutes, each side, until lightly charred and crisp (but not burnt) and the filling is warm and gooey. Remove from grill and let cool for 2–3 minutes before cutting each into 2–3 wedges. Dust quesadilla wedges with a little icing sugar and serve drizzled with caramel and Smoked Chocolate Sauce.

Special equipment: 4 bamboo skewers, presoaked in water for 1 hour

1 cup mini marshmallows
1 cup Oreo cookie pieces
1/4 cup Nutella
1/4 cup chunky peanut butter, at room temperature
11 small flour tortillas (6 to 8 in diameter)
1/4 cup icing sugar
1/4 cup caramel sauce
1/4 cup Smoked Chocolate Sauce (p. 228)

Serves 10 as a sweet appetizer or 5 as a dessert

SMOKED CHOCOLATE

Special equipment: Smoker

2 lb milk, dark or white chocolate bars (at least 1 in thick)

I use this ingredient so often in my desserts, I always make several large batches and freeze for up to 3 months.

Remove top rack of smoker and line with foil. Place chocolate on the wrapped rack. Prepare your smoker according to manufacturer's instructions, to a temperature of 110° to 125°F. Fill the water tray with ice and a few cups of cold water. (This will help keep the temperature low and the smoke cool.) Return foil-lined rack with the chocolate to smoker, and place in the highest position — as far away from the heat source as possible. Close the lid. Smoke chocolate until it is soft but before it begins to melt, 35–45 minutes. Watch it carefully. To maintain the temperature, periodically add ice to water tray.

Remove softened chocolate from smoker and allow to cool. Once cooled, place in a resealable plastic bag and transfer to freezer or refrigerator until ready to use (will keep for 1 month, refrigerated, or 3 months, frozen).

SMOKED CHOCOLATE SAUCE

2/3 cup sugar
4 oz Smoked Chocolate, cut into small pieces
1/2 cup whipping cream

Makes about 2 cups

This sauce is great to have in the refrigerator for quick desserts. If needed, the fastest, easiest way to heat up Smoked Chocolate Sauce is in the microwave on low for 1–3 minutes, stirring frequently.

Bring 1 cup water and sugar to a boil in a small, heavy saucepan over high heat; continue boiling for 4–5 minutes, or until sugar dissolves. Add smoked chocolate, whisking to incorporate, and return to a boil. Remove from heat and whisk in cream. Serve the sauce hot or transfer to an airtight container and refrigerate, covered, until needed.

SMOKED CHOCOLATE BUTTER FROSTING

Spread this on Vanilla Coke Rocky Road Cake, or on your favorite vanilla or chocolate cake.

Melt the Smoked Chocolate in the top of a double boiler. Heat vanilla cognac in a microwave-safe dish on medium heat for 15–20 seconds in microwave. Remove and pour into pan of melted chocolate, stirring until mixed. Cover pan to keep chocolate-cognac mixture warm and remove from heat. Using a stand mixer, cream together butter and salt. Add sugar, 1/2 cup at a time, and beat thoroughly until sugar has dissolved. Pour in warm chocolate-cognac mixture and beat until frosting is smooth and chocolatey. If necessary, add a little milk to give frosting a more spreadable consistency.

3 oz Smoked Milk Chocolate (p. 228)
1 oz vanilla cognac
1/3 cup unsalted butter
Pinch salt
1 1/2 cups confectioner's sugar
1/4 cup whole milk

Makes about 2 1/2 cups

BANANA FRITTERS WITH SMOKED CHOCOLATE SAUCE

Kids love these yummy banana pops, but omit the Frangelico when you're making the recipe for them.

Preheat grill to medium (about 350°F). Slice bananas on an angle into 3/4-in segments and place in a large bowl. Sprinkle with sugar, cinnamon and nutmeg. Using a spatula, gently toss to coat. Lightly spray coated banana slices with nonstick cooking spray and place directly on grill. Grill for 1–2 minutes each side, until lightly charred. Remove from grill and chill quickly in freezer. Drizzle chilled bananas with Frangelico liqueur and set aside.

In a large pot, at least 8 in deep, or in a deep fryer, heat oil to 350°F (if using a pot, you'll need to insert a thermometer to check temperature). Carefully insert 1 bamboo skewer, lengthwise, through each banana slice, so that it resembles a lollipop. Repeat with remaining banana slices and skewers. Keep cool in refrigerator.

In a medium bowl, sift together 1 cup flour, baking powder and salt. Whisk in egg and 1 cup cold water until smooth. Place remaining 1/2 cup of flour in a shallow dish. Dredge each skewered banana pop in flour, making sure all sides are coated. Shake off excess flour before dipping into batter. Carefully immerse batter-coated banana pops in hot oil. Fry for 3–4 minutes, or until coating is golden brown and crisp. Remove from oil and drain on paper towel–lined tray. Dust Banana Fritters with icing sugar and serve immediately with Smoked Chocolate Sauce for dipping.

Special equipment: 20 (6 in) bamboo skewers, presoaked in water for about 1 hour

4 just-ripe bananas, peeled
2 tbsp sugar
1 tsp ground cinnamon
Pinch of ground nutmeg
1/4 cup Frangelico liqueur
1 cup + 1/2 cup all-purpose flour
1/2 tsp baking powder
Pinch of salt
1 large egg
1 qt vegetable oil, for frying
1/4 cup icing sugar
2 cups Smoked Chocolate Sauce (p. 228)

Serves 6 to 8

ERIC'S BBQ PEARS

Special equipment: 12 sheets aluminum foil, cut into 12 x 12-in squares

6 Bosc pears
6 tbsp brown sugar
6 tbsp Grand Marnier
1 1/2 tsp dried orange peel
1/2 bunch fresh mint sprigs

Serves 6

This recipe comes from my neighbor Eric, who has a love of food that is almost as serious as mine. Grilled pears with orange peel, Grand Marnier and mint are truly spectacular. Follow with a bottle of grappa.

Preheat grill to medium-high (about 400°F). Place 2 sheets of foil (1 on top of the other) on a flat surface. Add 1 tbsp brown sugar in the center of the foil square. Place pear, upright, on top of sugar. Drizzle pear with Grand Marnier and garnish with orange peel and 2 sprigs of mint. Bring the corners of the foil square to the center and crimp to make a bundle. Repeat with remaining pears.

Place bundles on grill, away from direct heat, close lid and grill-roast for 30–45 minutes, or until pears are hot and tender. Remove bundles from grill and carefully open. Drizzle with a little extra Grand Marnier and serve with ice cream, fresh raspberries and a shot of grappa.

VANILLA COKE ROCKY ROAD CAKE

20 to 24 large marshmallows
3/4 cup brown sugar, firmly packed
3/4 cup cocoa powder
1 cup flat vanilla Coca-Cola
1/4 cup coffee cream
1 tsp vanilla extract
1/2 cup vegetable shortening
1/4 cup sugar
3 large eggs
2 1/4 cups cake flour
1 tsp baking powder
1/2 tsp baking soda
Pinch salt
2 1/2 cups Smoked Chocolate Butter Frosting (p. 229)
1/2 cup crushed unsalted peanuts

Makes 1 8-in layer cake

Okay, now this is ridiculous! Yeah, but it's also delicious.

Preheat oven to 350°F. Using scissors, cut marshmallows in half and rinse in cold water. Spread evenly on a waxed paper–lined baking sheet and set aside.

In a mixing bowl, combine brown sugar and cocoa powder; set aside.

In a heavy, small saucepan, bring Coke, cream and vanilla to a boil. Immediately remove from heat and add to sugar-cocoa mixture. Using an electric mixer or hand blender, beat until smooth; set aside to cool completely.

Using a stand mixer, cream shortening. Add sugar in a steady stream and continue mixing until mixture is light and fluffy. Add eggs, one at a time, and beat until fully incorporated. Sift flour, baking powder, soda and salt together, 3 times. Add the sifted dry ingredients, alternating with the cocoa-and-cola mixture, into the egg mixture, beating until smooth. Pour batter into two greased 8-in cake pans. Bake 30–35 minutes, or until an inserted toothpick comes out clean. Cool in pans for 10 minutes. Invert 1 cake onto a cooling rack and remove pan.

While cake is still warm, place marshmallow pieces in an even layer over the surface of the first cake. Invert the second cake onto the marshmallow-topped cake. Allow second cake layer to cool. Once cooled, cover with Smoked Chocolate Butter Frosting, sprinkle with peanuts and serve.

GRILLED LEMON PIE

This is like a Key lime pie, except with sweet, tangy grill-roasted lemons instead of limes.

Grilled Lemon Juice

12 lemons, cut in half

Cashew Graham Cracker Crust

1 1/2 cups graham cracker crumbs
3 tbsp sugar
2/3 stick unsalted butter, melted
1/4 cup ground cashews

Baked Grilled Lemon Layer

1 can sweetened condensed milk
3/4 cup Grilled Lemon Juice
4 large eggs

Chilled Cream Cheese Layer

8 oz cream cheese, room temperature
1/2 can sweetened condensed milk
2 tbsp sugar
1/3 cup Grilled Lemon Juice
1/2 tsp pure vanilla extract

Serves 8 to 10

To prepare the Grilled Lemon Juice: Preheat grill to medium-high (about 400°F). Place lemons on grill, cut side down, and grill for 5–8 minutes, until lightly charred. Do not move lemons once you have placed them on the grill. Remove from heat and let cool before squeezing the juice into a bowl. Strain juice to remove seeds and pulp; set aside.

To prepare the Cashew Graham Cracker Crust: In a large bowl, combine all crust ingredients. Firmly press into an ovenproof pie dish to create an even crust. Reduce grill temperature to medium (about 350°F). Transfer dish to grill and bake for 8–10 minutes, or until crust is just golden. Remove from grill and let cool.

To prepare the Baked Grilled Lemon Layer: In a medium bowl, mix together all lemon-layer ingredients. Pour over cooled crust. Reduce grill temperature to 325°F. Transfer pie dish to grill and bake for 15 minutes. Remove from grill and let cool.

To prepare the Chilled Cream Cheese Layer: In a food processor, process cream cheese until completely smooth. Add condensed milk, sugar and 1/3 cup of Grilled Lemon Juice. Process until fully combined. Immediately pour over cooled baked layer, cover and refrigerate to chill completely.

Remove chilled pie from refrigerator, cut into squares, and serve with whipped cream and some Grand Marnier–marinated berries, if desired.

GRILLED PINEAPPLE RUM BAKED ALASKA

Special equipment: 1 untreated cedar plank, presoaked in water for 1 hour

1/2 large fresh pineapple, peeled, cored and cut into 1/4-in-thick rings
1 store-bought lemon-flavored pound cake
1 qt ice cream — vanilla or rum raisin
6 tbsp pineapple jam

Meringue
16 egg whites
1 tsp cream of tartar
1 cup sugar

1 oz 151-proof rum

Serves 6

A gooey covering of golden meringue makes this one impressive dessert.

Preheat grill to high (about 500°F). Spray pineapple rings with nonstick cooking spray and grill for 2–3 minutes, each side, or until tender and lightly charred. Remove slices from grill, cut in half and store in a covered container in refrigerator until ready to use.

Using a serrated knife, slice pound cake, lengthwise, into 4 equal pieces. Place 1 slice in center of a cedar plank. Top slice with a scoop of ice cream and spread to form a 1-in layer. Top ice cream–cake slice with another layer of cake and press to seal. Spread 3 tbsp of pineapple jam onto second cake slice; top preserves with grilled pineapple slices.

Spread another 3 tbsp jam onto a third cake slice and press onto plank stack, jam side down. Spread top of third cake slice with another even layer of ice cream, about 1 in thick. Top with fourth and final layer of cake. Cover loosely with plastic wrap and place in freezer until ready to grill.

To prepare the Meringue: In a large, chilled stainless steel bowl, using a hand blender, whip egg whites, cream of tartar and sugar until stiff peaks form. (This should take about 4–5 minutes on high speed.) Set aside.

Preheat grill to very high (about 600°F). Remove cake from freezer. Using a spatula, frost cake on all sides with meringue, forming peaks and making sure there are no gaps. Place plank in center of grill and close lid. Check after 2 minutes: As soon as meringue peaks begin to brown, remove planked cake from grill and place on a second, unused cedar plank. Drizzle with rum and ignite with a Scripto BBQ lighter. (Don't even think of using one of those crappy little plastic ones.)

Place planked Alaska in the center of the table and spoon, slice or attack it in whichever fashion you prefer. I recommend cutting vertical slices through all the layers with a hot knife and serving each piece with more than a drizzle of Smoked Chocolate Sauce (p. 228) and a dusting of icing sugar.

Note: Be sure to wipe your knife after each cut to get that clean and perfect slice every time.

CEDAR-PLANKED PEACH CRUMBLE WITH ICE CREAM

Grilling brings out all the sweetness in peaches, and once tossed with Southern Comfort and planked with a crunchy crumble top, they are to die for.

Preheat grill to high (about 500°F). Arrange peach halves, cut side up, on planks. Place planks on grill and close lid. When planks begin to crackle, reduce heat to medium (about 350°F) and continue to grill for 10–15 minutes, or until peaches are golden brown. Remove planks from grill and transfer peaches to a large bowl. Turn off grill. When peaches have cooled slightly, remove skin and slice into 1/4-in segments. Toss sliced peaches with Southern Comfort, vanilla extract and sugar. Cover bowl with plastic wrap and refrigerate for 1 hour or overnight.

In a large bowl, combine oats, brown sugar, flour and cinnamon. Cut in cold butter, using 2 table knives, until mixture is coarse and crumbly. Stir in beer nuts and set crumble topping aside.

Preheat grill to medium (about 350°F). Transfer chilled and marinated peach slices into a buttered 8-in cast-iron pan. Sprinkle crumble topping over peach slices and transfer pan to grill. Bake for 25–30 minutes, or until fruit is hot throughout and crumble is golden brown. Let stand for 10 minutes before slicing and serving with vanilla ice cream.

Special equipment: 3 untreated cedar planks, soaked in cold water for 1 hour

12 peaches, pitted and cut in half
1/4 cup Southern Comfort
1 tsp pure vanilla extract
1/4 cup sugar
1 cup rolled oats
1 cup brown sugar, firmly packed
1/2 cup all-purpose flour
1/2 tsp ground cinnamon
1/2 cup cold unsalted butter
1/2 cup beer nuts, chopped

Makes 1 crumble

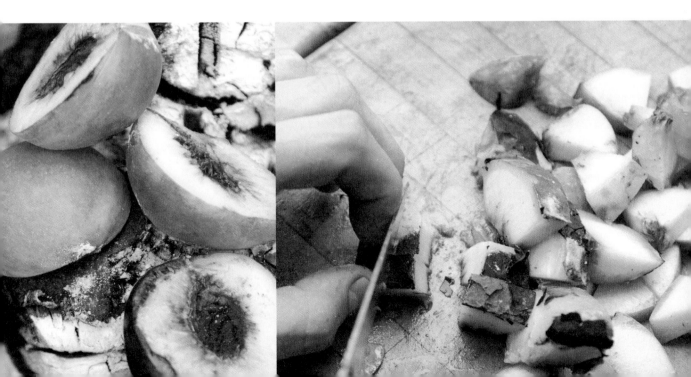

BREAKFAST

THE MOST IMPORTANT meal of the day is breakfast, and what better way to start the day than by firing up your grill? If you're at the cottage, in your backyard or on the deck of a fabulous yacht, nothing gets the morning going like a hearty grilled breakfast.

Some may be satisfied with fresh fruit and yogurt, or a bowl of cold cereal, but that's just not hearty enough for the King of the **Q**.

If you're like me, you may want Coil Sausage with Maple Whiskey Glaze, or some grilled French toast stuffed with cream cheese or maybe scrambled eggs made with Triple-Smoked Bacon. (Whether your grill is gas or charcoal, the side burner and griddle accessories come in handy for preparing breakfast.) So, start the day the King of the **Q** way: Have yourself a pot of hot coffee, then grill up a hearty meal.

TRIPLE-SMOKED BACON

Special equipment: Smoker

1 whole pork belly
2% Ready Cure
Bonedust Seasoning (p. 22)

Serves a bunch of bacon-lovin' barbecue nuts

You'll need more than 7 days to cure the bacon before smoking. Ready Cure is a curing salt made up of salt, sodium nitrite and sodium bicarbonate. The package recommends using 2% Ready Cure for a dry rub (i.e., 2 lb Ready Cure for every 100 lb meat). Get out your calculator and scale for this one: It's worth it.

Cut the pork belly into 2 to 4 large pieces, to fit your smoker. Weigh each piece and plug the combined weight into your calculator; multiply by 0.02 or 2 per cent. This will give you the amount (by weight) of Ready Cure to use. Now multiply the weight of the belly by 0.005 or .5 per cent. This will give you the amount (by weight) of Bonedust Seasoning needed.

In a large bowl, combine the calculated amounts of Ready Cure and Bonedust Seasoning. Mix well to combine. Rub the belly pieces with the Ready Cure–Bonedust mixture, pressing the cure into the meat to adhere. Cover tightly with plastic wrap and place in a large pan or foil tray to catch moisture. Store in refrigerator and allow to cure for 7 days.

When pork belly is fully cured, prepare smoker for a hot smoke (about 180° to 240°F), following manufacturer's instructions. Be sure to include a pan of water to add moisture. Remove cured belly from refrigerator and rinse thoroughly. Pat dry with a paper towel. Rub with 1 1/2 cups of Bonedust Seasoning. Place seasoned cured bellies in the smoker, and smoke for 2 hours at 240°F. Reduce heat to 180°F and continue to smoke for another 2 hours. Raise temperature to 220°F and continue smoking for another 2 hours.

Remove bacon from smoker and let cool at room temperature. Tightly wrap cooled bacon in plastic wrap or vacuum seal, and refrigerate for up to 2 weeks or freeze for up to 3 months.

Note: You can eat this smoked bacon without further cooking — or you can fry it, grill it or roast it.

Pork belly in the smoker (right), and BBQ
Coil Sausage on the grill (far right)

BBQ COIL SAUSAGE WITH MAPLE WHISKEY GLAZE

Coil sausage — a long sausage that has been rolled into a circle to resemble a patty — can be found in specialty food shops, butcher shops and most supermarkets.

Preheat grill to medium (about 350°F). Skewer each coil sausage with 2 bamboo skewers in an X pattern. Liberally sprinkle with Bayou Bite Cajun Seasoning, so that sausages are thoroughly coated.

To prepare the Maple Whiskey Glaze: In a small bowl, combine maple syrup, Jack Daniel's, brown sugar and barbecue sauce; mix well, until sugar is dissolved. Grill sausages for 8–10 minutes, each side, basting liberally with Maple Whiskey Glaze, until fully cooked and golden.

Top each grilled coil sausage with a fried egg, sunny side up, and serve with toast or hash browns.

Special equipment: 8 (6 in) bamboo skewers

4 (4 to 6 oz) pork coil sausages
2 tbsp Bayou Bite Cajun Seasoning (p. 23)

Maple Whiskey Glaze
2 tbsp maple syrup
1 oz Jack Daniel's whiskey
1 tbsp packed brown sugar
3 tbsp gourmet barbecue sauce

Serves 4

WESTERN BBQ SCRAMBLE

Serve this zesty egg dish with your favorite home fries.

8 slices Triple-Smoked Bacon
(p. 238), cut 1/4 in thick
1 large onion, quartered
1 large green bell pepper, cut in half
and seeded
3 tsp Bonedust Seasoning (p. 22)
1 jalapeño pepper, seeded and diced
1 cup diced smoked ham
2 tbsp chopped fresh coriander
1/2 tsp crushed red pepper flakes
12 large eggs
1/3 cup heavy cream
Salt and freshly ground black pepper
2 cups grated pepper Jack cheese

Serves 6

Preheat grill to medium-high (about 400°F). In a medium bowl, toss bacon, onion and green pepper with Bonedust Seasoning. Grill bacon, onion and green pepper for 3–5 minutes per side, until bacon is just crispy and onion and green pepper are lightly charred and tender. Remove from grill and cool slightly. Dice bacon and set aside. Slice onion and green pepper and set aside.

In a large bowl, combine bacon, onion, green pepper, jalapeño pepper, ham, coriander and crushed red pepper flakes; set aside. In another large bowl, beat eggs and cream together until smooth. Season with salt and pepper, to taste, adding extra Bonedust Seasoning, if necessary.

Liberally spray a cast-iron pan with nonstick cooking spray. Place pan in the center of the grill and heat for 3–5 minutes. Add bacon-and-onion mixture to eggs and combine; pour into pan. Stir over heat until eggs are almost cooked, then add cheese.

Once the eggs are just cooked and the cheese has melted, remove from grill and serve, drizzled with 1 tbsp of your favorite salsa.

CREAMY WHITE GRITS WITH BACON AND WILD MUSHROOMS

These are particularly good when served with Beer-Poached Eggs (p. 242) and a drizzle of hot pepper sauce.

1 1/4 cups coarse white grits
1 tsp salt
1 tbsp unsalted butter
2 cloves garlic, minced
1/2 cup bacon, grilled and diced
1 medium Vidalia onion,
grilled and diced
1 cup coarsely chopped Grilled Oyster
Mushrooms (p. 216)
Salt and freshly ground black pepper

Serves 4 to 6

In a large saucepan, bring 4 cups water to a boil. Add grits and salt, stirring constantly, until water returns to a boil. Reduce heat to low and simmer, covered, for 20 minutes, or until grits are thick; every 3–4 minutes uncover to stir. When thickened, remove pot from heat and set aside.

Melt butter in a large sauté pan over medium heat and cook for 2–3 minutes, or until butter is foamy and light brown in color. Add garlic, grilled bacon, onion and mushrooms; sauté until onion is translucent, about 2–3 minutes. Stir bacon mixture into grits mixture. Season with salt and pepper to taste and serve immediately.

BEER-POACHED EGGS

What better way to poach eggs?

1 (12 oz) bottle beer
2 tbsp white vinegar
4 large eggs

Serves 4

In a medium saucepan, combine beer, 3 cups of water and vinegar; bring to a boil. Reduce heat to medium-low, until mixture is just simmering.

Gently crack each egg into 1 of 4 small cups or dishes, taking care not to break the yolk. Using a wooden spoon, stir liquid in the pot to create a whirlpool effect and carefully slip eggs, 1 at a time, into the center of the whirlpool. Cover and simmer for 2–3 minutes for runny yolks; poach 1 minute longer for a slightly firmer but still soft-cooked egg. Using a slotted spoon, remove poached eggs from pot and drain on a paper towel. Serve immediately.

SALMON TOASTS WITH COTTAGE CHEESE AND SPRING ONION TOPPING

For when you need something a little more elaborate, these toasts are always a hit.

Cottage Cheese and Spring
Onion Topping

2 cups cottage cheese
1 cup sour cream
4 green onions, thinly sliced on the bias
2 tbsp chopped flat-leaf parsley or
fresh dill
1 tsp fresh lemon juice
Sea salt and freshly ground black
pepper to taste

8 thick slices firm but ripe beefsteak
tomatoes, about 1/2 in thick
2 tbsp extra-virgin olive oil
Salt and freshly ground black pepper
4 thick slices caraway rye bread
4 tsp butter
Freshly ground black pepper
4 leaves Boston Bibb lettuce
2 cups Cucumber Slaw (p. 74)
8 to 12 slices 24-Hour Jack Daniel's
Salmon Gravlax (p. 47)

Serves 4

To prepare the Cottage Cheese and Spring Onion Topping: In a large bowl, combine cottage cheese, sour cream, green onion, parsley and lemon juice. Season with salt and pepper to taste. Cover and refrigerate to chill.

Preheat grill to medium-high (about 400°F). Brush both sides of tomato slices with olive oil and season with salt and pepper to taste. Grill tomatoes for 1–2 minutes, each side, to lightly char; remove and set aside. Butter one side of each bread slice and lightly toast on grill, butter side down. Remove toast from grill and place each slice, butter side up, on one of 4 plates. Top with Boston Bibb lettuce, grilled tomato and Cucumber Slaw. Add a generous spoonful of Cottage Cheese and Spring Onion Topping and 2–3 slices of salmon before serving.

VANILLA CREAM CHEESE–STUFFED FRENCH TOAST WITH GRILLED PINEAPPLE

Although this recipe calls for grilled pineapple (basted in rum, if you like!), you can add any grilled fruit as garnish.

Preheat grill to medium-high (about 400°F). Using a sharp knife, cut a pocket down through the top crust of each French stick slice; be careful not to cut all the way through. In a small bowl, combine cream cheese and 1/2 tsp vanilla extract; mix well to combine. Spoon equal amounts of cream cheese mixture into pockets of French stick and set aside.

In a medium bowl, whisk together eggs, whipping cream and remaining tsp of vanilla extract. Add orange juice; mix well and set aside. In another medium bowl, combine cornflakes and brown sugar. Mix well and set aside.

Reduce grill temperature to low and place griddle on grill. Meanwhile, thoroughly coat each stuffed slice in egg mixture and set aside for about 10 minutes, allowing bread to absorb liquid. Dredge each stuffed and coated bread slice in cornflake mixture. Place 1 tbsp of butter on heated griddle and add toast, cut side down. Grill for 2–3 minutes, on all sides, until browned and stuffing is thoroughly melted.

Grill pineapple slices, 10 minutes per side, until golden brown and tender; baste with a bit of rum, if using. Place stuffed French toast on plate and garnish with grilled pineapple and chocolate shavings.

1 French stick, sliced diagonally into 1-in-thick slices
4 tbsp softened cream cheese
1/2 tsp + 1 tsp vanilla extract
6 large eggs
1/4 cup whipping cream
Juice of 1 orange
1 cup cornflakes
2 tbsp brown sugar, firmly packed
1 to 2 tbsp softened butter
Pineapple slices
Rum for basting (optional)
1 cup chocolate shavings, for garnish

Serves 4

GRILLED CANADIAN BACON HASH

For the best hash, cook potatoes one day ahead.

1 lb mini Yukon Gold potatoes
1 tbsp salt
4 tbsp softened butter
1 tbsp + 1 tbsp Bonedust Seasoning (p. 22)
1 large onion, diced
1 (1 lb) piece Canadian-style peameal bacon, in 8 slices, about 1/2 to 1 in-thick

Serves 4

In a large pot, cover potatoes with cold water and bring to a boil. Add salt, reduce heat to medium-low, and simmer for 12–15 minutes, or until potatoes are fully cooked and tender. Drain and let cool completely. Once potatoes have cooled, gently press with a fork to slightly mash.

Preheat a griddle over medium-high heat (about 400°F). Melt 2 tbsp of butter on griddle and add potatoes. Using a large spatula, fry, flipping mash occasionally, until crisp and golden on all sides, about 20 minutes; add 1–2 tbsp more of butter, as required. Sprinkle with 1 tbsp Bonedust Seasoning and add onion; continue frying and flipping for 5 minutes more.

Meanwhile, place 8 slices of bacon on the grill. Season with remaining tbsp of Bonedust Seasoning and grill for 5–10 minutes, or until bacon is firm and cooked through. Remove from grill and cut into 1/2-in-thick pieces. Transfer potato-onion hash to a serving platter and top with bacon pieces. Drizzle with barbecue sauce and serve with your favorite eggs.

Onions and potatoes on the grill, along with bacon (right)

SHRIMP CAKES AND REDFISH FILLETS ON BACON AND EGGS

Shrimp Cakes

2 cups mashed potatoes

1/4 cup shredded mozzarella cheese

1 cup baby shrimp, cooked

1 small red onion, diced

1 tbsp chopped fresh basil

Salt and freshly ground black pepper

2 tbsp softened butter

2 tbsp melted butter

2 (4 to 6 oz) redfish fillets, skin on

2 tbsp melted butter

Salt and freshly ground black pepper

4 to 6 slices bacon

2 large eggs

2 to 4 tbsp softened butter

2 slices bread

Serves 2

I first made this recipe while filming the TV show Fishing the Flats. When these cheesy, tasty shrimp cakes came off the grill, the crew devoured them!

To prepare the Shrimp Cakes: In a large bowl, combine mashed potatoes, cheese, shrimp, onion, basil, salt and pepper; mix well. Cover, and chill in refrigerator for 1 hour. When fully chilled, remove shrimp mixture from fridge and, using your hands, form into 2 balls. Press each to form a cake about 2 in across. In a griddle pan, melt 2 tbsp of butter over medium-high heat. Place shrimp cakes in pan and cook for about 10–15 minutes, turning once, until each side is crispy and cooked through. Baste grilled shrimp cakes with melted butter and set to one side of griddle pan to keep warm.

Brush redfish fillets with butter and season with salt and pepper. On medium-high (about 450° to 500°F), grill fillets, turning once, for about 6–8 minutes, or until fish flakes easily with a fork. Remove fillets from grill and set aside, keeping warm.

Place bacon on griddle pan and grill for 5–6 minutes on medium-high heat, or until fully cooked and crisp. Move bacon to sides of griddle pan. Add more butter and crack eggs into pan. Season with salt and pepper to taste and grill to desired doneness. Spread remaining butter on bread and grill toast for 1–2 minutes, until lightly charred on both sides and warmed through.

To assemble, remove toast from grill and top each slice with a shrimp cake, grilled redfish fillet, bacon and egg. Serve immediately.

SAUCES
CONDIMENTS
AND STOCKS

SAUCES AND CONDIMENTS make a simple dish great, and a great dish even better. These sauces and condiments can be made ahead of time, and kept in the refrigerator, for whenever a simple grilled chicken breast or steak needs a pick-me-up. These sauces are also really versatile — Spicy Ginger Glazing Sauce and Dragon BBQ Sauce make phenomenal dipping sauces for appetizers and hors d'oeuvres.

As well, I use many of these recipes, such as my Hot Sauce, Fire-Roasted Tomato Sauce and smoked stocks, as bases in a lot of other dishes. Fresh, homemade, tasty basics are the building blocks for more complicated recipes, and with a little preparation you can have these on hand and ready to go any time inspiration hits. You'll never have a boring meal again!

TEDDY'S HOT SAUCE

3 cups finger chili peppers, stems and
seeds removed
2 red Scotch bonnet peppers, stems
and seeds removed
2 red bell peppers, stems and
seeds removed
1 head garlic
1 medium onion, cut in quarters
1 cup vinegar
5 tsp salt

Makes about 6 jars

This is a very hot hot sauce since it calls for red Scotch bonnet peppers; handle with care.

Preheat grill to medium-high (about 400°F). In a grill basket, grill-roast finger chilis, Scotch bonnets, bell peppers, garlic and onion for 8–10 minutes or until tender and lightly charred. Remove from grill. Place all the peppers in a large pot. Peel head of garlic and add to pot. Coarsely chop and add grilled onion, vinegar, 1/2 cup water and salt. Bring to a boil over medium-high heat. Reduce heat to low and simmer for 40 minutes, stirring occasionally to keep mixture from sticking to pot.

After 40 minutes, remove from heat and let cool slightly. Using a hand blender, purée mixture until smooth. Ladle sauce into hot, sterilized preserving jars, leaving 1/2 in headspace. Top with disk and apply screw band until fingertip tight. Process sealed jars for 30 minutes in a boiling water bath, with water 2 in above jar tops. Remove jars and place them upright on a rack to cool. (Do not tighten screw bands once processed.) Label and store in a cool, dark and dry place. Once opened, this sauce will keep for 1 month refrigerated.

FIRE-ROASTED TOMATO SAUCE

1 large onion, sliced in 1/4-in rounds
2 large red bell peppers, halved, with
seeds and stems removed
20 plum tomatoes, cut in
half lengthwise
1 tbsp Bonedust Seasoning (p. 22)
2 tbsp + 1 tbsp olive oil
6 cloves garlic, minced
1 (28 oz) can plum tomatoes, coarsely
chopped and juice reserved
3 tbsp chopped fresh basil
Splash of balsamic vinegar
Salt and freshly ground black pepper

Makes about 2 quarts

Better than plain old ketchup, any day.

Preheat grill to medium-high (about 400°F). In a large bowl, toss onion, peppers and tomatoes in Bonedust Seasoning and 2 tbsp olive oil. Place tomatoes on grill, skin side down, and roast for 10 minutes, or until skins are charred and blistered. Meanwhile, grill onion and peppers for 6–8 minutes, or until tender and lightly charred. Remove vegetables from grill and cool slightly. Coarsely chop tomatoes, onion and peppers, and set aside.

In a large saucepan over medium heat, sauté garlic in remaining tbsp of olive oil for 1–2 minutes. Add chopped grilled onion, peppers and tomatoes, and plum tomatoes with juice; stir to combine and bring to a boil. Reduce heat to medium-low and simmer for 30–40 minutes. Remove from heat and, using a hand blender, purée sauce until smooth. Stir in basil and vinegar, and season with salt and pepper to taste. When cooled, transfer to an airtight container and store, covered, in refrigerator for up to 4 days or in freezer for up to 3 months.

SPICY GINGER GLAZING SAUCE

This can also be used as a dipping sauce for appetizers, and is great on grilled fish.

1/4 cup mirin

Juice of 2 limes

Juice of 1 lemon

1 1/2 cup fresh ginger, peeled and thinly sliced

7 bird chilis (also known as Thai chili peppers)

2 tsp Cochin Curry Masala Seasoning (p. 24)

1 tsp salt

1/2 tsp black peppercorns

2 tsp cornstarch

Makes about 2 cups

In a heavy, medium-sized saucepan over medium heat, combine 2 cups water, mirin, lime juice, lemon juice, ginger, bird chilis, Cochin Curry Masala Seasoning, salt and peppercorns; mix well and bring to a boil. Reduce heat to low and simmer, stirring occasionally, for 20 minutes, or until sauce thickens. Remove from heat and, using a hand blender, purée until smooth. Strain sauce over a bowl and discard solids. Return strained sauce to saucepan.

In a small bowl, stir 1 tbsp water and cornstarch together to form a paste. Add cornstarch paste to pan and return to boil; boil for 1 minute more. Remove from heat and let cool. Transfer to an airtight container, cover, and refrigerate for up to 3 weeks.

MANGO MOJITO BASTING SAUCE

This sweet and limey sauce is great over fish and shellfish, especially shrimp.

1 ripe mango, peeled and with pulp scraped from pit

2 heads garlic, peeled

3 green onions, coarsely chopped

1/4 cup chopped fresh oregano

1/4 cup corn syrup

1/4 cup vegetable oil

Juice of 3 large limes (about 3/4 cup)

3 tbsp thawed frozen concentrated lemonade

2 tsp garlic powder

1 tsp smoked paprika

1 tsp salt

Makes about 3 cups

In a food processor, combine all ingredients; process until smooth. Transfer to an airtight container, cover, and refrigerate for up to 1 week.

Mango Mojito Basting Sauce

WASABI BALSAMIC GLAZING SAUCE

Great on meat and fish.

1 1/2 cups balsamic vinegar
1 tbsp softened unsalted butter
1 small onion, finely diced
3 cloves garlic, minced
1/2 cup apple jam or jelly
1/4 cup brown sugar, firmly packed
3 tbsp soy sauce
1 tbsp prepared horseradish
2 to 3 tsp wasabi paste
1 tsp cracked black peppercorns
Salt

Makes about 1 cup

In a small saucepan over medium-high heat, bring vinegar to a vigorous boil and continue boiling for 2 minutes. Reduce heat to medium-low and simmer until vinegar has reduced by half. Set aside.

In a small, heavy pot, melt butter over high heat. Add onion and garlic and sauté for 2–3 minutes, or until tender. Reduce heat to low and stir in apple jam, brown sugar, soy sauce, horseradish, wasabi paste, cracked pepper and salt to taste. Add reduced vinegar and bring mixture to a slow boil while stirring constantly. Reduce heat and simmer until sauce is thick enough to coat the back of a wooden spoon.

Remove from heat and let cool. Transfer to an airtight container, cover, and store in refrigerator for up to 2 weeks.

DIRTY MARTINI BBQ SAUCE

This martini-style sauce is perfect on grilled fish, seafood, steaks, chops and chicken. Make a batch and store in the refrigerator. It will solidify, so when you're ready to use it, just place the desired amount in a small pot over low heat, until it melts.

1 cup jalapeño-stuffed green olives
2 tbsp juice from jalapeño-stuffed green olives
1/2 bunch fresh coriander, chopped
1/2 bunch flat-leaf parsley, chopped
3 cloves garlic, minced
2 tbsp minced capers
2 anchovy fillets
Juice of 1/2 lemon
1/2 oz pepper-spiced vodka or regular vodka
3 sticks butter (3/4 lb)
Salt and coarsely ground black pepper

Makes about 3 cups

In a food processor, combine olives, olive juice, coriander, parsley, garlic, capers, anchovies, lemon juice and vodka; process until smooth. Add butter, and salt and pepper to taste. Process until butter is fully incorporated in the olive-vodka mixture. Transfer to an airtight container, cover, and refrigerate for up to 2 weeks.

DRAGON BBQ SAUCE

This is a great dipping sauce for wings and spring rolls. Watch out, though, this is hot stuff.

In a large bowl, whisk together all ingredients. Transfer to an airtight container, cover, and refrigerate for up to 2 weeks.

1/2 cup Sriracha hot chili sauce
1/4 cup sambal oelek chili sauce
1/2 cup Thai sweet chili sauce
1/4 cup ketchup
3 tbsp mirin
3 tbsp rice wine vinegar
2 tbsp Thai fish sauce
2 tbsp chopped fresh coriander
1 green onion, minced

Makes about 2 cups

GUAVA BBQ SAUCE

The guava is an oval-shaped, fragrant tropical fruit. Guava paste and guava jam — popular in the Caribbean — can be found in most ethnic food markets.

In a small saucepan over medium heat, combine all ingredients. Bring to a low boil, stirring constantly, until sauce thickens. Remove from heat, and let cool. Transfer to an airtight container, cover, and refrigerate for up to 2 weeks.

3/4 cup ketchup
1 cup guava jam
1/2 cup guava paste (this is different from the jam)
3 tbsp brown sugar, firmly packed
Juice of 1 orange
2 tbsp fresh lime juice
2 bird chilis
1 tbsp Bonedust Seasoning (p. 22)
Salt and freshly ground black pepper

Makes about 2 cups

TAMARIND BBQ SAUCE

Tamarind pulp, sold in bottles or "bricks," is available in most Asian and East Indian food markets.

Place tamarind pulp and water in a medium saucepan over medium-high heat; stir until pulp dissolves. Strain mixture through a sieve into a bowl. Discard solids and return strained tamarind liquid to saucepan and add remaining ingredients; bring to a boil. Reduce heat to low and simmer for 10 minutes, stirring occasionally, until sauce is thick enough to coat the back of a wooden spoon. Transfer to an airtight container, cover, and refrigerate for up to 2 weeks.

1/2 cup tamarind pulp
2 cups water
1 cup packed brown sugar
1 Scotch bonnet pepper, chopped
2 sprigs fresh thyme
2 cloves garlic, minced
1 cup honey
1/2 cup ketchup
2 tsp Indonesian Cinnamon Rub (p. 24)

Makes about 3 cups

SALSA VERDE

6 tomatillos, rinsed and chopped
2 poblano chili peppers, roasted, peeled, seeded and diced
2 jalapeño peppers, seeded and diced
1 small yellow onion, finely diced
4 cloves garlic, minced
4 green onions, finely chopped
1/4 cup chopped fresh coriander
2 tbsp vinegar
2 tbsp extra-virgin olive oil
Pinch of ground cumin
Salt and freshly ground black pepper

Makes about 2 cups

The tomatillo — a Latin American cousin to the tomato — is a small green fruit that looks exactly like a small green tomato except that it is covered by a paper-thin husk.

In a medium bowl, combine tomatillo, poblano and jalapeño peppers with onion, garlic, green onion, coriander, vinegar and olive oil. Mix well, and season with cumin, salt and pepper. Cover and refrigerate for up to 1 week.

GUACAMOLE

2 large, ripe but still firm avocados
2 ripe tomatoes
Juice of 2 limes or 1 lemon
1 clove garlic, minced
2 tbsp chopped fresh coriander
3 canned green chilis, diced
2 to 3 pickled jalapeño or serrano peppers, minced (optional)
Kosher salt

Makes about 2 1/2 cups

Classic guacamole is perfect served with appetizers.

Peel avocados and remove pits. Coarsely chop the tomatoes and avocados and transfer to medium bowl. Add lime juice, garlic, coriander and green chili and jalapeño peppers. Mix well and season with salt to taste. (This does not keep well; prepare just before burgers are put on the grill.)

MELON RELISH

1/2 cup shallots, diced
2 tbsp extra-virgin olive oil
1 cup diced onion
1 large red bell pepper, diced
2 cups diced honeydew melon
2 cups diced cantaloupe
1/2 cup apple cider vinegar
1/4 cup white wine
2 tbsp brown sugar
2 tbsp sugar
2 tsp hot mustard powder
1/2 cup Thai sweet chili sauce
1/8 cup chopped fresh mint
1/8 cup chopped fresh basil
Salt and freshly ground black pepper

Makes about 4 cups

This relish is great on burgers.

In a large pot over medium heat, sauté shallots in olive oil. Add onion and sauté for 1–2 minutes, or until translucent. Add bell pepper, honeydew and cantaloupe, and continue sautéing for 1 minute. Stir in vinegar, wine, both sugars and hot mustard powder. Remove from heat and stir in chili sauce, mint and basil; season with salt and pepper to taste and set aside to cool. Transfer to a container and refrigerate, covered, for up to 2 weeks.

Salsa Verde

MRS. FIELD'S (NO, NOT THE COOKIE LADY) MUSTARD PICKLE RELISH

2 cups chopped yellow onion

2 cups bottled pickled pearl onions, drained and rinsed

4 cups finely chopped pickling cucumbers

2 cups finely chopped cauliflower

2 cups diced celery

1 red bell pepper, diced

1 green bell pepper, diced

1/2 cup salt

3/4 cup all-purpose flour

5 cups granulated sugar

3 tsp mustard powder

3/4 tsp celery seeds

3/4 tsp mustard seeds

1 tbsp turmeric

2 1/2 cups apple cider vinegar

Makes about 7 to 9 pint jars

Mrs. Field is my best bud's mom. And her Mustard Pickle Relish is perfect with hot dogs, sausages, burgers, sandwiches and any smoked meat. But make sure to give yourself enough time to make this. The vegetables have to be marinated overnight.

In a large bowl, combine onion, pearl onions, cucumbers, cauliflower, celery and bell peppers. In a smaller bowl, whisk together salt and 1 1/2 qt water until well combined. Pour salted water (brine) over vegetable mixture; cover bowl with plastic wrap, and marinate overnight in refrigerator.

When fully brined, drain vegetables in a large colander. Rinse in cold water about 5–6 times. Drain well and transfer to a large bowl. In a medium bowl, combine flour, sugar, mustard powder, celery seed, mustard seed and turmeric. Whisk in vinegar until well incorporated and sugar has dissolved. Pour over rinsed vegetables in large bowl and toss. Transfer vegetable-vinegar mixture to a heavy, large saucepan. Bring to a low boil over low-to-medium heat, stirring often. Boil for 15–20 minutes, or until relish thickens.

Ladle relish into hot, clean preserving jars, leaving 1/2 in headspace. Top with disk and apply screw band until fingertip tight. Process sealed jars for 10 minutes in a boiling water bath, with water 2 in above jar tops. Remove jars and place them upright on a rack to cool. (Do not tighten screw bands once processed.) Label and store in a cool, dark and dry place.

GRILLED CORN RELISH

1 tbsp mustard powder

1 cup Smoked Chicken Stock (p. 261)

2 stalks celery, trimmed and diced

1 yellow bell pepper, diced

1 white onion, diced

8 cups fresh sweet bicolor corn
kernels, cut from about 8 ears

2 tbsp all-purpose flour

2 tbsp Bonedust Seasoning (p. 22)

1 cup sugar

1 cup vinegar

1/2 tsp toasted celery seeds

1 tbsp turmeric

1 tbsp Smoked Salt Steak Rub (p. 28)

Makes about 5 cups

My take on the classic corn relish.

In a small saucepan, combine mustard powder and 1/4 cup Smoked Chicken Stock; whisk until powder has dissolved. Bring to a boil, reduce heat and simmer for 1–2 minutes. Remove from heat and add diced celery, pepper, onion and corn; set aside.

In another small saucepan, sprinkle flour to evenly coat bottom of pan. Cook over medium heat until golden brown, about 3–4 minutes, shaking pan to brown flour evenly. Remove from heat and set aside.

Meanwhile, return mustard–chicken stock–vegetable pot to stovetop. Add Bonedust Seasoning, sugar, vinegar, celery seeds, turmeric, Smoked Salt Steak Rub and remaining 3/4 cup Smoked Chicken Stock to pot; bring to a boil over medium-high heat. Reduce heat to low and simmer for 2–3 minutes. Add browned flour to simmering pot and increase heat to medium-high. When mixture returns to a boil, reduce heat and simmer for 2–3 minutes, stirring often. Transfer to a container and let cool slightly. Cover and refrigerate until needed, or pour relish into sterilized jars, seal and refrigerate for up to 2 weeks, or freeze for up to 3 months.

CORIANDER CASHEW PESTO

This is an inspired variation on traditional pesto. (When washing coriander, use a salad spinner to thoroughly dry before processing.)

In a food processor, combine coriander, chili, roasted garlic, olive oil and lemon juice; process until smooth. Add cashews and continue to process until smooth. Season to taste with salt and transfer to a bowl; cover and refrigerate for up to 1 week.

1 bunch coriander leaves, picked from stems, washed and well dried
1 green Thai chili pepper, seeded
1 head Grill-Roasted Garlic (p. 219)
1/4 cup extra-virgin olive oil
Juice of 1 lemon
1/2 cup salted, roasted cashews
Salt

Makes approximately 2 cups

SMOKED CHICKEN STOCK

Smoked chicken adds an extra kick to this stock — and it's an essential base for many other recipes.

In a large stockpot, combine all ingredients. Add enough cold water to cover vegetables and bring to a rolling boil, uncovered. Do not stir. Skim any gray scum from the surface. Reduce heat to medium low and simmer, without stirring, for 2 hours, skimming the surface when necessary.

After 2 hours, strain the stock and let cool. Stock will keep, covered, in refrigerator for up to 7 days, or in the freezer for up to 3 months.

2 lb smoked chicken wings
(see p. 175 for smoking method)
8 cloves garlic, smashed
1 large onion, chopped
2 medium carrots, chopped
2 stalks celery, chopped
8 black peppercorns
2 sprigs fresh thyme
2 sprigs flat-leaf parsley
2 sprigs fresh sage or rosemary
2 bay leaves

Makes 12 to 16 cups

SMOKED BEEF STOCK

Another basic that adds extra richness to soups.

Preheat oven to 400°F. Place bones in a large roasting pan and roast for 1 hour, turning regularly to get an even, dark golden brown color. Add celery, carrots, onions and leek; roast for 30 minutes more. Remove from heat and let cool slightly before transferring to a large stockpot. In stockpot, add smoked brisket, thyme, parsley, bay leaves, peppercorns and salt. Cover with cold water and bring to a rolling boil over high heat, skimming gray foam from surface. Do not stir. Reduce heat to medium-low and simmer, without stirring, for 4 hours.

Let stock cool slightly before gently straining through a fine-mesh strainer: Be careful not to press the solids through the strainer. Discard solids and set stock aside to cool completely. The stock will keep, covered, in refrigerator for up to 7 days, or in the freezer for up to 3 months.

10 lb beef or veal bones, including knuckles
4 stalks celery, cut into 2-in pieces
3 large carrots, cut into 1-in pieces
2 large onions, quartered
1 large leek, cut into 1-in pieces
1 lb BBQ Beef Brisket (p. 122)
1/2 bunch fresh thyme
1/2 bunch flat-leaf parsley
2 bay leaves
1 tbsp black peppercorns
1 tbsp salt

Makes about 16 cups

ACKNOWLEDGMENTS

Special thanks to Pamela, my true love, and Team Barbecue's director of operations. Your strength and love are what keep me focused. Forever pure, you make me shine. I love you.

Thanks also to Sigal, my assistant, who over the years has impressively managed not to pull out most of her hair. From Sigal, we hear lines such as, "I hear sirens, if you do that"; or "I smell a lawsuit"; or "I don't want to blow up"; or my favorite, "Do you want me to be a puddle of goo?" Sigal puts up with all my shit and keeps on trucking. Without her this book would never have been completed. Thanks Sigal, you rock.

Chef Mike: You've made the marshmallow salad, you've smoked bubblegum and you've made Spam croutons. I know some days you wonder: How did I get here? Well, you're here, and I'm glad. Your loyalty and devotion to my world are righteous things. Thank you. Now, can you please make me a chicken with chocolate stuffing?

Joanne, a.k.a. Jo Jo, Freak Show Jo, Barnacle Betty, Suzie Shoes — and the list of nicknames goes on. Thank you for always looking after me, making sure that I live on something more than tequila and Cokes. You are an extremely talented chef, with a passionate heart. Thank you for being part of my adventure. Now, if we could only get you to be on time.

Sara Angel, of Angel Editions. Thanks for believing in me and this book. You've been able to isolate the essence of me and my world. You believe. Cheers! Amy Hick. Pushy, pushy! Thanks. We got it done.

Edward Pond. Not "Ed" or "Eddy," but Edward...Pond. The Bond of the camera. "Do something cool," or "What ya gonna do now?" (The last I saw of Edward, he was skipping down the beach in the Dominican Republic. He'd had a lot of rum at the time.)

Bill Douglas of The Bang Design, who has captured the King of the Q world with his design, and created a gorgeous-lookin' book.

Nicole de Montbrun. This is the fifth book that I have done with you, Nicole. Thanks for all your awesome help and support.

Special thanks to Kirsten Hanson and Iris Tupholme at HarperCollins Canada, for their incredible support of this project.

Thank you to:
Kirk Sharpley of King of the Q Television
Ron McAvan of Outstanding Foods
And my sponsors:
★ McCain
★ Napoleon
★ Jack Daniel's
★ Scripto
★ Chef Revival
★ Reynolds
★ Wet Ones
★ King of the Q Sauces and Seasoning Rubs

Thanks to all those grill guys who have kindly donated a grill to my passion:
* Napoleon BBQ (Ingrid, Wolfgang and David)
* Big Green Egg (John & Brian: The Grill Guys)
* Primo Grill
* Freedom Grill
* Traeger Grills

And to all those who have supported me and my crazy barbecue endeavors:
* Steven and Robert Mintz from Uni Foods, Rupari Food Services and Plumrose USA
* Martha Chin and Leanne Wiens. You two have been a huge help in getting it done at my catering company, called We Hate Catering.com
* Mark Barr of Seaforth Creamery

Thanks to all my grilling and barbecuing buddies:
* Ray Lampe
* Vince of 2 Men & A Hog
* Earl
* The Smokin' Eh Team
* BBQ Boys
* Chef Luther Miller
* Mike Zaborsky, one of my biggest fans, and his gang at Argosuck.com

Special thanks to my tasting panel of friends:
* Wendy
* T-Bone
* Lorne and Louise
* Christine Chamberlain
* Carol Chapman
* Jud Currie
* Rob McCann
* Dale McCarthy
* Olaf and his crew
* Eric, Pina, Adriana, Sophia and Daniella
* and many more

Thanks to my family — Ma, Pa, Janie and Crew and Edward and Crew

Thanks, and get sticky!

Love you all,
Teddy

INDEX

King of the Q's Blue Plate BBQ is an Angel Edition
Created under the editorial and creative direction of Sara Angel

Project Editor
AMY HICK

Editors
NICOLE DE MONTBRUN
SARA ANGEL
PATRICIA HOLTZ
AMY HICK

Copy Editor
PATRICIA HOLTZ

Index
LAURIE COULTER

Book Design
BILL DOUGLAS AT THE BANG

Production
LUKE DESPATIE